THE RETURN OF THE TALIBAN

Hassan Abbas is Distinguished Professor of International Relations at the Near East South Asia Strategic Studies Center, National Defense University, Washington, DC. He is the author of numerous books, including *The Taliban Revival* and *The Prophet's Heir*.

Further praise for *The Return of the Taliban*:

"An informative and persuasive book to help make sense of the origins and ideology of Afghanistan's new rulers." Farah Adeed, *Dawn*

"A distinct approach . . . The book places its primary focus on the potential for a more pragmatic and hopeful future." Adam Weinstein, *Foreign Policy*

"As always in political movements, there is nuance that does not end up in the policies . . . Abbas describes how Taliban factions formed through twenty years of fighting." Suzanne Raine, *Engelsberg Ideas*

"The first book-length analysis of the Taliban after they returned to power." Kristian Berg Harpviken, *Journal of Peace Research*

"*The Return of the Taliban* draws upon Abbas' wealth of personal experiences and engagement with key players in the Afghanistan con   'w

"Abbas' narrative fills in the picture with analytical detail mined diligently from a number of sources." T.C.A. Raghavan, *Wire*

"A masterly, riveting account of the return of the Taliban! A work of inspiring and profound scholarship." Amitabh Mattoo, Professor of Disarmament Studies, Jawaharlal Nehru University

"This highly readable book by Hassan Abbas is rich in revealing pivotal decisions leading to the Taliban's seizure of power and in describing how as rulers the Taliban struggle to reconcile pressures for transition with their rigid ideology. The book furnishes valuable insight into who the Taliban are and how best the West can engage them." Marvin Weinbaum, author of *Pakistan and Afghanistan*

"This is a very informative and readable book, providing a comprehensive analysis of the Taliban's return to power from insurgency to governance. It succinctly traces and diagnoses the Taliban's trajectory from 1.0 to 2.0 to 3.0. Its perspective deserves to be widely read and understood." Amin Saikal, author of *Modern Afghanistan*

"Hassan Abbas has written the definitive account of the Taliban's return to power in Afghanistan. The book tells a compelling story of US policy failure in the region and sheds light on the inner workings of the new Taliban regime. Well researched, rigorous and insightful, the book is a must-read for anyone interested in contemporary world affairs." Anne Likuski, author of *Al-Qaida in Afghanistan*

THE RETURN OF THE TALIBAN

AFGHANISTAN AFTER THE AMERICANS LEFT

UPDATED EDITION

Hassan Abbas

YALE UNIVERSITY PRESS
NEW HAVEN AND LONDON

For information about this and other Yale University Press publications, please contact:
U.S. Office: sales.press@yale.edu   yalebooks.com
Europe Office: sales@yaleup.co.uk   yalebooks.co.uk

Set in Minion Pro by IDSUK (DataConnection) Ltd
Printed in Great Britain by Clays Ltd, Elcograf S.p.A

Library of Congress Control Number: 2024934833

ISBN 978-0-300-26788-4 (hbk)
ISBN 978-0-300-27871-2 (pbk)

A catalogue record for this book is available from the British Library.

10 9 8 7 6 5 4 3 2 1

MIX
Paper | Supporting responsible forestry
FSC
www.fsc.org
FSC® C018072

For the women of Afghanistan

Contents

CONTENTS

Illustrations

7. A Taliban Humvee, Kabul, August 2021. Voice of America News.

8. Taliban fighters, Kabul, August 2021. Voice of America News.

9. Afghan citizens being transported from Kabul on a US C-17, August 15, 2021. Air Mobility Command Public Affairs.

10. Taliban spokesperson Zabihullah Mujahid at the Taliban's first press conference after taking power, August 17, 2021. Photo by Hoshang Hashimi / AFP via Getty Images.

11. The Taliban flag flying atop the Shrine of the Prophet's Cloak, Kandahar. © Jake Simkin.

12. Taliban interior minister Sirajuddin Haqqani reviews new Afghan police recruits during their graduation ceremony, Kabul, March 5, 2022. Photo by Wakil Kohsar / AFP via Getty Images.

13. Mullah Yaqoob, Mullah Baradar and Bashir Noorzai, Kabul, September 19, 2022. Photo by Wakil Kohsar / AFP via Getty Images.

14. Afghan women at a "Stop Hazara genocide" protest, Kabul, October 1, 2022. Photo by AFP via Getty Images.

15. Taliban fighters stand guard at the Karte Sakhi shrine on the first day of *Nowruz*, Kabul, March 21, 2022. Photo by Ahmad Sahel Arman / AFP via Getty Images.

Maps and Charts

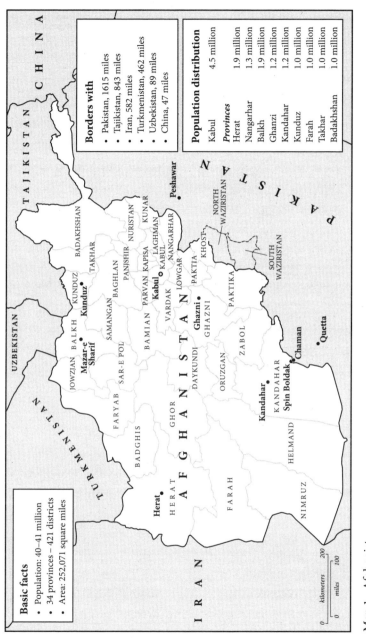

Basic facts

- Population: 40–41 million
- 34 provinces – 421 districts
- Area: 252,071 square miles

Borders with

- Pakistan, 1615 miles
- Tajikistan, 843 miles
- Iran, 582 miles
- Turkmenistan, 462 miles
- Uzbekistan, 89 miles
- China, 47 miles

Population distribution

Kabul	4.5 million
Provinces	
Herat	1.9 million
Nangarhar	1.3 million
Balkh	1.9 million
Ghanzi	1.2 million
Kandahar	1.2 million
Kunduz	1.0 million
Farah	1.0 million
Takhar	1.0 million
Badakhshan	1.0 million

Map 1. Afghanistan

Introduction
History Repeats Itself

August 15, 2021—Just how the mighty had fallen in Kabul depended on who you considered mighty. When the moment arrived, the supposedly most powerful man in Afghanistan—its twice-elected president Ashraf Ghani—had now found himself to be the most vulnerable. The divisive Afghan politics of which he was an integral part had paralyzed Kabul for years. The regional strongmen and their patronage networks had systematically weakened the state by dismembering whatever semblance of rule of law ever existed in the country. But this was all history now. In early August 2021, Ghani knew the Taliban were at the gates of the city, and he also knew the biggest target in the world was on his back. When he asked his military commanders about the situation, they told him the last thing he would have wanted to hear: many of the villages surrounding Kabul had cut deals as protective measures, offering no resistance when the Taliban paid them visits. Effectively, Kabul was on its way down.

Ghani did consider putting up military resistance to the Taliban, but like most of his thoughts, that consideration was short-lived. After the February 2020 US–Taliban "peace" deal, his hope had started to dwindle. From that point forward, everything went downhill. Zalmay Khalilzad, the US special envoy spearheading the negotiations between America and the Taliban leaders, tried to convince Ghani on more than one occasion to work with the Taliban. Ghani made it clear that was inconceivable and rejected the suggestion outright. In his final days in Kabul, Ghani had become quite conspiratorial in his thinking. He was convinced that former president Hamid Karzai, his political rival Abdullah Abdullah and Khalilzad were all conspiring to remove him from office and were paving the way for the Taliban takeover of Kabul under one of their leaders, Mullah Abdul Ghani Baradar. When in his mind he concluded that he could no longer avert such a plan, he shared critical security information with rival Taliban leader Sirajuddin Haqqani, to help him make a move on Kabul ahead of other Taliban factions, especially Mullah Baradar.[1] That was both Ghani's way of taking revenge on Khalilzad for "planning" his ouster as well as a belated expression of gratitude to the Haqqani network for its support of his 2014 presidential campaign. As incredible as the story may sound, two Afghan insiders confirmed it to me. Former Afghan intelligence chief Rahmatullah Nabil also corroborates the Ghani–Haqqani election understanding in 2014.[2] Pakistan's premier intelligence outfit, the Inter-Services Intelligence (ISI), had sponsored the arrangement.[3]

By 2021 Afghanistan had been at war for twenty years. The government in Kabul had become so used to getting big checks from the US that two-thirds of the Afghan budget—if not more—was coming through direct US financing. Other allies, including the European Union, were making additional contributions. Afghanistan had no legs of its own to stand on, and ultimately Ghani was in no position to think he could make decisions about Afghanistan independently once the Americans had declared their desire to leave the country by September 2021. He refused to accept that fact as well, and in his stubbornness killed any hope of cooperation with the US team. However, he was correct in assuming that the Taliban would never work with him or truly cooperate with any democratic setup. They had spent decades being the greatest enemy of the Afghan constitution—why would they work with it now? Ghani, alongside many of his cabinet members, vividly remembered the Taliban atrocities of the 1990s. In their heads they replayed the terrible memories from that time, when bigotry and violence ruled the country, with cruelty toward women and minorities the law of the land. Ghani believed that working with the Taliban in any foolish attempt at a power-sharing arrangement would mean the effective end of the Afghan republic. He was entitled to his own views, of course, but nevertheless, he should not have made promises he had little chance of keeping. Only a short while before he fled, he told US Secretary Antony Blinken on the phone he would fight to the death. Of course this was not to be.

The last thing one could want to deal with during a life-or-death crisis is a quarrel. Unfortunately for Ghani, every meeting with his two closest counsellors was affected by the fact that they hated each other's guts. They were Hamdullah Mohib, his national security advisor—a bright 38-year-old Western-educated Afghan who earlier served as Afghanistan's ambassador to the US, arguably Ghani's most loyal man—and Amrullah Saleh, the assertive vice president of Afghanistan, known more for his highly critical views of Pakistan and fervent attachment to the idea that the Taliban are an extension of Pakistan's ISI.

Both these men spent day and night with Ghani during the fateful days before the Taliban takeover of Kabul. On August 14, 2021, a mere day before the Taliban marched into the city, Ghani was having conversations with the two of them regarding the deteriorating situation they were confronted with. Expectedly, they offered opposite views on how to deal with the crisis. In the midst of the conversation, however, their disagreement became the least source of tension for them. Mohib received a call on his mobile from Khalil Haqqani, a leading member of the Haqqani clan that is highly influential within the Taliban hierarchy, offering advice in a firm but friendly tone: "Give up and get out."[4]

As soon as Mohib had this brief conversation, he worriedly shared with Ghani that it was all over. Without a moment's hesitation, Ghani responded with an almost casual rejection of the idea. He explained that the Americans had told him the Taliban would not march into Kabul and that he would have received a warning if something had changed. Ghani was told that one of his top aides, Salam Rahimi, who for days was engaged in back-channel communications with the Taliban, had brokered an arrangement that ensured that the Taliban would "refrain from taking over the city by force, in exchange for an interim power-sharing deal."[5] He was now hoping that these parleys in Qatar would lead to some kind of face-saving deal. Whether this naivety and ignorance was a coping mechanism or sheer stupidity, his failure to take any decisive action—in making any move to secure Kabul or strategize about options—would be disastrous.

On the morning of August 15, news of the Taliban entering Kabul started pouring in. Deep in thought, Ghani now instructed Mohib to contact the US ambassador to confirm what they were hearing. Mohib had a rough time with the Americans since he had blasted Zalmay Khalilzad by calling him an overly ambitious player who aspired to become a "viceroy" in Afghanistan.[6] After being blocked by the US from all bilateral engagements, he had only recently reestablished himself after a pardon from Khalilzad on Ghani's special request. Mohib had a different idea about who to call. Rather than the US ambassador, he made a call to the CIA station chief, whose assessment was quite pessimistic. Mohib told Ghani things were indeed gloomy. Ghani's close associates had in fact already packed up their belongings in anticipation of the deepening crisis.

Ghani had no way of knowing if it was actually the CIA station chief on the other end of the line, but Mohib was insistent it was time to leave. Amrullah Saleh had already been missing for a day or so. As rash as he was in his opinions, Saleh was also a brave man, having survived multiple suicide bombing attacks by the Taliban, and remaining unscathed. It would be unfair to call him a coward for escaping as the Taliban would likely have him tortured to death given his ruthless anti-Taliban campaign that had also targeted many Taliban families. Upon realizing Ghani was a lost cause, unable to make any decision on his own, he had left Kabul swiftly and silently. All we know is that a local cab came to the doors of the palace and he was seen getting into it, wearing a cap and glasses. The choice of a cab was obviously to avoid being spotted and by now he had already reached the Panjshir valley, around 30 miles from Kabul, where he thought he would be safer.[7]

With Saleh missing, Mohib became even more convinced that a quick evacuation was the only way to save their lives. An insider confirmed to the BBC, "Mohib told Ghani that the Taliban were on their way and that they would capture him and kill him."[8] The moment they had discussed yet barely planned for had been thrust upon them in the final hour. Even then unable to accept the reality unfolding before him, Ghani was shepherded by Mohib toward two helicopters waiting for them. There was one last hurdle though—a handful of stressed-out palace guards awaited them; a shouting match ensued but someone in the fleeing party had thought through the final steps. They were paid to get out of the way. The helicopter set off for Uzbekistan where Ghani's second ride for the United Arab Emirates was waiting. A humiliating rushed exit, without a backward glance, would be President Ghani's farewell to his nation.

In Kabul, none of the notorious warlords of yesteryear, including Abdul Rashid Dostum, Ismail Khan and Atta Mohammad Noor, who remained close allies of presidents Hamid Karzai and Ashraf Ghani, were to be found. They too had abandoned their promises—fake promises as it turned out—of fighting to the death. Ghani can be condemned for poor decision-making, but for him, there was nothing left to be commanded. Afghan security forces, many of whom had not been paid for weeks if not months, saw the writing on the wall early on and escaped the possible bloodbath. Ghani had little credibility in the eyes of his people. All he had at the end was a small coterie of confidants who ensured that he was receiving highly filtered information. Dissent was deemed crime. As journalist Kathy Gannon aptly summed up: "Ghani's style of rule was often characterized as cantankerous and arrogant, rarely heeding the advice of his government and often publicly berating those who challenged him."[9] A good leader truly would have made a difference in that dark hour. A good leader was what the Afghan people deserved.

Hearing the news of Ghani's escape was a real disappointment for Washington, but not necessarily a surprise. In my conversation with a White House official that day, I heard an interesting sentiment: "If these guys aren't still ready to fight for their country and fleeing in every direction, are they really worth our support?"[10] On August 16, 2021, President Biden while defending his decision of total withdrawal, reemphasized this point in his public address:

American troops cannot and should not be fighting in a war and dying in a war that Afghan forces are not willing to fight for themselves. . . . We spent over a trillion dollars. . . . We gave them every tool they could need. . . . What we could not provide them was the will to fight for that future.[11]

There is a point here indeed, and a valid one, but still it is so convenient to say this from the comfort of Washington. The US and its allies just cannot brush off their complicity in hand-picking and empowering inept and corrupt leaders in Afghanistan.

The unfortunate reality is that since 2002 the Taliban gradually reemerged as the biggest gang and largest militia in Afghanistan with no local group or organized force having the capacity to challenge them. Taliban resilience leading to their revival is quite well documented.[12] To be fair to the Afghan security forces, the number of their casualties in the months leading up to the fall of Kabul were reported as "shockingly high."[13] At least they fared better than the political elite in Kabul. It is also worth remembering that Ghani had become so paranoid toward the end that he dismissed many of his key police and military commanders thinking they were disloyal, a move that, according to a May 2022 report from US congressional watchdog group, Special Inspector General for Afghanistan Reconstruction, or SIGAR, not only undermined the morale of Afghan security forces but also confused the war effort.[14] It is a mystery why SIGAR reports, often disseminating hard truths, could not see sunlight in Washington.

To make sense of the Taliban's complex history, we can simplify it by dividing it into three phases. Beginning with the group's genesis and emergence in 1994 and ending with their 2001 fall at the hands of the US military, we have Taliban 1.0, a period spanning from their birth to their first stint in power, and their eventual downfall after 9/11. This was followed by one or two years where they were dormant, effectively in the wilderness and on the run. Subsequently, the Taliban regrouped, reenergized and reframed their aims, galvanizing the cadres from their base in the mountains of the Afghanistan–Pakistan frontier—Pakistan's erstwhile Federally Administered Tribal

Areas (FATA). The strategizing and plotting was happening in Pakistan's city of Quetta, where the Taliban leadership council was now comfortably housed. Thus was born their second phase—from 2003 to 2018 we have Taliban 2.0—the movement turning into a forceful insurgency across Afghanistan. Finally, that brings us to today. When Taliban leaders started their negotiations with the US around 2018–19, Taliban 3.0 was born in the modern-day meeting rooms of Qatar's capital Doha. Taliban 3.0 is their reincarnation unraveling before our eyes: even if they haven't changed ideologically, Afghanistan has—and they have no choice but to adapt, whether they like it or not. They will have to learn to stop acting as morality police and as puritans, and divert their energies toward becoming efficient administrators and dependable leaders— an entirely new ballgame, to put it mildly. With the new generation and new exposure to authority, their task is to reimagine and redefine themselves. Their identity as Taliban 3.0 and the length of their time in power will be determined by whether they can accomplish this herculean task—and if they have it in them at all.

For almost three decades now, we have watched this extremist group in Afghanistan, presenting itself to the world as "the Taliban," the students from Islamic seminaries. The truth is that only top leaders holding senior political offices, Rahbari *shura* (leadership council) members and some of the second-tier leaders of the organization studied in the seminaries of Afghanistan and Pakistan. A great majority of Taliban foot soldiers and ordinary members are peasants, farmers and small-scale traders who have never gone through anything that resembles a religious training.

Tribal culture and ethnic politics are at least as relevant to their identity as their religious orientation.

Viewed through the prism of their rigidity and bigotry, and now of their triumph, many lay observers fail to fully comprehend the divergences among the varieties of Taliban. The obscure nature of their organization made them mysterious as well. While the Taliban may have presented an image of unity and even simplicity earlier on, few things in history are so black and white. The truth is that most things, and people too, are a medley of different shades of gray. The Taliban have proven to be no exception. While it is easy for a lay observer to view them as a cohesive entity, they too have rips in the fabric of their unity, which have been growing since they tasted power again. During the insurgency phase, the differences were adding up but went unmentioned, as they were totally dedicated to making Afghanistan chaotic and ungovernable. The differences in their vision for Afghanistan's future are now coming out into the open.

The most important factor causing the fall of Kabul in August 2021 was how the Taliban strategized their return to power through a combination of hard bargaining on the negotiation table with the US, while ramping up pressure on Kabul through increased violence, including targeted suicide attacks. And it is really intriguing, how the Taliban, under the cover of these two elements, surreptitiously reached out to influential tribes and groups across the country to convince them—and coerce or bribe them where necessary—to opt for "peace" deals with the Taliban to avoid any reprisals afterwards. The Taliban knew this art well—of brokering surrenders—having employed it from its earlier time in power. As Jack Watling aptly says, "A lot of people, because they lacked confidence that Kabul would be able to save them, capitulated."[15] More so, with media flashing headlines about the progress in Taliban–US negotiations in Doha, the Taliban's capacity to throw around its weight increased. It helped the Taliban to effectively project the inevitability of their return to Kabul.

The Taliban, over the years, had mastered the use of sophisticated social media tools, as evident from the fact that its chief spokesperson in Doha, Suhail Shaheen, had over 350,000 Twitter followers in August 2021 (it has nearly doubled since then).[16] Similarly, the official Twitter account of the spokesman for the Islamic Emirate of Afghanistan, Zabihullah Mujahid, has over 740,000 followers.[17] The Taliban were on YouTube from 2009, on Twitter and Facebook from 2011, and on Instagram from 2016. Intriguingly, the Taliban had hired one or possibly more public relations firms during their insurgency years to facilitate their social media presence by projecting their key ideas, using hashtags, amplifying messages across platforms and helping them to create potentially viral images and video clips.[18] In 2018, according to a credible study, the Taliban even posted more messages on Twitter than Afghanistan's Ministry of Defense, and in more languages![19]

An adaptable and agile force, the Taliban had started their final campaign in 2021 approaching Kabul from all directions; first solidifying their presence in the areas of their strength—roughly one-third of the country—and then capturing the surrounding districts of these hubs. The second stage was seizure of districts in northern areas, which came as a surprise for everyone and was highly demoralizing for the Ghani government. The third phase strategically took control of border crossings with Iran, Pakistan and Tajikistan. All along they avoided capturing provincial capitals to avoid direct major confrontations with Afghan forces stationed in these locations.[20] On the side, the Taliban co-opted local elders in many locations to convince Afghan security forces to surrender or abandon their posts in order to avoid bloodshed. The Taliban were offering $150 to government security officials (mostly without salaries for months now) to surrender and join them.[21] All of this not only helped the Taliban gain momentum but also created an impression that Afghan forces were offering little to no resistance—or even joining Taliban ranks.[22] This raised the morale of the Taliban's roughly 60,000 to 65,000 foot soldiers. The numbers even swelled when victory started looking imminent, as many Pashtuns from the south and east now greedily awaited the spoils of war. By early August, the Taliban felt confident enough to move on provincial capitals and successfully targeted the takeover of important cities—Jalalabad, Kunduz and Mazar-e-Sharif—in the north. More than half of 421 districts were now under Taliban control. They were simply unstoppable now.

Most Western watchers and analysts (including me) thought that at least Kabul would not fall, assuming that all Afghan security forces would converge to defend it. It was not known then how the Taliban had already pre-positioned its assets and materials around Kabul, besides successfully placing its intelligence operators in important institutions of Kabul and getting regular feeds. Spies from the Haqqani group had infiltrated many ministries and critical security organizations, including Kabul airport's security command center.[23] Various private businesses and international donor agencies in Kabul also had Taliban spies. Clearly, the Taliban had orchestrated their path to power with diligence. It was a remarkable operation and it clearly took everyone opposed to their return by surprise.

Moving on to the present, the most formidable challenge the Taliban faced on taking over the reins of power on August 15, 2021, was how to transition from an insurgent group to a political group running a government. The organization needed a change of mindset and, even though they had governed Afghanistan before, they are now struggling with the realization that Afghanistan has changed, even if they have not. And it would be wrong to assume that the Taliban were not affected by change in so many arenas, from modes of communication, especially social media, to the influence of Afghans' exposure to, and engagements with, modern institutions.

The Taliban's primary asset continues to be the tools required by a militant movement. Good governance requires an entirely different skill set, and a different approach. Warriors are neither trained nor often accustomed to serve as administrators and public servants. Such transitions can be time-consuming as well as disruptive of leadership hierarchies. Kamran Bokhari, a scholar specializing in militant organizations, goes a step further; during a conversation with me he argued that: "the whole experience of ruling and governing can potentially dilute the ideological component of the Taliban's thinking."[24] Their very reality is in direct conflict with governing a polity, and until these elements can be reconciled, their future looks rough, in his opinion. This perspective and its nuances are reflected in the story of a young Taliban soldier, whom I will call Khalid here. I engaged with him on various topics over the last year.

At 21 years old, Khalid only knew his country under American forces. He had no memory of the Taliban's vicious rule in the 1990s, no knowledge of their atrocities except through spoken accounts. So, as he entered Kabul on August 15, 2021, jubilant and empowered, he was still unsure of what exactly he was walking into. All he knew was that his boss, who could not have been much older than him but, regardless, had higher credentials because of being wounded in combat earlier, had received a message on a walkie-talkie that they had grabbed from the local Afghan security: "go in—fast." The destination, they were told, was the presidential palace. Khalid, riding his Honda motorbike, followed his boss, without even knowing where he was.

This was a city he had surveilled before, one where he had even participated in the funeral of a suicide bomber. That was where his knowledge of the city ended, besides the fact that it was a city owned by the Americans. And, of course, that everything they were fighting for was to win it back, as a matter of honor. He walked into the palace with an entourage of others, greeted by an expectant security official still wearing Afghan military fatigues—probably a Taliban sympathizer who had penetrated presidential security or someone who had joined the Taliban at just the right moment out of fear of being killed at their hands. Through the doors of the palace before him lay a new world, and a new future. When he was told, in the evening, to find himself a place in the palace to sleep, he was taken by surprise. He, along with his two friends, were anxiously waiting for orders to burn down the building and they had been thinking of where to start! He little realized that now his new task was to secure the building. Their new role indeed came as a surprise, as well as shock, for many Taliban foot soldiers, as they know little about what governance entails. All they knew was how to destroy. They don't know how to build.

The purpose of this book is to tell the story of the Taliban's transition, from the old world of self-styled clerics to the new world of young, mobile-holding, tech-savvy morality police with the world as their oyster. When they look in the mirror, they see empowered heroes who defeated a mighty global power and saved their nation from the tyranny of unwelcome intruders. This book is also about those not seen in the reflection: the plight of those on the receiving end of their intolerant policies—ordinary Afghans, women, children and minorities. For the Taliban, it does not matter if you are a Muslim—if you do not agree with and obey them, you are the other. And being the other may amount to a death sentence. This book is just as much about ordinary Afghans as it is about the Taliban—I want to reveal the true plight of the people unfairly consigned to that fate: those Afghans who, for decades, were told, along with the rest of the world, that they would be saved by the West and politicians in Kabul—only to be put in the exact same situation twenty years later, and abandoned without a second thought.

This book aims to capture the idea of religion gone sour—and also that of tribalism, mixed with patriarchy, a toxic

dose of nationalism and ethnic rivalry. In short, a combination of all those things that hold the deadly power of making
human beings rigid and narrow-minded in their worldview.
It was this concoction that created the superficial perception
that the Taliban are the soldiers of God—a God in desperate
need of violent defense. These are the people (predominantly men) willing to do anything they can to secure a
ticket to heaven, and they will act to take everyone else
there too—or condemn them to their own hell on earth.
The degeneration of Islamic seminary education, especially
in South Asia, has created this gigantic problem, linked to
heightened sectarianism as well as the politicization of
religious principles. An argument can be made that, for all
practical purposes, the prevalent Taliban ideology falls
under the category of "new religious movements."

How Afghanistan—a home to Sufi mystics—went
through a forced ideological transformation is also briefly
probed in the book. Afghanistan was once soaked in the
radiance and spiritualism of mysticism; this is indisputable.
Not just that though—local poetry and languages are
strongly connected to Sufism's path through the country.
Some of the most notable Pashto and Dari/Persian language
poets were prominent mystics, whose poetry revolved
around humanism, tolerance, divine love and mercy. Thus,
Pashtun as well as Afghan identity were also strongly influenced by the light of Sufism and Irfan (spiritual knowledge).
This mystical tradition of Afghanistan is now reeling under
an existential threat.

This book is also about the glorious myth of the ability of
foreign intervention to install a democratic order. This

deceptive idea has reached its dying breath in the past few years, with Afghanistan striking the final blow. It is as much about misplaced idealism as it is about self-deception funded by a dangerous amount of money.

The aggressive geopolitical contest in broader Southwest Asia—from triangular Saudi Arabia–Iran–Turkey competition to India versus Pakistan rivalry—which is deeply impacting Afghanistan, is another theme explored in the book. The Qatar versus United Arab Emirates (UAE) competition to exert influence over the Taliban has added a further layer to an already complex scene. Whether China will ultimately play a larger role in stabilizing Afghanistan is another issue worth probing.

It is no secret that the India–Pakistan rivalry and their proxy warfare have played a crucial role in bringing Afghanistan to where it stands today—on the verge of another bout of isolation and potentially again turning into a hub of international terrorism. India, which has no common border with Afghanistan but has a historical relationship with the country, wanted to be part of the solution over the last two decades, through development aid. It also wanted to check Pakistan's influence in the country as anti-India militants, sponsored by Pakistan, had flourished in Afghanistan when the Taliban were in control earlier. With the rise of Indian influence in Kabul during 2001–21, Pakistan felt encircled and vulnerable. India had not shied away from supporting anti-Pakistan elements, using its influence in Kabul. For Pakistan all of this amounted to an existential threat—at least, that is what its military establishment would like everyone to believe. Hence, for Pakistan, supporting the Taliban served various purposes—from pushing back against and scaring India to ensuring that Afghanistan serves as Pakistan's backyard. It was also concerned that Pashtuns, divided between Afghanistan and Pakistan via the Durand Line, might pursue the dream of creating a sovereign state, often touted as *Pashtunistan*. Such an eventuality would be Pakistan's nightmare, so it naturally want to avoid it at all costs.

Even during the heyday of US–Pakistan counterterrorism cooperation, Islamabad was not deterred from emboldening and even empowering the Taliban as much as possible. Pakistan's open support for the Taliban was never really a secret project—it was not meant to be, it appears. Hosting millions of Afghan refugees over the years and exporting thousands of madrassa-educated Pakistanis to Afghanistan made the project feasible. In fact, the whole exercise was geared toward establishing strategic depth for Pakistan within Afghanistan, in the words of one of Pakistan's former army chiefs.[25] Pakistan, through such poorly conceived agendas, gifted the Taliban inroads into its own heartland with disastrous security implications. Many new militant organizations—labeled as "Pakistani Taliban" and "Punjabi Taliban," and later their offshoots—created havoc in Pakistan between 2007 and 2014. These Taliban-affiliated groups operating across Pakistan received a serious beating at the hands of Pakistan military after 2014 and were severely degraded, though not decimated. With the resurgence of the Afghan Taliban, they too are staging a comeback in the Pakistan–Afghanistan frontier area. This was indeed predictable and was accurately forecast by many, including myself.[26]

Another major theme explored in the book is societal as well as demographic transformation in the Pashtun-dominated areas of both Afghanistan and Pakistan. The fall and rise of the Taliban since 2001 has left a deep imprint, especially on Pakistan's Pashtun majority areas, the area that produced such a luminary as Ghaffar Khan, who spearheaded a progressive and secular movement that survives to this day in Pakistan's Khyber Pukhtunkhwa (KPK) province. Khan was a deeply religious man and had worked and prayed with India's legendary Mohandas Karamchand Gandhi without becoming insecure about his Islamic roots. He had redefined the Pashtun identity, adding a progressive element to a tradition known already for its graciousness, hospitality and cultural pride. The tragic irony of the Talibanization that has taken place is that it has led to a squeezing of the space for pluralism held so sacred by many Pashtuns across Afghanistan and Pakistan.

The loss of art and culture anywhere is a tragedy for humankind. These societal transformations have been directly and darkly impacted by the evaporating space for pluralism, music and poetry. Progressive literature is still being produced in the area—it never stopped. But changes in the Pakistan–Afghanistan tribal belt especially proved to be deep-rooted and devastating. The adoption of an extremist identity—where religious militancy emerges as the new norm and the old cultural values of respect for elders and emphasis on reconciliation through dialogue were thrown out the window—has embedded itself.

What the Pakistani state failed to realize, despite witnessing these dynamics, was that they could not be friends with one kind of Taliban and enemies with the other. They could see the signs clearly before their eyes but resisted accepting this. In the process they lost tens of thousands of people, including soldiers, scholars, clergy and ordinary people. It looks as though hardly any lessons were learned.

This book investigates how the old Taliban maintain their relevance for the new generation and asks whether this is really a "new" Taliban, or more of the same? Can the Taliban unite the state and society, and how will they deal with rivals, both political and religious? To understand these dynamics, it is critical to be clear about various factions and groupings within the Taliban. Finally, how are other extremist Islamic groups, both like-minded ones and rivals, interpreting the return of the Taliban, and what message are they are taking from their revival? How do they want to interact with them? Do they want to help the Taliban avoid failure? Will the Taliban listen to their advice and believe that their success equals the success of political Islam?

These issues are probed while recognizing that the circumstances, environment and context of the Taliban have changed in multiple ways. For instance, the exposure and level of awareness of the Taliban today is no match for what they were in the mid-1990s. The digital revolution has changed many things, and even the regional political land-scape is rapidly changing. The Taliban cannot stay unchanged in the midst of all that.

This book seeks answers to the above questions through interviews with the Taliban and many of their friends in Pakistan, Iran and the Gulf countries. It greatly benefits from excellent reporting in the regional as well as international media. Independent journalists today have far more access to Afghanistan in comparison to when the Taliban last ruled Kabul in the 1990s.

Like much of the world, many Taliban leaders, or their staff at least, have a social media presence. They have accounts on Twitter, Facebook and even Instagram, as mentioned earlier. Also, many former Afghan government officials have chosen to stay in Afghanistan, trying to interpret what the Taliban are doing, and they are sharing their insights through social media platforms. This study benefits from an analysis of all such content. Essentially, then, this is also an attempt to understand them through their self-projected public narrative. It offers a window into their thinking and some trends are obvious from following these regularly.

The Taliban might have run their victory lap, but they have a long way ahead of them still. Their real test starts now. Just as we watch curiously as an audience, they too must confront the looming questions of their capability. Do these men, trained in religion and weaponry, have the capacity to sustain the institutions they inherited? And, more than that, with little experience, can they build entirely new ones? If they want to go far, they will need training wheels, for certain, and a starting push. But only if they are willing to receive help will they get it from the outside. Going by the signals they have put out at the time of writing (late 2022), though, it seems that they want to.

Lastly, the underlying thesis tested here is that the return of the Taliban to power warrants a rebirth of the group in a way—as they are not immune to the changing tides of time.

The Taliban have not changed much in ideological sense but today's Taliban are different from the last time they were in power. They have learned important lessons over the last two decades from fighting the United States and its allies. As evident from their approach and performance in the Doha negotiations, the Taliban are capable of making compromises and even transforming some of their rigidly held political views. My research finds they are adapting to their new reality of governing Afghanistan and, in certain sectors, they seem to be breaking from commonly held assumptions about them. The Taliban have proven to be pragmatic, but they refuse to make any policy adjustment which they think will threaten their internal cohesion or weaken their political base. However, the battle lines between the relatively pragmatic Taliban in Kabul and their highly conservative counterparts in Afghanistan's second largest city, Kandahar, the spiritual and political hub of the Taliban, are drawn, already causing policy paralysis. If this division and rivalry continue to worsen, they may turn out to be devastating for the Taliban. Cruel restrictions on women's education and employment suggest that narrow-minded elements are still strong—a bad sign.

The Taliban, for sure, have a newfound sense of international relations and thus foreign policy is among the priorities for the contemporary movement, something not seen in the 1990s. Taliban 3.0 are also susceptible to outside influence—primarily because the new economic infrastructure of Afghanistan cannot operate in isolation. They recognize the need to engage regionally and globally; they want their banks to connect with the global banking system; they need high-speed internet, and they need better connectivity between government organizations, etc. All of this potentially will have a modernizing effect on them, whether they like it or not. Though how they will manage this—and, even more so, whether they will let the young handle this—will ultimately define the future of the Taliban.

The book makes a strong case for engagement, which does not in any sense equate with endorsement. However, the growing urgency of communication between the Taliban and the international community must be realized—if only for the betterment of ordinary Afghan lives. Dialogue, at the very least, will open a door for a new beginning, a new lifeline, for those most impacted by the debilitating situation. We must not allow our stubborn attachments to the past to obstruct the goodness of tomorrow. As my professor, the late Roger Fisher, eloquently put it in his book *Getting to Yes*: "The challenge is not to eliminate conflict but to transform it. It is to change the way we deal with our differences."[27] Let us open our minds enough to transform the situation we have found ourselves in into one of hope, potential and possibility. Refusing to even engage automatically eliminates these necessary aspects; and what a great travesty that would be. Engaging with the Taliban will, at the very worst, result in the inflation of their egos—and at best will restore life to a nation and people who have long deserved peace and prosperity.

It is also very important to continue to study the Taliban both as a religio-political movement, and as a militant group. In terms of categorization, they fall in the middle, though not neatly. Four books provided me with immense insight into the group and their contemporary politics and strategy. The first is Carter Malkasian's *The American War in Afghanistan: A History*, an outstanding contribution based on firsthand accounts and interviews with those in the know, especially about the ins and outs of the Doha negotiations. The second is Craig Whitlock's *The Afghanistan Papers*, which offers valuable background about policy blunders that contributed toward the Taliban's return to power. The third is a book penned by the new chief justice of Afghanistan, Mullah Hakim—whose work, with the introduction by supreme leader Hibatullah, is a window into Taliban thinking today.[28] The fourth and final one is by Afghan historian Abdul Hai Mutma'in titled, *Taliban: A Critical History from Within*, offering analysis of the history of the modern Taliban, filling many gaps. Additionally, remarkably insightful reports from Afghanistan Analysts Network and United States Institute of Peace (USIP), especially those written by Andrew Watkins and Asfandyar Mir, were of great help. Last but not least, reports on the Islamic State in Khorasan (ISK) and Pakistani Taliban by Amira Jadoon and Abdul Sayed for *CTC Sentinel*, an excellent research publication very ably edited by Paul Cruickshank, provided a great deal of information and brilliant analysis. Those interviewed for the book are thanked in the Acknowledgments but three experts were instrumental in helping me understand Taliban dynamics today: Mohammad Israr Madani, a former teacher at Dar ul Uloom Haqqania and an interfaith dialogue advocate; Ambassador Robin Raphel, a former US diplomat par excellence; and an Afghan Taliban insider who wishes to remain anonymous.

As a disclaimer, I must share that I lived, studied and worked with Pashtuns of Pakistan during the early 1980s and then the late 1990s. I briefly served in two districts of KPK (then known as North-West Frontier province) in 1997–98 as a federal police officer (assistant superintendent of police) before moving to the United States for higher education in early 2001. While I was studying for my doctoral degree at Tufts University's Fletcher School of Law and Diplomacy, I published my first major work in 2004 titled *Pakistan's Drift into Extremism: Allah, the Army, and America's War on Terror,* shedding light on how the anti-Soviet "Afghan Jihad" changed the socio-political dynamics in the region leading to radicalization trends. In 2014, Yale University Press published my academic research titled *The Taliban Revival: Violence and Extremism on the Pakistan–Afghanistan Frontier,* where I shared my field experiences, assessments and findings focusing on extremism trends in the region. I have been researching and teaching about security, politics and religion in South Asia, including Afghanistan, at the National Defense University in Washington DC and earlier at Columbia University, and Harvard Kennedy School, for over a decade and a half now. This latest work builds on my earlier research and brings the story to the present.

1

The Road to Kabul

The Secret Deal, the New Taliban and a House of Cards

The Taliban's return to Kabul looked imminent after the news of Afghan President Ashraf Ghani's escape had spread across Afghanistan like wildfire. However one spins it, the reality is that the US–Taliban peace deal of February 2020 enabled and empowered the Taliban in a major way. This chapter investigates the circumstances leading up to the deal and the dynamics at play during the negotiations. The deal was widely seen in Afghanistan, and elsewhere too, as a pact highly advantageous to the Taliban. The reclusive Taliban supreme leader Mullah Hibatullah Akhundzada had declared the deal, "a collective victory of the entire Muslim and Mujahid [fighter] nation"—quite an exaggerated claim.[1] Still, the Taliban had no intention of marching on Kabul anytime soon. It was also the failure of the poorly conceived intra-Afghan dialogue—the negotiations between the Ghani government and the Taliban after the US–Taliban deal—that paved the way for the Taliban's return to power. The Taliban were soon to reemerge as the sole arbiter of Afghanistan's destiny.

The one factor that had helped the Taliban more than anything else during the final phase of the insurgency was the release of roughly 5,000 of its fighters from prisons, including several hundred highly dangerous lawbreakers who were found to have been involved in murders, kidnappings, drug trafficking and even terrorism. While Ghani attempted to resist, the Trump administration served as an ardent advocate for the Taliban's demand for prisoner release as per the deal. During a phone conversation, Mullah Abdul Ghani Baradar, a top Taliban leader also spearheading the negotiation team in Doha, asked Trump to intervene, complaining about Ghani, which triggered Trump to threaten Ghani by saying, "if there is a perception that the big picture is being sacrificed for small matters then we are ready to change our relationship."[2] Ghani complied. What went in the Taliban's favor was the fact that they had already done their part, with the timely release of around 1,000 Afghan security personnel in their custody in accordance with the deal. The release of Taliban prisoners unquestionably gave a boost to Taliban morale and aided them through the additional human resource made available for their various battlefronts at a crucial time. On the intra-Afghan negotiation table, both sides stonewalled each other to the best of their ability.[3] Zalmay Khalilzad, and more so his team, wanted the final US withdrawal to be conditional on success of the intra-Afghan negotiations, but Trump insisted on sticking to the timeline.[4] Biden followed that path even more rigorously.

Those opposed to the Taliban were understandably more frightened now, seeing the Taliban resurgence unfold before their eyes, and many succumbed to pressure when the Taliban

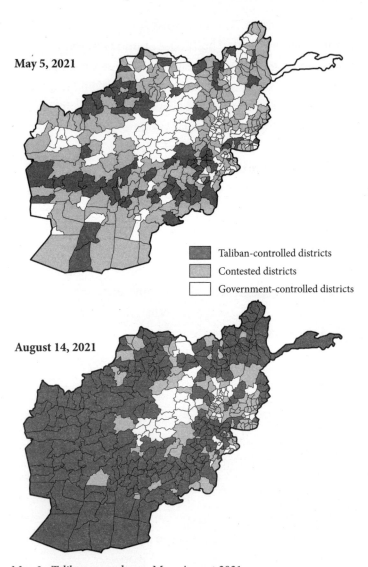

May 5, 2021

August 14, 2021

Taliban-controlled districts
Contested districts
Government-controlled districts

Map 2. Taliban ascendance, May–August 2021

Sources: Various local and international media reports including *The Economist* and *Aljazeera*

demanded obedience. Their lives and those of their family members were at stake. The Taliban's military successes on the ground were swifter and more devastating as a result, even in the north which had never been their stronghold. The psychological impact of all this was visible and tangible; encouraging for the Taliban and depressing for their opponents.

Taliban Leadership Transitions

At this testing hour of startling transition in 2020, Afghanistan was basically leaderless. President Ghani was losing credibility and control while no Taliban leader had been in a position to really fill the shoes of Mullah Mohammad Omar (b. 1960), the charismatic founder of the Taliban movement, since his mysterious death in 2013. The supreme leader or *Ameer ul-Momineen* (henceforth Emir) of Afghanistan during the first Taliban government (1996–2001), Mullah Omar had resurrected the movement as an insurgency in the aftermath of the US invasion in October 2001. The Taliban had been completely uprooted from Kabul in late 2001 and, for a brief time, it seemed as if they would be ingloriously consigned to the dustbin of history. In such difficult circumstances, Mullah Omar had inspired and organized a massive Taliban resurgence in the face of the most powerful military coalition in the world. For the Taliban, it was a David and Goliath situation—and they were the triumphant David.

The loss of such an iconic figure as Mullah Omar was devastating for the Taliban. Any ordinary movement would have been totally demoralized, and likely died out completely, after facing such intense challenges. The story of the Taliban's resilience is no ordinary tale in that sense. Given his legendary status in Taliban rank and file, Mullah Omar's death in a Karachi hospital on April 23, 2013 was kept top secret by Taliban leaders for over two years—until July 2015—before Afghan intelligence made it public.[5] The feted leader had two influential deputies during his lifetime— Mullah Abdul Ghani Baradar, one of the four co-founders of the Taliban movement, and former defense minister, Mullah Ubaidullah Akhund. The latter had died of a heart attack in a jail in Pakistan in 2010 after his arrest in 2007 under suspicion of having close ties with Osama Bin Laden, leaving Mullah Baradar as the top candidate for the vacancy of Emir.

The only problem was that Mullah Baradar (b. 1968) was now out of favor with Pakistan. Besides his credentials as Mullah Omar's top lieutenant and a remarkable military commander, he was also Mullah Omar's brother-in-law. After the Taliban's fall in November 2001, he was in practice the operational commander of the insurgency. He was pragmatic enough though to realize that the Taliban could at best achieve a military stalemate on the ground, given the strong US military presence in the country, leading him to become a supporter of reconciliation with the Kabul government. To pursue this path, he was in secret communication with the then Afghan President Hamid Karzai's brother Wali Karzai.[6] This is what led to his arrest by Pakistani security forces in 2010. This was no ordinary operation—not in the least.

A joint ISI–CIA operation in Karachi was planned at the request of the CIA. Pakistani intelligence, initially, was in the dark about the identity of the target. Interestingly, both intelligence agencies were working at cross-purposes in this case. This became painfully obvious when the ISI refused to allow CIA officials to interrogate Baradar.[7] From the point of view of Pakistani intelligence, Mullah Baradar was not supposed to make any decisions on his own free will! He was after all, a "guest" enjoying Pakistani hospitality and support. He remained in a jail until 2013 and was then moved to an ISI "guest house." His punishment? To stay in the not so comfortable custody of Pakistani intelligence for years to come. Almost fifty of his close associates would receive the same humiliating treatment.[8] Baradar was too intelligent and influential to be away from the action for long, but his wings were clipped severely—restricting his potential to fly for some time to come.

Thus, luck would smile on another candidate—the relatively young 47-year-old Mullah Mansour Akhtar, a Taliban leader who had been managing the day-to-day affairs of the Taliban as the operational chief of the movement since 2013. His career had been unremarkable till then, with various roles in the first Taliban government (1996–2001)— including serving as security manager of Kandahar airport, as aviation and transportation minister, and as envoy to Europe for acquiring military equipment.[9] Besides business interests—primarily drug trafficking, according to United Nations (UN) reports—he also served as "shadow" governor of Kandahar.[10] His frequent trips to Dubai (and at least one to Bahrain) between 2006 and 2012 on a Pakistani passport using the pseudonym Wali Muhammad, remain somewhat of a mystery.[11]

Mullah Mansour was not exactly the most popular of leaders among the top options. Lacking charisma and clerical credentials, he was basically a power-hungry man known mostly for his business acumen and his network in the Gulf. The most interesting thing about him, in the words of a former US intelligence analyst, was his "famed perfume shopping trips to Dubai, where he stayed comfortably in the embraces of Russian prostitutes and royal protection."[12]

He was of course close to the Pakistani intelligence service, a requisite credential for those aspiring to rise in the senior ranks of the Taliban, especially during the insurgency years when their sanctuary in Pakistan was a crucial lifeline for them.[13] It was hard to beat this combination. Mullah Mansour was officially appointed the new Taliban Emir (leader) by the Taliban *Rahbari Shura* (leadership council) which met near Quetta in Pakistan in July 2015. Mullah Mansour was keen to take the job but it was yet to be seen if the Taliban's rank and file were ready to accept him. Some senior Taliban leaders had serious reservations about him. Syed Mohammad Tayyab Agha, chief of the Qatar-based Taliban Political Commission, resigned after registering his strong objection to the holding of such a crucial meeting in Pakistan rather than Afghanistan, indicating serious dissent within the group.[14] The Taliban Political Commission had been operating in Doha, Qatar, since January 2012, using this neutral space for discreet contacts and negotiations between any and all parties involved in the Afghan conflict.

It took months, and many interventions from senior clerics aligned with the Taliban, for Mullah Mansour to gain legitimacy as the Taliban chief.[15] In an effort to consolidate his grip over the various Taliban factions that had now emerged, he quickly expanded military operations across Afghanistan, including an emphasis on hit-and-run guerrilla tactics and widening the recruitment base to non-Pashtuns.[16] His success in hoisting the Taliban's white flag over the northern Afghan city of Kunduz in September 2015 cemented his leadership position—it was after all the first provincial capital of Afghanistan to fall to the Taliban in 14 years of insurgency.[17] He appointed two deputies, who were to play a crucial role in the future: highly conservative cleric and former judge, Mullah Hibatullah Akhundzada, and Sirajuddin Haqqani, the influential military commander from the Haqqani network, a group famously deemed by the US Chairman of the Joint Chiefs of Staff, Admiral Mike Mullen, "as a veritable arm of the Pakistani intelligence."[18] Politically speaking, these were smart choices for him. Hibatullah was also the one who had sanctioned keeping Mullah Omar's death in 2013 a secret by issuing a fatwa (religious decree). That made it possible for Mullah Mansour to lead on behalf of the deceased Mullah Omar till his actual assumption of the leadership position in 2015.[19]

Destiny, however, had something else in store for him. The tenure of Mullah Mansour turned out to be short-lived as his friendly outreach to Iran proved to be an overstretch with deadly consequences. Mullah Mansour was killed on May 21, 2016 by a 6 a.m. US drone strike in the Nushki district, about 140 kilometers from Quetta, the capital city of Pakistan's Baluchistan province. The official response from Pakistan was a standard press release saying, "the drone attack was a violation of its sovereignty," while an official also maintained that this would not hurt the security and intelligence cooperation between the US and Pakistan.[20]

Contradictory statements from Pakistan about the US drone strikes were quite the norm by then, but Islamabad's muted condemnation here was still surprising given that this happened well inside Baluchistan province. In fact, the strike occurred near the Taliban's "Quetta Shura" headquarters, unlike regular drone strikes in the Pashtun tribal belt in Pakistan's then semi-autonomous Federally Administered Tribal Areas (FATA), where leaders of Tehrik-i-Taliban Pakistan (TTP) and Al-Qaeda were often targeted. Things were awry, for certain. Pakistan was hiding something.

The ensuing statement from the then US Secretary of State John Kerry offered some insights. It said, "He [Mansour] was directly opposed to peace negotiations and to the reconciliation process."[21] Details of any US-sponsored reconciliation efforts with the Taliban were not widely known at the time, while Pakistan was separately trying to kick-start peace talks between the Taliban and the Afghan government. What Kerry kept to himself, though, was that Mansour was hit on his return drive from Iran, where he spent more than seven weeks, and had settled his family there. Pakistani intelligence were naturally turning suspicious of Mansour, believing that they had lost their grip on him. Still, they were sad to see him depart to the next world. In fact, a senior Pakistani official who knew him well and had interacted with him regularly still sounded sad when I broached the topic in a conversation with him in September 2022. He gave a few details about him that are as intriguing as they are insightful. He maintained that, contrary to the US intelligence assessments, in his view Mansour was willing to opt for a settlement with the Kabul government and later the US also regretted taking him out. More insightfully, he said that the US was sharing drone targeting details with the Pakistani intelligence service. For instance, initially the strike was planned for when Mansour stopped at a market for a tea and toilet break on his way to Quetta, but attacking him at that location would have taken the lives of dozens of people around him. Finally, he was targeted an hour later, when he was in his car with only a driver and a family member. This level of detailed sharing of information indicates that Pakistan was cooperating with the US in this operation.

During this conversation, I asked the official whether Pakistan was curious as to why Mullah Mansour was traveling from Quetta to Dubai quite regularly. He reminded me that Mansour's connection to Dubai dated all the way back to the first government of the Taliban in the 1990s, when he served as an aviation minister. He would regularly host sheikhs from the region for falcon hunting in Afghanistan, and eventually developed a close friendship with the royal family of Dubai. The favors were returned in the form of private jet journeys to Dubai and all the attendant luxuries as a respected royal guest!

The above narrative chimes well with a follow-up story from a highly knowledgeable person in Washington DC who closely followed Taliban activities as part of his job at the time. Convinced that Mansour was a major hurdle in the peace process, and with violence against US troops at an all-time high around this time (2015–16), the US was closely watching this resourceful and well-networked Taliban chief making regular trips to Dubai—and something was not adding up. So Susan Rice, the US National Security Advisor, reputed to be sharp and tough-minded, made a call to the Sheikh of Dubai in late March 2016, asking for a small favor. The sheikh would not answer the phone, apparently playing a game of golf so serious he could not face any interruption. When eventually he did answer, the conversation was not very pleasant, to say the least. Rice explained the US's request to the sheikh—that Mansour be detained and arrested in Dubai to be handed over to the US authorities already waiting in the country. The sheikh apologized before telling her that he could not be of much help, as Mansour was already on a plane to Iran. When Rice asked to have the plane stopped, he replied that it was a private plane, and so could not be turned around. Persisting, Rice asked if UAE fighter jets could be employed, to which the sheikh retorted that there was not enough time, and that it would be too problematic diplomatically. This sufficiently explains the extent of the protection Mullah Mansour enjoyed. Personal networks at times can conveniently transcend state-to-state relations.

These inside stories show that these Taliban figures we often consider as some kind of conservative cave-dwellers, going between mosque and madrassa, are actually politicians, pure and simple. They too love their alcohol and paid trips, women and private jets. Their clerical titles are mere titles, and they are less holy than they sound. They do the same things they declare their enemies must be killed for. No surprise there, though.

The choice of the next Taliban Emir was to prove far more important than the leadership council then realized. The possibility that the chosen leader would ultimately follow in the footsteps of Mullah Omar by holding court in Kandahar was at best a hypothetical proposition at the time, given the strong US and NATO presence in Afghanistan. Tens of billions of dollars from Western capitals were still flowing toward building Afghan institutions. And yet, despite that, the US state-building project in Afghanistan was proving to be a disaster in the making, with hardly anyone possessing the courage to admit it. American policymakers were either not reading the damning reports regularly produced by the Special Inspector General for Afghanistan Reconstruction (SIGAR), or had difficulty focusing given the seemingly unending nature of this war. Everyone was growing weary of Afghanistan, it seemed—everyone except the Taliban.

On Sunday, May 22, 2016, a day after the assassination, Mullah Mansour's associates hurriedly got together near Quetta to search for his replacement—but without success. The rival Taliban splinter group led by former Talban-era governor of Nimroz, Mullah Rasool closely watched the proceedings.[22] On the sidelines, US intelligence was also anxiously weighing up the prospect of Sirajuddin Haqqani as the new Emir.[23] It was too soon to expect such a move, even though the influence of Haqqanis within the Taliban movement was on the rise. It's no wonder that US intelligence assessments gauging the Taliban's motivations and momentum on the battlefield in Afghanistan were lacking, to put it mildly.

The Rise of Mullah Hibatullah Akhundzada—the Taliban's New Supreme Leader

Just a few days after Mullah Mansour's killing, a new Emir had been chosen. The role would go to none other than Mullah

Hibatullah Akhundzada, a 55-year-old highly reserved cleric hailing from the Taliban's spiritual heartland of Kandahar. Who would have guessed that five years later, he would be the supreme commander of the Taliban's new government in Afghanistan? Known for his hardline fatwas, he had also previously served as the deputy chief of Afghanistan's Supreme Court under the first Taliban government.[24] Earlier, he held judicial roles in many provincial and military courts, which made him eligible for such a senior position. For a movement that boasts of religion as its main identifier but is short of scholars well-versed in their proclaimed beliefs—those belonging to the Sunni-Hanafi-Deobandi sect—Hibatullah's knowledge of Islamic law/Sharia and theological background is a valuable qualification. Of course, the Taliban who wear beards and appropriately colored turbans, keeping their hands busy with rosary beads to play perfectly the part of faithful men, are a dime a dozen. Those who actually possess the ability to quote chapter and verse from scripture (even if we ignore their controversial interpretations) are fewer. In Taliban circles, Hibatullah is also known as "Shaykh al-Hadith," a title reserved for those with extensive knowledge of the sayings and actions of the Prophet of Islam. A tragic irony is this—whatever interpretation of hadith he subscribes to differs greatly from that of the majority of Muslims worldwide. Nevertheless, his prestige among the Taliban is thus understood in the context of his sought-after qualifications.

With this background, Hibatullah is admittedly a giant among the Taliban—his Kandahari roots would only add to his standing among them in years to come. His stature was further reinforced by the death of his 23-year-old son Abdur

Rahman—who carried out a suicide bombing at an Afghan military base in Helmand in July 2017—earning him even more respect among his peers.[25]

The Taliban's new top leader appears to be cut from the same cloth as Mullah Omar in every regard: rigid in his religious approach, calm in his demeanor, and with a palpable dislike for publicity and fanfare. He has a reputation as a strict disciplinarian, a trait that augmented his status as a principled leader. If there is any one thing required for such a personality cult to take root, it is most certainly a leader's no-nonsense aura. More so, this persona is only amplified through the mullah's physical appearance—he has a stern look and long grayish beard, aligning the inner man with the his outside appearance. Those who know Mullah Hibatullah firsthand say he does not like to be photographed and does not even know how to use a mobile phone.[26] If nothing else, he can hold on to at least some personal security in the age of electronic surveillance, where it seems impossible to do so! It is precisely these details that make these figures so interesting—they fit almost dangerously well into stereotypes. The nuances of their reality can be perplexing at times.

It appears that Mullah Hibatullah mostly resided near Quetta in Pakistan after the Taliban were dislodged from Kabul in November 2001, and remained a core part of the Quetta Shura.[27] Serving as a deputy to Mullah Mansour during the years 2013–16 kept him fully informed on the important organizational and command decisions pertaining to the insurgency in Afghanistan. But Hibatullah's heart is not in the battlefield—he acts more as a strategist when it comes to spearheading the Taliban campaign. Behind the scenes but ever so involved, he directs as the film plays out in front of him. Before emerging as the Emir, he spent years managing a small seminary near Quetta, preparing new cadres of Taliban leaders. This occupation allowed him to practice and stay in touch with his primary skill as a theologian, something he cherished. He is extreme in his religious worldview but open to dialogue and debate, even on issues where he has strong views.[28]

Maintaining direct control over the insurgency in Afghanistan while based near Quetta in Pakistan was increasingly difficult, especially during the last and crucial phase of the insurgency (roughly 2016–21). He thus granted greater autonomy to his military commanders in Afghanistan for the sake of efficiency, even though there was a risk that his command could be weakened as a result.[29] Still, he was fully informed of what was transpiring on the ground and would even travel inside Afghanistan, against all the odds, to consult with his commanders and issue instructions. In late 2017 he, along with some members of the Quetta Shura, visited Helmand to reassess Taliban strategy as they were facing stiff resistance from US and Afghan forces.[30] His cleverness showed through in his deep understanding of the realities on the ground that led him to revise the Taliban *modus operandi*: they began to target Afghan posts at night, avoiding direct combat with Afghan security forces, especially in Afghan government strongholds, and, importantly, increasing suicide attacks and assassination campaigns in cities.[31]

The suicide bombing phenomenon, a deadly weapon, had assumed a life of its own by now. Interestingly, this was never a part of the traditional Taliban toolkit as the first suicide bombing in Afghanistan was conducted only in 2003.[32] From there on it was incorporated in Taliban motivational materials, borrowing a great deal from Arab sources. Mullah Hibatullah had advised Mullah Omar as early as 2008 to adopt this dreadful tactic more widely.[33] A decade later he had to convince nobody, as he was the one calling the shots. This change of tactics surely worked in the Taliban's favor, adding to Hibatullah's reputation as a leader.

His choice of deputies had played an important role in his decision-making. Through them he had ensured that he would not be out of the loop on anything crucial. He retained Sirajuddin Haqqani, the most lethal and dominant military commander, as deputy to the office of the Emir, and invited Mullah Yaqoob (b. 1990), the 26-year-old son of Mullah Omar, to be his second deputy. Yaqoob had studied in Islamic seminaries in Pakistan's port city of Karachi and was also popular among the younger Taliban members. Being the son of Mullah Omar afforded him a constituency of his own. Hibatullah and Yaqoob had a good relationship, especially after Omar's death in 2013.

Mullah Yaqoob's time spent in Karachi added value to his credentials and influenced his leanings. Members of the Quetta Shura had started relocating from Quetta to Karachi in 2009–10 to avoid being targeted, and Mullah Omar himself was moved by the Pakistani intelligence to Karachi after he suffered a heart attack in 2011.[34] He remained hospitalized there, with Yaqoob acting as his loyal carer throughout the illness. In fact, it was Yaqoob who had dismissed rumors of Mullah Omar's unnatural death and had thereby come to prominence in Taliban circles. More recently, Yaqoob had a chance to serve as the acting leader of the Taliban when Hibatullah became infected with Covid-19 in May 2020.[35]

In another crucial development, Mullah Hibatullah added a third deputy to his team in 2018—it could be no one else but Mullah Baradar, who was released from a Pakistani prison in October 2018 after US pressure had mounted. The direct US–Taliban negotiations in Doha, Qatar, under the auspices of the Taliban Political Commission, was gaining momentum and Baradar's inclusion in the Taliban negotiating team added a lot of credibility to the process. Respecting the Taliban's preference, the US had asked Qatar to provide space for a Taliban political office in 2012, and since then over two dozen Taliban leaders had moved to Doha, along with their families.[36] It was inconceivable that this had happened without Mullah Omar's approval. In fact, it was his former personal secretary, Tayyab Agha, who was picked to lead the political office in Doha. Not only was Mullah Omar fully on board, he even tasked the Taliban team in Doha to report directly to him.[37] He had just one condition: a clear US commitment to withdraw its forces from Afghanistan. This issue was so fundamental to the Taliban that all his successors loyally followed this basic negotiating condition.

It is worth mentioning that, for many within Taliban circles, the Doha office was viewed with a certain amount of suspicion. Abdul Hai Mutma'in, a former advisor to Mullah Omar and Mullah Mansour, maintains in his book that Tayyab Agha had manipulated a conditional approval out of Mullah Omar and handpicked his own and Mullah Abdul Salam Zaeef's friends to join him in Doha. He also claimed that the Qatar initiative was basically sponsored by German and US intelligence.[38] Such perceptions created mistrust between Taliban field commanders and all those engaged by the Taliban Doha office for years.

Inside the Secret US–Taliban Negotiations in Doha (2018–21)

After many false starts and disruptions manufactured in Kabul and Islamabad, the direct US–Taliban negotiations finally kicked off during the Donald Trump presidency (2017–21). The Taliban's open letter addressed to the American people on February 14, 2018, conveying a readiness to enter direct peace talks with the United States (on the condition that the current regime in Kabul was excluded) was an invitation that was hard to ignore.[39] The carefully crafted 2,800-word letter quoting US and UN statistics about high casualties of US and NATO forces and rising heroin production also sounded a clear warning:

> If the policy of using force is continued for another one hundred years, the outcome will be the same . . . as you have observed over the last six months since the initiation of Trump's new strategy.[40]

The letter was a powerful combination of a few twisted facts, a touch of sarcasm and some straight talk. It taunted the US about how its resources amounting to "tens of billions of dollars" were being wasted on "thieves and murderers" in Kabul, provoking a Western official to put it quite bluntly:

"I hate to say it, but they [the Taliban] have started to hit where it hurts simply by telling the truth."[41] The timing of the letter was perfect as, after some initial dithering, Trump was now making it abundantly clear to all power centers in Washington DC that he was really serious about negotiating a deal with the Taliban. He was convinced that nothing else was working. He was not that far off the mark!

Washington was indeed finding itself in a bit of a quandary by 2018. The media as well as the think-tank community were now repeatedly asking: was the American plan working? Top officials, analysts and ordinary taxpayers alike debated whether the US policies set in place to rebuild Afghanistan and defeat the Taliban were effective and efficient at all. The truth nobody seemed ready to accept then was that for twenty years the US had been throwing money at the problem while many of the politicians and officials in Kabul tasked with managing that money were drowning themselves in corruption. Then there was denial about the fact that the very presence of NATO and the US was a potent factor inspiring the Taliban. For any reader of history, it was no secret that the only time Afghanistan was united was when they were kicking out foreigners. Whether it came down to *Pashtunwali* (Pushtun code of honor) and tribal ethos, or religious ideology, everything was rooted in a deep pride attached to an entrenched sense of honor and independence. If that meant hunger or underdevelopment sweeping the nation—as irrational as it may sound—anything could be sacrificed in its name. Nothing was indispensable. The truth is that it is an exploitative sense of honor, selective as well as self-serving, and the Taliban are a true reflection of this.

To give credit where it is due, even if solely based on his "America first" policy or economic concerns, Trump seemed not overawed by the Afghanistan challenge. He was neither ideologically focused on counterterrorism like Bush, nor hesitant like Obama—he did not hold back in pushing hard on the military. He was upfront and clear, telling them straight to their face that their strategy was not working and something needed to change drastically. His level of trust in US intelligence assessments of the Taliban was very low to begin with and the CIA, in particular, failed to impress him. Trump was simply not ready to blindly sign up to an endless commitment in Afghanistan.

President Trump had initially (2017–18) adopted an aggressive posture in Afghanistan allowing US military commanders to go on the offensive against the Taliban.[42] A harsher Pakistan policy was crafted in parallel, in an effort to compel it to stop supporting the Taliban. The Afghan Air Force received more combat helicopters as well as ammunition, and the number of air strikes targeting the Taliban (real or perceived) also increased many-fold, but in the midst of this the number of civilian casualties jumped as well.[43] The Taliban felt the heat but their support base remained intact. The Ghani government's poor governance offered little incentive to Taliban supporters to switch sides. The Taliban under Mullah Hibatullah, meanwhile, adapted quickly and decided to focus more on suicide bombings and targeted assassinations of government officials in towns and cities to disrupt official proceedings and instill a new wave of fear in Kabul.[44] The policy succeeded in creating more frustration in Kabul as well as in the White House. Nothing seemed to really work against the Taliban.

Ashraf Ghani, then President of Afghanistan, wanted to be more than a spectator in all of this and intelligently thought of offering the Taliban a ceasefire during Eid, the Muslim holiday, around mid-June 2018. Taliban IED (improvised explosive device) attacks on Afghan security forces, regularly ambushing government officials, and suicide attacks in and around Kabul, had unnerved the government. To everyone's surprise, Mullah Hibatullah reciprocated by directing his foot soldiers to avoid any confrontation with Kabul forces during the holidays (three days generally). What happened after that was unprecedented: ordinary people, police officials and Taliban all mingled happily, praying, eating and celebrating together at that time, without any fear or hesitation. The media understandably went berserk over it, with images of the Taliban flashing all across the newspaper headlines and television news broadcasts. The battle lines vanished into thin air, it seemed, and suddenly there was hope for a calmer future. Peace was possible after all.

The spontaneity of people coming together to engage with the Taliban, and the ease with which the Taliban communicated with all and sundry, including their opponents, was a good omen. This brought the Ghani government under pressure as it was not ready to compromise on its fundamental demands from the Taliban. Kabul wanted the Taliban to accept the new political and constitutional system in place and operate within it, while the Taliban were not ready to really talk peace while Americans were still stationed in Afghanistan. After the third day of the ceasefire, Taliban spokesperson Zabihullah Mujahid simply ignored Ghani's announcement of an extension of the ceasefire and categorically declared that, "Our fighters will now resume their operations across the country against the foreign invaders and their internal puppets," making their intentions pretty clear.[45] For the Taliban the ceasefire had achieved two goals: creating public goodwill across the country and, more strategically, establishing publicly in front of the US that the Taliban were a cohesive force and their leaders were in control. Washington was listening intently as Trump was impatiently looking for a pathway to a settlement—a deal that would save him $27 billion a year in military spending in Afghanistan.[46] He was even heard shouting at his White House staff, "Where is my deal?"[47]

Trump wasted no further time in appointing an envoy for peace talks. In September 2018, he appointed Zalmay Khalilzad, a well-known American with Afghan roots, to pursue a peace deal in his new role as the US Special Representative for Afghanistan Reconciliation. Known as Zal in Washington policy circles, he had a background in academia and the world of diplomacy and had earlier served as a negotiator of the Bonn agreement, the arrangement that created the "new" Afghanistan after the 9/11 attacks. He had remained deeply involved in crafting US policy toward Afghanistan since then, and even seriously contemplated running for the top office in Afghanistan. His ambition was palpable. Known as a tireless and energetic individual, he was ready for the job without a doubt.

Zal was handed a clear mandate and a free hand to cut a peace deal with the Taliban in a short span of nine months. America's romance with state-building in Afghanistan was coming to a shabby end. For those enjoying its fruits, it looked like a sudden and abrupt ending, but the reality is that two decades and tens of billions of dollars were consumed to pursue this dream. It was time to let it go. If done correctly, the impact of the investment would eventually show somehow. Still, this was a torturous route for those who had fought against the Taliban or contributed toward Afghanistan's rebuilding effort in any way. Despite initial skepticism and hurdles, Zal was lucky to receive support from all sides—diplomats, generals, spies as well as politicians. He was assisted by senior officials from the State Department, the Pentagon and the White House in the US negotiating team. Few, though, were completely in the picture as to how far he was ready—and empowered—to go.

Zal started shuttling between Doha, Kabul, Islamabad and Washington, in a whirlwind it seemed, trying to make everyone feel that they were part of the peace effort. Except for the governing regime in Kabul, everyone fell in line right away. Doha, the hub where the direct US–Taliban conversations were taking place, was the center of attention now. And the Taliban negotiating team also soon started earning frequent flyer points (mostly with Qatar Airways), but more slowly than Zal as their route was much shorter: on Doha–Islamabad return flights.[48] This was the safest way for the Taliban negotiators to receive guidance and directives from the Taliban Shura and Mullah Hibatullah. The American team was content with this because without the top Taliban leadership's involvement, there was no point to the whole exercise.

Yet, for the Americans, there were many assumptions and concerns at play about factionalism within the Taliban and a potential fragmentation that could complicate any settlement prospects.[49] The most crucial and sensitive question was whether all the field commanders in Afghanistan were loyal to Quetta- and Doha-based leaders. Taliban leaders in Quetta reportedly consulted a few commanders on the ground in Afghanistan about their response to a peace deal and, to their surprise, found that only half of them would accept such an outcome.[50] The remaining half wanted to continue to fight. So, the most critical question was not if a US–Taliban peace deal could be secured, but rather, whether Taliban leaders could sell such an agreement to their ranks.

In Doha, the conversations were not easy either. The Taliban were convinced that they were winning and Zal had little inclination to make them think otherwise. He was obviously wary that the US exit from Afghanistan should not look like a surrender and, to that end, he had a list of conditions. How hard he was willing to push for these, no one knew. The Taliban team on the other end was better prepared and more organized than anyone expected.

The profiles of the Taliban negotiation team are quite instructive, offering a peek into Taliban strategy for negotiations as well as its plans for the future of Afghanistan. This roughly 20-member team, all men unsurprisingly, was full of seasoned commanders with battlefield experience against the Soviets as well as the US-led coalition in Afghanistan.[51] In the initial phase, Sher Mohammad Abbas Stanikzai, a high-profile member of the Taliban's Doha political office, was picked to perform the role of an executive manager of the Taliban negotiation team and serve as the lead negotiator. With a Master's degree in political science and fluent in English, he was known more for his skills in diplomacy than on the battlefield. During the first Taliban government (1996–2001), he had served as deputy foreign minister and was often tasked with communicating with foreign visitors.[52] Interestingly, he was a graduate of the Indian Military Academy (IMA) in Dehradun in the 1980s.[53] This last qualification, though, was enough to make him a suspect in the eyes of Pakistan's intelligence services as they never trusted him fully even though he worked closely with them at times. For the US, he appeared sufficiently independent and that helped his credentials as a negotiator.

Many initial meetings between the two sides in late 2018 were consumed in debating the ground rules. The Taliban totally refused to accept any conditions about the future system of government in Afghanistan and insisted that it was for Afghans (meaning themselves) to decide while also making it categorically clear that it would be an "Islamic Emirate," whatever that meant. The US side soon realized that there was no point in getting bogged down in such conversations and they would be better off making it clear that for the US, terrorism threats emanating from Afghanistan were of paramount concern. Conversations became more meaningful from that point onward.[54]

The negotiations further warmed up toward the beginning of 2019. The US team was first to show flexibility, in fact radical flexibility. In the beginning, the US goals were: Taliban renunciation of Al-Qaeda, end of hostilities and political settlement in Afghanistan, and long-term presence of US intelligence assets and counterterrorism capacity inside

Afghanistan.[55] For the Taliban, complete US withdrawal was the core objective and they had every intention of enforcing their own model of government as soon as that happened. They kept the latter part of the objective very close to their heart and never made it obvious. Yet all those who never anticipated such a scenario were lacking in their understanding of the Taliban.

The Taliban kept on insisting on a quick and complete withdrawal of the US troops. Zal initially only agreed to a gradual withdrawal of troops from Afghanistan in return for a Taliban pledge that no international terrorist group would be allowed to operate from Afghanistan to launch attacks against the United States and its allies.[56] Pakistan was also pressured on the side to use all their influence on the Taliban to move quickly in this direction. Pakistan took their time as for them a Taliban-dominated Afghanistan meant the ouster of India from Afghanistan—their long-desired objective and fundamental motivation in supporting the Taliban from early on. Their policy was working well, so why would they be in a hurry? Zal worked hard to engage Pakistan closely and over time developed a good rapport with both military and civilian leaders in Pakistan. A senior Pakistani diplomat closely monitoring the Doha negotiations shared with me that while the US team indeed kept Pakistan in the loop about the major sticking points during the closed-doors conversations, Pakistan was separately getting regular and fuller briefs from their sources among the Taliban participating in the parleys.[57] It helped Pakistan strategize well.

In January 2019, something happened that was unexpected: US Secretary of State Michael Pompeo gave a surprising go-ahead to Zal "to negotiate a withdrawal of US forces to zero with the Taliban," postponing also any "Kabul-led" negotiations, as well as giving up any long-term presence of intelligence and counterterrorism forces inside Afghanistan.[58] It was Trump dictating this course, without a doubt. This was huge as it would not only fulfill the Taliban's prime demands but also reduce US leverage to impose any conditions necessary. It was, as well, a grudging acknowledgment that the US project in Afghanistan was over. Perhaps, Zal was supposed to offer these to Taliban gradually. To give him his due, Zal did ask for a peace settlement with Kabul and ceasefire but Abbas Stanikzai rejected those outright, as before. There was jubilation in the Taliban camp when Stanikzai shared the news that the US was basically ready to withdraw completely.

The Taliban read the US motives well and within days offered the US something they were looking for: "an offer to renounce external terrorism and implement any enforcement mechanisms that the US desired."[59] This was no small commitment but it was based on the clear assumption that the Taliban would be the new sheriff in town. Those holding power in Kabul were soon to become powerless—and to the US it did not really matter anymore. Washington had finally run out of patience with those at the helm of affairs in Kabul.

The signing of a deal was still some time away while Kabul was anxiously hoping to be invited to join the conversations in Doha. The Taliban, however, were unwilling to engage directly with Kabul until they reached an understanding with the US. This was a Taliban precondition and the US had agreed to it in July 2018.[60] In this process, the Taliban had gained a lot of political mileage from the recognition they were receiving as a sole negotiating partner with the US. They desperately needed such legitimacy and, to their good fortune, it was handed to them on a silver platter. While the Taliban tentatively agreed to engage with the government in Kabul, which they always referred to as illegitimate, for future power-sharing conversations, they cleverly delayed it to a point where Kabul's leverage was significantly reduced.

The year 2019 was crucial for negotiations as things were moving at a fast pace, too fast for Kabul's comfort, but both the US and Taliban now could see light at the end of the tunnel. The Taliban negotiating team now had the added advantage of being spearheaded by soft-spoken Mullah Baradar, who was long convinced that a negotiated settlement was the only way forward. His rational and reconciliatory approach, while sticking to core Taliban demands, elevated the level of discourse on the negotiating table. The US team was now more confident that the Taliban team they were negotiating with was truly representative of the influential elements within the Taliban ranks. This was important given the concerns about Taliban cohesion. Baradar was both highly respected among the Taliban rank and file and seen as someone who was quite independent of Pakistan.

The Taliban negotiating team had gone through a few expansion phases to raise its stature and credibility. The most interesting was the addition of five former Guantanamo prisoners who, in 2014, were exchanged for Sgt. Bowe Bergdahl, the American service member held by the Taliban as a prisoner of war. These included former top army commander Mullah Fazel Mazloom, accused of mass killings; former

Balkh commander Noorullah Noori; former governor and interior minister Mullah Khairullah Khairkhwa, accused of drug trafficking and association with Al-Qaeda; Abdul Haq Wasiq, former Taliban deputy minister of intelligence; and Mohammad Nabi Omari, accused of Al-Qaeda links and later of joining the Hamid Karzai government to spy for the Taliban.[61] Some of the charges are reported to be exaggerated accounts but the fact remains that these men survived very tough conditions at Guantanamo for over 12–14 years and were naturally bitter about it. Another prominent addition was the Quetta Shura's chief of staff Amir Khan Mottaqi, adding another layer of credibility for the ordinary Taliban who were following the negotiation news closely.

Now they were all sitting face to face with the American generals, diplomats and intelligence personnel. If there was ever a meeting to witness, it was this one in Doha in mid-March 2019. The Taliban seated at the table were not what most would expect them to be—some were the former Guantanamo inmates introduced above, some former prisoners in Pakistani jails, and among them were those who were moderate in their thinking, and flexible—and had earned the chance to be at the table with the US. Not only that, but some of them were notably communicative—ready to discuss ideas.

Sitting across the table from them was General Austin S. Miller, the commander of the American and NATO forces in Afghanistan, who at one point during the conversations told the Taliban that he respected them as fighters and further surprised everyone by saying: "We could keep fighting, killing each other, or, together, we could kill ISIS."[62] This was a major shift quite hard for many observers to immediately absorb and decipher, but nonetheless a sign of hope for a peace deal. Seeing Baradar and Zal joking with each other, too, helped ease the atmosphere in the room.[63] By mid-2019, with both sides having gone through seven rounds of negotiations, major differences had already been resolved, but suddenly it seemed that the Taliban had started to retract on some crucial points. For instance, the Taliban narrative on Al-Qaeda started changing; becoming more defensive and even trying to deny that the terrorist organization was responsible for the 9/11 attacks. When the US team pushed back hard, they grudgingly again committed to ensure that Al-Qaeda would not be allowed to misuse Afghan soil for staging terrorist operations against the US and its allies, but now they began to backslide on pursuing a settlement with Ghani and Kabul.

I had a chance to speak to an individual present in the meeting hall during a segment of the negotiations. He said he first walked into the room without a good understanding of who the Taliban were—with a perception of them as aggressive warriors unable to string a sentence together. He was totally surprised to observe their discipline: none of them contradicted or interrupted each other, they were clear and concise, respectful of each other's views, and they stated their arguments eloquently.[64]

In Kabul, Ghani was not in the full picture as to the scale and even the developing scope of conversations in Doha. He was increasingly out of touch with reality, having surrounded himself with an incompetent coterie of confidants. He had utterly failed to unite the country and to work together with like-minded political players as he abhorred sharing power.

His poor choice of military and police leaders was another serious problem, and even though he opted to institute reforms in 2017–18, planning a gradual retirement of over 5,000 over-age and unqualified senior military officers, it was too late to rescue the collapsing security institutions.[65] Nepotism and total disregard for merit had ruined the Afghan security infrastructure.[66] Furthermore, Ghani disagreed in principle with Zal's approach of direct US–Taliban negotiations. Earlier in February 2018, Ghani had offered unconditional direct talks to the Taliban, even agreeing to recognize them as a political party, but the Taliban categorically refused, as they viewed the government in Kabul as illegitimate and the country as being under occupation.[67] Zal was now giving up on Ghani and, by extension, on the government in Kabul.

What made the negotiations and ultimately the settlement so fascinating was the variety of elements that were driving this process: dramatic personality clashes, policy U-turns, hard bargaining and surprising meetings of minds, such as between Zal and Baradar, that were all essential pieces of this huge puzzle. Early on, this became not just a negotiation to end a war, but a desperate attempt to satisfy people's egos—if anything, it was that more than all else. The war was ending just as it had begun—as a struggle littered with attempts to find the right allies, over-indulgence in the use of force, and ignorance about the Afghan way of war. Hotel rooms and group chats filled with the weight of disagreements served as the backdrop to what was meant to be a genuine attempt at searching for a reasonable compromise. But if history has taught us anything, it is that this is the nature of politics—an all-out contest for power.

Countless times, history books have detailed fascinating instances where personal relationships and all their twisted dynamics have had the power to influence international politics. The story of how America's longest war finally ended proves to be no exception.

It was no secret that Zal Khalilzad and Ashraf Ghani did not get along well with each other. However, this deal was not the first time they had worked together—or apart, rather. In fact, the two had known each other for over fifty years before meeting again for these conversations. As per his job description, Zal had been keeping President Ghani in the loop, but the extent of the information he actually conveyed was declining significantly over time. It was at this juncture that Ghani made his fatal misstep, naively believing it impossible that the US would actually completely withdraw from Afghanistan in the foreseeable future. As long as the US had a presence in Afghanistan, Ghani believed, he remained relevant. Zal, on the other hand, let him stay in his bubble while meeting with just about everyone else to make sure America got out as soon as possible.

Ghani and Zal had first met around 1965 or so, as exchange program students in the United States, later crossing paths again at the American University in Beirut, one of the finest universities in the Middle East.[68] With a crisis brewing in Afghanistan in the late 1970s, they both eventually immigrated to the United States. Their paths diverged, but only briefly: Zal proceeded to the University of Chicago for his doctorate as Ghani landed at Columbia University for his (studying cultural anthropology). Later on, Zal found his way to Columbia University as well, as an assistant professor. Both had a feeling, as the years went on, that their pattern of coincidental meetings would not end any time soon—and though they were right, surely neither could predict just how catastrophic a turn it would take.

Despite their obvious similarities in background and interests in scholarship, the two could not be more different. Ghani was socialist-oriented while Zal was capitalist, Ghani was an introvert while Zal was an extrovert, Ghani was a bit rigid while Zal was flexible and ready to find a middle path when faced with a daunting challenge. In a story brilliantly detailing this old relationship, *The New York Times*'s Mujib Mashal says that there always was a "fundamental clash in how they operate."[69] It seems that dynamic has carried on over the decades, as we know now that the two of them had dramatically different approaches to the crisis facing their country. Ghani wanted to lead negotiations with the Taliban, while Zal pursued a more direct understanding between the US and the Taliban. Of course, both believed themselves to have the winning approach.

Zal, to be fair to him, had truly managed to make the idea of negotiating with Taliban work—he was likely the best choice to be in that role. While some place blame on him for giving in to Taliban demands, it is not likely the Taliban would have gone that far in negotiations with any other American. After all, he did not look like the enemy they had been so accustomed to—he looked like them.

While the US and Taliban teams were still talking and arguing, arrangements were made to kick-start the Kabul–Taliban track of negotiations, dubbed then the "intra-Afghan conference," to be held in Norway. The time had come for what was deemed a crucial and difficult part of the whole engagement. With their eyes firmly set on the formal deal with the US, knowing that was what mattered the most, the Taliban began parleys with Afghan civil society representatives quite informally and a bit half-heartedly in Doha, as a prelude, setting the stage for more formal conversations with the Ghani government later. With no schooling in diplomacy or negotiation skills, the Taliban's steps were shrewdly planned throughout.

In one such informal conversation in July 2019 between Taliban negotiators and a private group of over forty Afghans, including women representing various sectors, some unprecedented scenes were witnessed.[70] A few Afghan officials had also joined this dialogue. During the proceedings, a female participant learned about a terrorist attack on a school in Ghazni that injured two of her young orphan nephews (aged 7 and 8), who had recently moved with their grandmother to the area to be far away from the violence that had taken the life of their father. She had helped them go to this school targeted by the Taliban. She was naturally devastated and while sharing the sad news with the group, with tears flowing on her cheeks, she bluntly asked the Taliban: "Why are you killing us?" To her total surprise she saw many of her Taliban negotiators were also saddened. They had children too! At the end of this dialogue, the Taliban negotiators agreed to include in the joint public statement, a clear commitment to reducing civilian casualties to zero. These confidence-building steps were helpful for both sides and Zal became further convinced that the Taliban would ultimately enter meaningful negotiations with the government in Kabul. It seemed like a reasonable expectation at the time.

By September 2019, a draft accord was ready and things looked so positive that President Trump had ordered arrangements to be made at Camp David for a deal-signing with the Taliban and all the attendant media fanfare.[71] Ghani too was supposed to attend. Neither the Taliban nor Ghani were amused, but it was members of the US Congress who created an uproar, leading to the demise of the idea. The understanding had indeed reached an advanced stage but the moment for it to be signed and announced had not yet arrived. Some details of the draft agreement were leaked indicating that the US withdrawal would be completed in a year and a half—by March or April 2021. Both sides were still uncomfortable with making a few elements of the proposed deal public.

For the US, the details of the Taliban guarantees of safe passage for departing US forces were a sensitive topic. Further, the Taliban believed that the extent of the agreed upon US–Taliban cooperation in fighting their common enemy—the Islamic State in Khorasan (ISK), an affiliate of the Islamic State of Iraq and Syria (ISIS) that had emerged in Afghanistan since 2015—could be devastating for their public image. Such commitments and pronouncements had to stay confidential, whether on paper or not. Even without exposing the secret aspects, the news that trickled into the media led to some political backlash in the US. The strongest statement perhaps came from Senator Lindsey Graham and General (retired) Jack Keane, who both argued in a *Washington Post* opinion piece that the US must not outsource its security to the Taliban, while further warning that, "If we abandon

Afghanistan out of frustration and weariness, we pave the way for another 9/11."[72]

With all the intricacies involved and hurdles erected, things slowed down a bit. One real complicating factor was how the Taliban were simultaneously talking peace and killing people in Afghanistan. This was either a part of a choreographed strategy to increase leverage on the table by showing strength on the battlefield, or an indication that Taliban negotiators were not fully in control of the field commanders who were calling the shots on the ground. While this doubt lingered in the minds of the American team, the Taliban only gained more space—territorially as well as on the negotiation table in Doha. The truth, often ignored in Western analysis, is that the Taliban field commanders were partly reacting to the rising number of military operations, including airstrikes conducted by the Afghan and US forces, targeting Taliban strongholds. Controversial night raids spearheaded by CIA-sponsored Afghan groups that operated independently of both the Afghan and US militaries likely caused more public anger than disruption to Taliban activities.[73]

A new and complicating dimension of the crisis meanwhile manifested itself through ISK's deadly suicide bombings. At times it was hard to figure out who was behind the violence in certain cases, and to what end. Ordinary Afghans had lost count of the dead and had little idea who was doing what, basically losing the capacity to distinguish between a friend and a foe. The pain they were feeling was deep and seemed endless. All of this was also having a deep psychological impact, sure to show itself in the times to come in ways no one could predict.

Another factor—perhaps a decisive factor in determining the pace of negotiations—scarcely known about at the time to people outside the top layers of the US government—was Trump's nine-month ultimatum given to his top aides in July 2019 to pull out all US forces from Afghanistan.[74] The message conveyed through Secretary Pompeo to Zal was loud and clear. He knew that he had a limited time span as Trump's timetable was obviously linked to the fast-approaching presidential elections in November 2020. With no prospects of an Iran deal despite "maximum pressure" and the assassination of Iran's ace military strategist Qasim Solemani, and nothing to show for the North Korea nuclear gambit except the weird photoshoot with the North Korean leader Kim Jung-un, Trump needed something to shore up his dealmaker image. Here luck was on the side of the Taliban.

Even with some ups and downs due to Trump's mood swings and political compulsions, the major issues stood resolved, and only the exact timeline for US withdrawal and ceasefire details were pending. The fact that Trump was in a hurry was no secret and the Taliban were well prepared to use this information to the full. Agreeing to a ceasefire, as logical as it may sound as a part of this peace deal, was not something the Taliban were ready to commit to. Their reluctance even led to halting the negotiations (from September to December 2019), and even then all they offered was a temporary reduction in violence after the deal was announced. With regard to the Taliban reasoning behind their reluctance to halt attacks, a Taliban negotiator insightfully told Carter Malkasian:

We need the United States to announce a withdrawal in order to prove to our fighters that jihad has been won. Otherwise what was sacrifice for? We are very worried that fighters will go to Daesh or other groups.[75]

The US team was understanding, for want of a better word, as it decided to resume the negotiations in December 2019, and that surely helped the Taliban negotiators led by Baradar, allowing him to impress upon the Quetta Shura and Mullah Hibatullah (at Taliban headquarters) that the Taliban must show some flexibility on this point. They did, offering a week-long reduction in the violence before the signing of the deal. By early February 2020, things had started to look very promising for the peace deal to be finalized within weeks. Both sides wrestled with the idea of a week-long reduction in violence either before or after the signing of the deal. On a positive note, there was a significant decline in violence when the time came to implement the agreement, establishing that the Taliban were a cohesive force capable of delivering what they committed to.

The Hibatullah–Baradar dynamic remains a largely unknown part of internal Taliban politics. Both have tremendous respect for each other but their paths had diverged after 2001, impacting their worldviews. Hibatullah grew more conservative while enjoying some freedom in Pakistan to do so, whereas Baradar lived through tougher environments in Pakistani custody while his health deteriorated due to suffering from diabetes. Baradar spent his time thinking and rethinking while Hibatullah was either strategizing about upping the level of violence in Afghanistan or reading.

His choice of books, given his clerical background, was not expected to help him think outside the box. All the more so as Hibatullah had to keep the conservative elements of the movement happy (since they were the ideological backbone of the movement) while also juggling with management of the field commanders. Baradar, with incarceration experience and broader exposure, had become more pragmatic and he was more of a politician, adept at making compromises to make things work. Baradar's "patience and willingness to champion peace" indeed had a positive influence on thinking in the Taliban camp.[76] At the end of the day, Hibatullah and Baradar made a great team for the Taliban. Zal shared with an interviewer that while Baradar was easy to talk to and seemingly flexible on minor issues, he would always ask for time to seek guidance from Hibatullah and Co. whenever a critical matter came up.[77]

Sensing victory, Taliban deputy leader Sirajuddin Haqqani penned an opinion piece that—of all places—found space on the editorial page of *The New York Times* on February 20, 2020. He was a "specially designated international terrorist," according to the FBI, with the US Department of State offering a reward of up to $10 million for information that would bring him to justice. While aptly arguing that, "Everyone is tired of War" and "that the killing and the maiming must stop," he hinted at Taliban readiness for making the compromises necessary to develop a consensus on the form of future government in Afghanistan. The deliberate choice of words, such as making a commitment "to working with other parties in a consultative manner of genuine respect to agree on a new, inclusive political system in which the voice of every Afghan is reflected and where no Afghan feels excluded," clearly sounded democracy-leaning to those who had no clue about Taliban ideology. References to a "right to work" and a "right to education" for women sounded equally empowering. Separately in Doha negotiations, Taliban leader Shahabuddin Delavar had provided categorical assurances about permission for women's education and work. Kabul was stunned; but they were now yesterday's men.

On February 29, 2020, the US and the Taliban finally signed the landmark "Agreement for Bringing Peace to Afghanistan" in the Sheraton Hotel, Doha, with dozens of diplomats from across the world in attendance. The US Secretary of State Mike Pompeo looked on while Zal and Baradar inked the deal. In the words of Carter Malkasian, Trump "heedlessly" pressed "for withdrawal instead of giving Khalilzad [Zal] the time to wring more out of Taliban."[78] The very first paragraph of the agreement maintained that the comprehensive peace agreement offers "Guarantees and enforcement mechanisms that will prevent the use of the soil of Afghanistan by any group or individual against the security of the United States and its allies."[79] This was the most critical American concern. By May 2021, all US combat troops would leave Afghanistan if the Taliban repudiated Al-Qaeda and other terrorist groups, entered negotiations with Kabul, and endeavored to reduce violence. The Taliban, for their part, committed not to attack US and NATO troops. With foresight, no such commitment was given about the Afghan security forces as that was left to be negotiated in the intra-Afghan conference.

The agreement had a handful of secret provisions as well. One of these barred the US forces from supporting or enabling Afghan troops in their targeted operations against the Taliban.[80] This could easily be termed as treacherous by Afghan forces, but for America safety of its personnel came first. Understandably so. The biggest prize for the Taliban though, after the withdrawal commitment, was the provision to release up to 5,000 of its prisoners languishing in Afghan prisons. Some of the most dangerous Taliban prisoners, those found to be involved in terrorist activity, were kept at the US's Bagram base—and there was nothing in the deal that would make them ineligible to benefit from this provision. The Taliban, too, were bound to release 1,000 Afghan security personnel they held in captivity.

The End

The truth is often hard to acknowledge, but the reality is that the Taliban outlasted the Americans. State-building takes time and the US invested tens of billions of dollars, but the Taliban's cost-effective measures to instill fear and disrupt development projects worked well for their goals. After the deal, ordinary Afghans started to prepare for the inevitable as it was obvious to them that the Taliban would be unstoppable now. With the US and international forces out of the picture, Kabul was unlikely to hold its ground. The Taliban strategy now was to impress upon the people of Afghanistan that submitting to their authority at this stage was in everyone's best interest. This was how the tide started turning—quietly and gradually, no village untouched. What helped the Taliban clinch the peace deal was precisely the same widely held belief that Afghans were exhausted after the war and ready to settle. Littered with the toxic remnants of war and tragedy, the Afghan soil needed new energy and vitality to revive itself. Whether Afghans could come together to offer hope in this unpromising scenario was yet to be seen.

The million-dollar question remained as to whether there could be a meaningful dialogue between the Taliban and the government in Kabul. Ghani was in no mood to negotiate with the Taliban and things stalled immediately due to differences over prisoner releases. There was little follow-up, as Ghani wanted peace on his terms only. His ignorance of the Taliban's rapid ascendance would put a nail in his own coffin. Kabul and Ghani were losing legitimacy due to these delays.

A date around mid-September 2020 was picked for the intra-Afghan dialogue to finally commence but in a surprising move, the Taliban announced a major shake-up in their negotiation team on September 5, 2020. Abdul Hakim Ishaqzai, a conservative senior cleric originally from Kandahar known to have the ear of Mullah Hibatullah, was the new chief negotiator, replacing Sher Abbas Stanikzai. Baradar, being head of the Doha political office, remained the overall leader of the Taliban negotiating team. Like Hibatullah, Abdul Hakim was running a madrassa, an Islamic seminary, near Quetta (named Darul Uloom Shariah in Kuchlak area) and served as a Taliban judge besides leading an influential council of clerics responsible for issuing religious edicts—fatwas—on important matters.[81] His seminary was targeted by an ISK suicide bomber on January 19, 2020, in which he lost his son and many students.[82] Importantly, he was also a graduate of the Darul Uloom Haqqania in Pakistan, a training ground for Taliban leaders. The Taliban were now ready to play hardball with Ghani and his team.

Zal wanted to usher the Taliban and Kabul toward finding an amicable power-sharing arrangement, but time was running out. The reality was that the Taliban and Kabul had been at each other's throats for too long, mercilessly killing each other. Neither side was going to forget that. Afghanistan needed a reconciliation commission on the lines of that which had helped heal the wounds in South Africa after apartheid was ended. And yet, no leader on either side had legendary Nelson Mandela's stature to make that work in Afghanistan.

Ghani had serious trouble accepting that the US and its allies were withdrawing their respective forces. He was basically completely deluded, and even asked his friends in DC to inquire if the US really was leaving, to which multiple US officials responded "Yes!" The US expectation was that the Taliban and Ghani would agree to a settlement for a neutral interim government with representatives of both sides, who would help the two sides find common ground. According to Zal, Ghani "hated that, because it means that he has to go."[83] The plan went awry.

The Taliban were now strategically surrounding provincial capitals and major city centers. Taliban spies, having penetrated deep into Afghan government bureaucracy, were providing vital information to Taliban leaders. All of this was transpiring while US forces were packing up in Afghanistan. The Taliban were creating no trouble, as promised. The coronavirus crisis had also taken its toll in the meantime and priorities everywhere were changing; around the world the domestic health emergency was the first thing states were concerned about. Work on international relations was put on the backburner.

On April 14, 2021 President Biden, three months after assuming office, announced that all US troops would be out of Afghanistan by September 11 the same year. For all practical purposes, he had inherited this policy direction from Trump—but it was his administration that would be held responsible for the planning and implementation of the withdrawal. The choice of September 11 was symbolic, implying that the American response to the terrorism attack that traumatized America two decades earlier was complete and over. In DC policy circles, Afghanistan was now seen as a "lost cause," and the longest war in American history was indeed coming to an unceremonious end as the Taliban were knocking at the gates of Kabul. On July 8, 2021, President Biden while making remarks on his decision to draw down forces in Afghanistan, all but confessed:

After 20 years—a trillion dollars spent training and equipping hundreds of thousands of Afghan National Security and Defense Forces, 2,448 Americans killed, 20,722 more wounded, and untold thousands coming home with unseen trauma to their mental health—I will not send another generation of Americans to war in Afghanistan with no reasonable expectation of achieving a different outcome.[84]

Biden had made up his mind to exit Afghanistan. Even as Obama's vice president earlier, he was known to be skeptical of what the US could accomplish in Afghanistan, and during internal White House deliberations he even "urged Obama to reject the expensive counterinsurgency strategy that expanded the war."[85] He was consistently pessimistic about the prospects for a stable Afghanistan and, public pronouncements aside, he was not hopeful that Ghani could pull it all together. During a press conference in January 2022, he defended his decision to withdraw, arguing that Afghanistan has been, "the graveyard of empires for a solid reason: It is not susceptible to unity . . ."[86]

The truth is that America was exhausted and Kabul was crumbling at the mere thought of facing the Taliban on its own. America's Afghan favorites, Ashraf Ghani being a chief example, had suddenly started looking too weak to stand on their own feet. Corruption and nepotism had eaten into the vitals of the Afghan state. With no prioritizing of institution-building, weak rule of law and reliance on war lords and drug dealers, things could not have ended differently. The new edifice of an overcentralized and unaccountable Afghan state was unsustainable. All of this had transpired on the US watch while (along with other international donors) it was paying for almost 80 percent of the Afghan national budget.

There had once been a time the US swore to never give up the Bagram base—it provided a secure footing in Afghanistan to maintain counterterrorism capacity, and also enabled the US to keep an eye on the Chinese. But eventually, even that idea was abandoned. To its discredit, the Biden administration had planned its withdrawal in the least efficient manner possible. American media was less charitable in its assessment of how things turned out. Renowned journalist Peter Bergen maintains:

> Compounding Biden's disastrous policy decision to completely pull out of Afghanistan was the botched handling of the withdrawal. . . . Biden patted himself on the back that the US military subsequently extracted 124,000 Afghans from Afghanistan, calling the operation an "extraordinary success," which was like an arsonist praising himself for helping to try to put out a fire that he had started.[87]

The future of the Taliban was yet to unravel, but Ghani took too long to realize that it was all over for him. What the Taliban had done to the Soviet-backed President Najibullah in 1996 after taking over Kabul was hard to forget. Najibullah was brutally killed and his body hanged from a traffic light post outside the presidential palace in Kabul. As described in the introduction, Ghani and his associates decided to flee to avoid a similar fate, and his government in Kabul, by now confined to the presidential palace and its immediate surroundings, simply fell like a house of cards. According to an insider, there was another option for Ghani as well. A plane was ready to take him and Abdullah to Qatar, leaving power in the hands of some of his ministers with whom the Taliban were ready to negotiate for an inclusive interim government. That could have created a different future but Ghani's insecurities led him to sabotage it instead.

2

From Insurgency to Governance

Who's Who in Afghanistan Today?

After two decades of waging a brutal insurgency, the Taliban triumphantly entered Kabul on August 15, 2021 unhindered and uninterrupted. With the presidential office of Afghanistan deserted, and cabinet members nowhere to be found, the Taliban literally drove into government buildings and facilities, mostly on their motorcycles, without a shot being fired. Initially, they were waiting at the entrance points to major cities trying to live up to their commitment at Doha that they would give intra-Afghan dialogue a real chance. Even on the eve of the fall of Kabul, a Taliban spokesman tweeted, "The Islamic Emirate instructs all its forces to stand at the gates of Kabul, not to try to enter the city."[1]

This was an iconic moment and a massive milestone, not only for the Taliban but also many Islamic militant movements across the world who would draw inspiration from it in times to come. For most Afghans, this was unimaginable, even a few months before this fateful day. They were not alone in this view. Even the US intelligence wildly underestimated the speed of the Taliban advance and, as late as mid-July 2021, they assessed the risk of an imminent Taliban takeover of Kabul as low.[2] By then, the Taliban were slowly but surely negotiating their way toward Kabul, cutting deals, resurrecting tribal alliances, and instilling terror where necessary. The unexpected, unwanted and undeniable was now a harsh reality staring everyone in the face.

The disoriented government in Kabul collapsed on live television with the world's eyes on them, as state institutions crumbled one after the other, triggering fear and chaos. A significant majority of provincial headquarters across Afghanistan had either surrendered to the Taliban or were fighting losing battles defending their territories. Important city and regional centers—including Kandahar, Herat, Kunduz and Mazar-e-Sharif—were already under the Taliban's control when they made a move into Kabul. It was a scene from a horror film—the suspense and anticipation was unbearable.

US President Joe Biden's call to Afghan leaders on August 10 to unite and "fight for their nation" had predictably fallen on deaf ears.[3] It was too late and the Biden administration knew that. For the Taliban to pull this off was no ordinary victory—it was utterly remarkable, in a way almost unbelievable. They had after all confronted a resourceful Kabul backed by a powerful international military coalition led by the United States for years on end. Now, with the US military withdrawal in its very final days, Taliban ascendance was all but guaranteed. Still, the rapid nationwide Taliban military advance was as stunning as it was surprising for global observers. The news of Taliban successes on the military front across the country was no secret, but hardly anyone projected the precipitous fall of Kabul to the Taliban. In the Taliban camp, there was relief all around—and belief in their holy cause was only strengthening.

It is beyond doubt that Kabul was unprepared for this sudden and dramatic change. The Ghani government was failing and struggling at many levels, but with Taliban in the driving seat, the idea of a democratic and modern Afghanistan, women working side by side with men, and young girls walking to schools, all now seemed like a dream—a tarnished dream. The world was watching their television screens in shock as the Taliban moved into the presidential palace, racing through the streets of the Green Zone, which housed heavily fortified embassies and offices of international organizations, without facing any resistance. Many of these buildings had been hurriedly evacuated in recent days, some hardly hours before. Afghan military and police—trained and equipped, and with tens of millions of dollars spent on their upkeep—were conspicuous by their absence, with not even a shot fired by them in the air, even out of anger. The silence was deafening.

Many security personnel had in fact changed into civilian clothes well ahead of the Taliban's march into the city and had either fled or were rushing to the airport in the hope of being evacuated by the US or one of its NATO allies. Meanwhile, Taliban fighters, with guns slung over their shoulders, wasted no time taking over checkpoints across Kabul. That is one thing they had proved to be really good at over the years. They had mastered the art of installing roadblocks and establishing checkpoints along major highways and rural roadways, extorting millions of dollars a month from truckers and travelers.[4] That skill was at work now establishing the writ of the government—the Taliban government.

Many Afghans, feeling helpless and frustrated, meanwhile switched sides, a sight not too uncommon in the country's history. Desperate times call for desperate measures indeed, and those measures only spoke to the intensity of the situation and the fear in people's hearts. For some, however, such desperate measures would mean a tragic betrayal. In fact, they first felt betrayal not only on the part of their political leaders but also the country's Western sponsors, who were seen as having cut a deal with the Taliban behind Kabul's back. When the news arrived that President Ashraf Ghani had shamelessly fled the country on the eve of the Taliban's imminent takeover of Kabul, the sense of being left in the lurch became more stinging. For all those who were still entertaining any hopes that Afghanistan could be saved, disappointment was all that awaited them. Ghani made a mockery of his repeated claims that he would stand with the Afghan people till the very end. He was not alone, though, in his fall from grace. He was accompanied in this dishonorable journey by many other Afghan leaders across ethnic and political divides. They had sufficient time to strategize a defense of the capital city Kabul at least, or could have put up a decent fight to stand for what they always declared to be worth fighting for. Former Afghan President Hamid Karzai and chief executive Abdullah Abdullah, though, proved to be honorable exceptions to the rule.

The plight of ordinary Afghans was the most tragic of all, as they fearfully locked themselves in their homes, not knowing what fate awaited them. It seemed the world was against them, and with their leader having fled, they felt nothing less than completely abandoned. They had no one to look up to, no one to help them, their only company was the most dreaded reality of uncertainty. As rumors of foreign evacuations spread like wildfire, thousands rushed toward Kabul airport with whatever little they could carry to flee the country.[5] The desperation of the scene was nothing less than heartbreaking. Others ran toward banks to withdraw cash—it was a scene of confusion and chaos. If there is one image that truly depicted the unraveling tragedy, it was the haunting photographs posted on social media of people clinging to a departing plane, tragically falling to their deaths after its take-off.[6] It was one of those moments in history—where it was as if time had stopped.

The Taliban had made best use of their time since the 2020 deal to strategically lay the groundwork for deals with tribes to choke Kabul. All their energies were directed at over-whelming the machinery of the Ghani government, which had lost the will to fight. As fractious and indecisive as they were, the political elite in Kabul were expected to rise to the challenge for their own survival if nothing else, but that was not to be. Marvin Weinbaum, a seasoned American scholar of South Asia, in a conversation with me insightfully projected that, "the Taliban, it should be understood, has come to the table not to argue about differences but to try to wear down the government side into conceding to its demands."[7]

The hard truth is that Afghan security forces had been severely demoralized since the 2020 Doha agreement, leading to defections that only boosted the Taliban drive to power. The US-trained Afghan military, hugely dependent on foreign contractors and air support, were now disheartened as well as clueless with that back-up missing. For many of them, it was now a choice between surrender or certain death. So they opted to live, which also meant that the Taliban could now lay their hands on Western military equipment and weapons. Corruption too had destroyed the capacity of the Afghan security forces, both military and police. Ghani's support base (which was not very large to begin with) was shrinking day by day. There were many additional contributing factors. It is hard to understand, for instance, the US decision to schedule the last phase of their forces' withdrawal in summer, when the Taliban are super-active and mobile, unlike in winter when harsh weather dampens their capacity to operate freely. The only positive news of sorts, under the circumstances, was that during the Taliban capture of the important cities of Herat, Kandahar and Mazar-e-Sharif in the first half of August, there were no reports of large-scale violence, massacres, or executions of captured Afghan officials. Taliban foot soldiers were not rampaging through these cities and were visibly operating in an organized, and somewhat careful, manner. Though far from offering a sense of relief to Kabul, the Taliban wanted to avoid chaos and panic, it seemed. On the morning of August 15, a Taliban spokesperson even had posted a statement online saying:

Because Kabul is a big city with a large population, the mujahedeen of the Islamic Emirate do not intend to enter by force, and negotiations are underway with the other side for a peaceful transfer of power.[8]

By evening, Taliban forces were sitting in the presidential palace in Kabul and their pictures and media briefing were on television screens across the world. Mullah Baradar, though jubilant, sounded as surprised as anyone else when he exclaimed in a video statement that, "the victory, which saw all of the country's major cities fall in a week, was unexpectedly swift and had no match in the world," while acknowledging that "the real test would begin now."[9] He had little idea at that moment about a personal test he was about to face. After leading the negotiations with the US to success with remarkable dexterity and precision, he was about to lose his influence within the Taliban at the hands of his jealous rivals.

With the US embassy nearly empty and all efforts geared toward evacuation of embassies and other staff of Western organizations, hapless Afghans were now getting ready for uncertain times. The only sure thing now was that Taliban momentum was unstoppable.

Inside Kabul: The Taliban Assumption of Power

With no Afghan security forces or US military back-up units to defend Kabul, two leading Taliban figures—Sirajuddin Haqqani, son of Jalaluddin Haqqani, the hero of the anti-Soviet Jihad years, and Mullah Yaqoob, son of Taliban founder Mullah Omar—dashed into Kabul on the evening of August 15, rushing their forces to the ministries of interior and defense—the two control centers. Whoever took charge of these would earn the right to tell Mullah Hibatullah that they had secured the most coveted power centers of all.

On approaching the Afghan presidential palace as well as other government buildings in Kabul, the Taliban had found literally no one even guarding these places.

While competition among various Taliban commanders in rushing toward Kabul helped speed up the military campaign, it was forces under the command of the Haqqani network that benefitted most from this situation.[10] Siraj's uncle Khalil Haqqani, known for his skills as an arbiter in tribal disputes and resourcefulness in organizing *jirga*—an assembly of tribal leaders—to find solutions to hard problems, had prepared the ground well.

As the insurgency raged on year after year, the nature of the challenge confronting them ensured that the Taliban were a cohesive unit when facing the enemy. Before the eyes of NATO and Afghan security forces, they were one. Behind the scenes, the divisions within their factions mounted, despite their common goal. What were these divides, though? Primarily, the factions existed along identity lines and can be broken down into five main categories. First, those seen as the "moderates" of the group, their public face—those who led negotiations in Doha. Second, the Quetta Shura—hardliners and old guard who fit into the mold of general perceptions about the group, the ideological brain. A parallel Taliban group that emerged in 2005—Peshawar Shura, managing the eastern provinces of Afghanistan—balanced the southern bias of the Quetta Shura. Third, those fighting on the ground, the veins of the group—field commanders running the physical show. Fourth, the notorious organized criminal groups made up of drug dealers who capitalized on the chaos for their own financial gain. And last, potentially the largest of the factions was made up of ordinary villagers, who, with tribal alliances and in their opposition to urbanites and Kabul, found themselves without much choice in "joining" the Taliban.

Matin Bek, a senior official in the Ghani government, supports an important element of the above classification. Mathieu Aikins quotes him saying, "True power within the movement . . . resided not with Baradar's group in Doha but with the military commanders on the ground and the senior leadership hiding in Pakistan."[11]

Noting these divisions, the question would arise—who would end up leading the government? In a complete *Game of Thrones* situation, the coveted Iron Throne lay vacant as the various factions differed over who had the greatest right to it. Just as things started to look irreconcilable, in flew a very important somebody from Islamabad on September 4. It was none other than the man pulling many strings—Lieutenant General Faiz Hameed, the head of Pakistan's Inter-Services Intelligence (ISI). His three-day stay in Afghanistan played an important role in cabinet formation. Only under the iron fist of the ISI chief could widening internal divisions be put aside and quarrels resolved, one would assume. Giving a quick interview in Kabul's Serena hotel lobby, he quipped: "Don't worry, everything will be okay."[12] An alternate reading might be: I will ensure that our favorites get important cabinet slots. This was an important goal for Pakistan as not all Taliban power centers were aligned with it. Hibatullah and his men— with his two powerful deputies, namely Siraj Haqqani and Mullah Yaqoob, now unofficially managing critical security ministries—would rule.

Whether Faiz Hameed fully succeeded in his mission or not, the photographs and video clips of him sipping tea in the Serena hotel went viral. For observers, these visuals provided evidence of the huge influence of Pakistan on the Taliban. Realizing the blunder, Pakistani news channels were instructed not to show these pictures.[13] But it was obviously too late. Earlier, Pakistan's foreign office had advised Faiz to stay in the Pakistan embassy in Kabul where all meetings would be arranged, but the overconfident spy chief dismissed it. Later, in November 2021, when he was questioned by a handful of Pakistani politicians (including Bilawal Bhutto Zardari) in a closed-door conversation in Pakistan's parliament about why he traveled to Kabul before the formation of the new Taliban government, he defended his actions by saying that the US and Chinese intelligence chiefs had also visited Kabul around then. One politician drily quipped, "Maybe they visited too, but you were the only one photographed!"[14]

During the meetings with the Taliban leaders where Faiz reportedly made a case for inclusive government, he was curtly told, "We will consider the suggestion but we cannot include people like Atta Mohammad Nur, who murdered so many Taliban."[15] Atta Nur, a Tajik, remained governor of Balkh province from 2004 until 2018 when President Ghani fired him. He was an important US ally. Interestingly, Atta Nur's son Khalid Nur, a graduate of the Royal Military Academy Sandhurst, had met the then prime minister Imran Khan and army chief General Qamar Bajwa on the morning of August 15, 2021 along with seven other non-Pashtun Afghan leaders seeking support to play a role in

Afghanistan's future.[16] Incidentally, I had a chance to interact with Atta Nur in a conference in Baghdad in late September 2022, where we were panelists discussing the future of Afghanistan under the Taliban. In his remarks, besides trashing the Taliban, he categorically placed all the blame for bringing the Taliban back into power on US shoulders. Times have changed, and so has Atta—following a treacherous Afghan elite norm.

The biggest victim in this power struggle was Mullah Baradar. The American favorite, as well as the preferred choice of many relatively moderate Taliban, officially lost his chance to be the new leader of Afghanistan. He was Mullah Omar's choice to be his successor but the wily Mullah Mansoor had robbed him of that opportunity years ago, and now it was others who conspired to push him aside. It was he who played a critical role in legitimizing the Doha negotiations and had convinced Mullah Hibatullah that negotiations were their best route to getting Kabul back. He also gave hope to the Americans that they could work with the Taliban. Along with Zal, he had figured out a way which offered the best-case scenario for the Taliban's future, but Ghani's intransigence destroyed the prospects of a power-sharing deal as well as a peace settlement that would have empowered the moderate Taliban under Baradar. Zal had a follow-up plan in mind—in his words: "I thought after the overthrow that we should use the leverage we had to get the Taliban off the terror list, gradually release funds, and reopen the embassy—so we could get what we wanted from them in exchange, which is counterterror cooperation, women's rights, and an inclusive government."[17] But now, Baradar was on the sidelines of the political powerplay, weary and waiting, as the situation on the ground changed for everyone.

To be seen as close to Americans was not expected to bring any benefits among the rank and file of the Taliban or generate any political capital in Afghanistan under the changed circumstances. And then there was the news of a "secret" meeting between CIA Director William Burns, a seasoned diplomat, with Mullah Baradar on August 23, 2021.[18] The reported conversation was about evacuation coordination and safety of US and Western personnel as per the Doha agreement (and probably some specific points related to the secret provisions of the deal). As important as it was for the US side, it turned out to be a death knell for Baradar's political prospects. A "secret" meeting should really have been kept secret if it was so important that the US was ready to risk Baradar's future. Baradar himself should have known better or maybe he was overconfident.

Taliban 3.0?

The Taliban started off their second stint in government with some positive messaging after an unexpectedly peaceful takeover of Kabul. Enamullah Samangani, a member of the Taliban's cultural commission, announced on August 17, 2021, a "general amnesty" for government workers across Afghanistan and surprisingly invited women to join its government.[19] This statement in the midst of a panic, where many were rushing to the airport to exit the country, soothed many a nerve—even if only temporarily.

While embassies were being vacated and Kabul airport was engulfed with chaos, many leading lights of the Taliban started to arrive in Kabul from Doha. In such circumstances, the Taliban did quite well to pull off their first official press conference on the eve of August 17, 2021. It was led by Taliban chief spokesman Zabihullah Mujahid. A graduate of Pakistan's Darul Uloom Haqqania, this relatively young 44-year-old spokesman is among the longest-serving Taliban media managers and his voice was quite familiar to international journalists as he had been regularly responding to media phone calls and managing Taliban social media accounts. Still, few recognized his face before this first public appearance. In fact, he had been so efficient at his job that there remained some confusion as to whether this was one individual or if a team of Taliban spokesmen were all using this one name to hide the identities of multiple people. The Taliban were not only good at building profiles of their stalwarts but were also adept at ensuring their safety as much as possible during an insurgency. Hence the choreographed mystery surrounding Zabihullah Mujahid, who was described as a "relatively moderate, pleasant man" by veteran BBC journalist John Simpson.[20]

A few short excerpts from the press conference give a flavor of the "new" Taliban thinking and the initial guiding principles that they committed to:

The Islamic Emirate, after freedom of this nation is not going to [seek] revenge [on] anybody, we don't have any grudges against anybody. . . . We have pardoned anyone, all those who had fought against us. . . .

I would like to assure the international community, including the United States that nobody will be harmed in Afghanistan. I would like to assure our neighbours, regional countries, we are not going to allow our territory to be used against anybody, any country in the world. . . .

We would like to assure you that nobody is going to knock on their door to inspect them, to ask them or to interrogate them as to who they have been working for or interpreting for . . .[21]

The Taliban, it seemed, earnestly aspired to focus on repairing their international image and even distanced themselves from their earlier policies. In response to a query on whether they had changed in terms of ideology, Mujahid insightfully argued:

Our nation is a Muslim nation, whether it was 20 years ago, or whether it was now. But when it comes to experience and maturity and vision, of course, there is a huge difference between us, in comparison to 20 years ago. There will be a difference when it comes to the actions we're going to take, this has been like a evolutionary, complimentary [sic] sort of process.[22]

This certainly gave the Taliban some breathing space to put their house in order—as much as possible at the time. A lot of activity was taking place in Kandahar where the Taliban top leader Mullah Hibatullah was now in consultation with senior Taliban figures to decide about the government formation. The first jolt for the Taliban, meanwhile, came from an internal enemy—the Islamic State in Khorasan (ISK), an affiliate of the terrorist organization ISIS, in the form of a suicide bombing attack on August 26, 2021 killing over 170 Afghans and 13 US troops at Kabul airport. Most of the casualties were Afghans who were waiting to be evacuated. ISK wanted to show its lethal capacity as well as disrupt the Taliban's consolidation. The Taliban later claimed that they had collected intelligence about ISK planning for such an attack and that is why they had postponed gatherings in public places and had advised their top leaders not to gather.[23]

Ironically, the Taliban had released the suicide bomber a few days earlier from the Parwan prison at Bagram air base. They had opened the gates of this prison as well as the city's main prison, at Pul-e-Charkhi, the day they took charge of Kabul, freeing more than 12,000 inmates, including senior leaders of Al-Qaeda and at least a thousand members of ISK, according to a report in *The New Yorker*.[24] It was a disastrous decision.

On September 7, 2021, Zabihullah Mujahid announced a 33-member, unsurprisingly all-men, "caretaker" cabinet (see Charts 1 and 2). In some ways, the new government follows the Iranian model in their prop of a supreme leader—finding their own Ayatollah Khamenei in Mullah Hibatullah. Until the real government could be solidified, they decided to build an interim government. Partly, it was intended to give the impression that the Taliban would seek legitimacy before introducing any new form of government, besides keeping all options open for any political collaboration if necessary. Except for the office of the supreme leader, every other position was supposedly temporary. The next important position was that of prime minister. It wound up going to one of the most unexpected players of all—as if they decided to pull a name out of a hat. The coveted position was given to nearly 70-year-old Mullah Mohammad Hassan Akhund, one of the founders of the Taliban, who had served as its deputy foreign minister from 1996 to 2001.[25] A graduate of a madrassa in Pakistan's Karachi, he was briefly elevated in the first Taliban government as deputy prime minister as well, but the position was symbolic rather than having any real authority. Hailing from Kandahar's Shah Walikot district, he was known more for his clerical status than for winning any laurels in the battlefield. Most importantly, besides his closeness to Hibatullah, he served as a member—and later as a leader and advisor—of the *Rahbari Shura* (leadership council), often called the Quetta Shura (since its inception in May 2002), and both these factors explain the reason he was chosen for this important position.[26] He also enjoyed good reputation within the Taliban circles and, according to Taliban members I talked to, he is not seen as someone who aimed, or used manipulation, to get this position.[27]

Prime Minister Akhund has two deputy prime ministers serving under him. Notably, one of them happened to be the man who would have been the top contender for the position of prime minister. This was, of course, Mullah Baradar. To say he "deserved" it would be an understatement—after all, it was he who had led negotiations and ensured their success—but among other hurdles discussed above, he was not seen favorably by Pakistan's intelligence services, and that at the time was sufficient grounds for disqualification from the top executive slot in Kabul. The second deputy, Mullah Abdul Salam Hanafi, is another senior Taliban

leader who served as a key member of the Taliban negotiation team in Doha. Associated with the Taliban movement
from its very early years, he served as the deputy education
minister during the first Taliban regime between 1996 and
2001. Being an ethnic Uzbek from Jawzjan province, he is
the among the very few non-Pashtuns holding any position
of significance in the Taliban hierarchy. Easygoing and frank
in his discourse, he is counted among the relatively moderate
elements of the Taliban.[28] He studied at several religious
seminaries in Afghanistan and Pakistan, including in Jamia
Darul Uloom, a famous Deobandi madrassa in Karachi. He
later taught at Kabul University. Like Mullah Baradar, he is
a well-traveled leader, having participated in Taliban parleys
in Moscow, Beijing and obviously in Doha.

In the new cabinet, almost mockingly, one of the most
important positions went to America's most wanted man—
Sirajuddin Haqqani (known as Siraj and Khalifa). Almost a
legend, for years all the US intelligence knew of him came
from one hazy side photo of him. He was appointed as the new
interior minister, including responsibility for Kabul's police
and security. When things went really south and many security forces abandoned their posts, his forces quickly moved in
and took up positions. Some of those who had fled quickly
returned to their jobs to merge with the Taliban, further
strengthening Haqqani's power.

The other prized position of defense minister went to
Mullah Omar's son Yaqoob, partly because he was a deputy
of Hibatullah and given the fact that he had led the Taliban
military campaign in recent years. The job was his to take.
He is deemed to be both a moderate and a favorite of Saudi

Arabia as well, according to knowledgeable Taliban expert Antonio Giustozzi.[29] The combination sounds a bit odd but the explanation offered for this makes sense: Yaqoob's predecessor (as Taliban army chief during the insurgency years), Ibrahim Sadr, had close links with Iran, and Saudi Arabia wanted to ensure that the next Taliban military chief would not have such inclinations. This became obvious with the emergence, soon after the US–Taliban peace deal was announced, of the breakaway Taliban faction Hezb-e Walayat-e Islami (Party of Islamic Guardianship). This faction included many supporters of Sadr.[30]

It deserves mention that both Siraj and Yaqoob were directly dealing with security affairs for some time. For administrative purposes, the Taliban had divided Afghanistan's 34 provinces into two wings, south and southeast. The south, comprising 14 provinces, fell under Mullah Yaqoob, and the southeast comprises the remaining 20 provinces, with Siraj Haqqani enjoying oversight and management responsibilities.[31]

Of the 33 cabinet slots, 30 had gone to Pashtuns and only two to Tajiks and one to an Uzbek, making it obvious that the Taliban's idea of diversity was almost meaningless. Almost all positions went to senior members of the Taliban movement and the cabinet portfolios largely reflected the tasks they had had in the leadership council.[32] Seeing the imbalance, even Pakistan's prime minister, Imran Khan, tweeted on September 18, 2021:

After mtgs in Dushanbe with leaders of Afghanistan's neighbours & especially a lengthy discussion with

Tajikistan's President Emomali Rahmon, I have initiated a dialogue with the Taliban for an inclusive Afghan govt to include Tajiks, Hazaras & Uzbeks.[33]

The Taliban expanded the cabinet on September 21, 2021 announcing a list of deputy ministers and then further added over two dozen names against cabinet positions on October 4, followed by an announcement on November 23, 2021.[34] These expansions (full list in Appendix I) also included names from Panjshir and Baghlan provinces with considerable Tajik and Uzbek populations, in a half-hearted attempt to send a message of inclusivity. The first cabinet meeting of the Taliban, on October 4, 2021, had added insult to the injury when it announced 38 new official appointments made by Taliban supreme leader Mullah Hibatullah Akhundzada—almost all religious clerics from Pashtun ethnicity.[35] A third deputy prime minister was also announced—Maulvi Abdul Kabir—perhaps reducing the importance of the position. A former governor of the Nangarhar province, he too is a member of the Taliban leadership council and hails from the Zadran tribe, the tribe of the Haqqanis.

While at least 14 members of the interim cabinet are on the UN Security Council terrorism blacklist, a few highly educated members were also inducted in the cabinet. One of them is Abdul Latif Nazari, as deputy minister of economy, and importantly he hails from the Hazara ethnicity and holds a PhD in political science. Besides his experience in media, he has published books on democracy, the rights and obligations of citizenship, and multilateralism in international relations—quite an impressive range of topics.[36] Another Hazara, Dr. Hassan Ghyasi, was also appointed as deputy minister of public health. Similarly, the commerce ministry is led by a Tajik minister, Haji Noor Uddin, and his two deputies, Muhammad Bashir and Azim Sultan, also from Tajik backgrounds. By Taliban standards, this is certainly progress, and at least deserves recognition.

An interesting case is that of the current Taliban minister for finance who goes by the name of Hidayatullah Badri—but that was not always the case. Few people know about the story behind his real name, Gul Agha Ishaqzai. The reason for this almost secret double identity is that after 9/11, having refused to cooperate and offer information, Agha was beaten and left to die by Pakistani intelligence in Quetta. Nobody assumed he would actually survive—so when he did, to avoid being handed over to the US he changed his name—bringing us to today. Now, for Gul Agha to have been appointed to this new position with his former history meant he had to have been forgiven by Pakistan. How that came to be tells us a lot: Taliban foreign minister Amir Khan Muttaqi personally took him to former Pakistan army chief, General Qamar Bajwa to extend the hand of friendship. Only Bajwa's favorable nod gave him the opportunity.

Besides a Pashtun background, another important qualification to land a job in the Taliban government is one's direct or indirect link with Pakistan, whether it is membership of the Quetta or Peshawar Shura or alumni status with Darul Uloom Haqqania seminary. The older generation of the Taliban had mostly gone to this seminary located about 60 kilometers from the Afghan border. It is one of Pakistan's oldest and most notorious seminaries. More Taliban leaders passed through its halls than any other seminary. At least eight prominent Taliban cabinet members today, and scores of military commanders and governors, are graduates of this school (see Appendix II). These include interior minister Siraj Haqqani, foreign minister Amir Khan Muttaqi and the former higher education minister Abdul Baqi Haqqani, among others.[37] Many of the alumni adopt the title Haqqani as a surname, as a badge of honor and that is how the "Haqqani" network is labeled, contrary to a misperception that Haqqani is the name of some Pashtun tribe. Even Pakistan's former prime minister, Imran Khan, was under this wrong impression when during a public speech he remarked that Haqqanis are a famous tribe.[38]

The Haqqanis today are part and parcel of the Taliban. The relationship started off as an alliance, and they kept separate identities to some degree but gradually they merged during the post-2001 insurgency phase. Siraj and his uncle Khalil Haqqani, now the minister for refugees, have been at the forefront as Taliban representatives in all important meetings since the August 2021 takeover. For all *jirgas* and reconciliation meetings, Khalil, known as an effective mediator, is often the leading facilitator. It is generally believed that Siraj Haqqani is Pakistan's greatest ally among the Taliban, but many insiders believe the vital spot actually belongs to Khalil Haqqani, Siraj's uncle. Foreign minister Muttaqi has also made many strides in meetings with Pakistani high command, as a highly influential Taliban representative.

Another influential and ultra-conservative member of the Taliban cabinet is Noor Mohammad Saqib, minister for Hajj affairs. A graduate and former top student of Darul Uloom Haqqania, he served in the first Taliban government as chief justice and is well known for his toxic sectarian views. He issued many anti-Shia fatwas—religious edicts—that led to atrocities against Hazara and other Shia communities in both Afghanistan and Pakistan. One of his former colleagues in an interview shared with me that Noor Saqib was cautioned even by his alma mater Haqqania to curb his Takfiri approach—excommunicating Muslims or declaring them apostates. He was responsible for many controversial legal decisions during the first Taliban government and though his new position reflects a downgrading, he retains enough influence to land a cabinet slot.

Some Taliban members from the younger generation have degrees from the International Islamic University in Islamabad—a relatively modern institution in terms of its teaching and research standards, funded partly by Saudi Arabia. Not a traditional madrassa, it saw some graduates end up getting second-tier positions in the Taliban cabinet (as deputy ministers). One would assume they are unlike the old-school traditional Taliban, perhaps more open-minded and well-read. Dr. Naeem Wardak, a PhD from this university, has been representing the Taliban in their political office in Doha since September 2020.

Perhaps the most interesting appointment of all is also the most unexpected, with a fascinating history behind it. If anything represents the generational and ideological shifts of the current Taliban government from the one a quarter of a century ago, it is this. The position of the head of the cricket board would become so hotly desired that literal

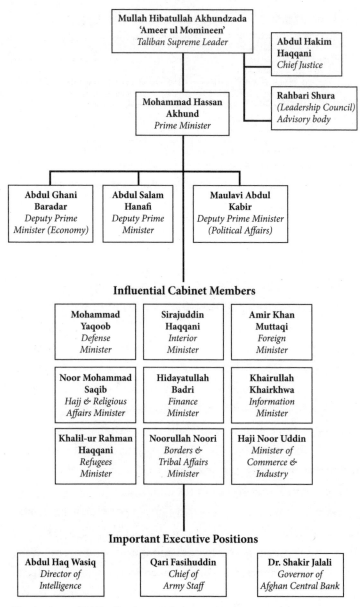

Mullah Hibatullah Akhundzada
'Ameer ul Momineen'
Taliban Supreme Leader

Abdul Hakim Haqqani
Chief Justice

Mohammad Hassan Akhund
Prime Minister

Rahbari Shura
(Leadership Council)
Advisory body

Abdul Ghani Baradar
Deputy Prime Minister (Economy)

Abdul Salam Hanafi
Deputy Prime Minister

Maulavi Abdul Kabir
Deputy Prime Minister (Political Affairs)

Influential Cabinet Members

Mohammad Yaqoob
Defense Minister

Sirajuddin Haqqani
Interior Minister

Amir Khan Muttaqi
Foreign Minister

Noor Mohammad Saqib
Hajj & Religious Affairs Minister

Hidayatullah Badri
Finance Minister

Khairullah Khairkhwa
Information Minister

Khalil-ur Rahman Haqqani
Refugees Minister

Noorullah Noori
Borders & Tribal Affairs Minister

Haji Noor Uddin
Minister of Commerce & Industry

Important Executive Positions

Abdul Haq Wasiq
Director of Intelligence

Qari Fasihuddin
Chief of Army Staff

Dr. Shakir Jalali
Governor of Afghan Central Bank

Chart 1. Key Taliban leaders in the caretaker government

Qari Din Mohammad Hanif, *Minister of Economy:*
a Tajik from Badakhshan province; studied in Peshawar

Abdul Baqi Haqqani, *Minister of Higher Education:*
he served as the governor of Khost and Paktika provinces during the Taliban's first government, 1996–2001. He was replaced by Nida Mohammad Nadim, a former police chief of the Nangarhar province, in October 2022

Najibullah Haqqani, *Minister of Communications*

Mohammad Khalid, *Minister for Irshaad and Dawaat*
(roughly meaning religious guidance and proselytization)

Hamidullah Akhundzada, *Minister of Civil Aviation and Transport*

Shahabuddin Delavar, *Minister of Mines and Petroleum*

Mohammad Abbas Akhund, *Minister of Disaster Management*

Habibullah Agha, *Minister of Education*

Abdul Manan Umeri, *Minister of Public Works:*
stepbrother of the founder of the Taliban movement, Muhammad Omar

Muhammad Younas Akhundzada, *Minister of Rural Rehabilitation and Development*

Abdul Latif Mansoor, *Minister of Water and Energy*

Muhammad Ishaq Asim, *Minister of Public Health*

Abdul Rahman Rashid, *Deputy Minister of Refugees and Repatriations*

Abdul Wali, *Minister of Labor and Social Affairs*

Abdul Majeed Akhund, *Minister of Martyrs and Disabled Affairs*

Nooruddin Turabi, *Minister for Prisons*

Mohammad Khalid Hanafi, *Minister for the Promotion of Virtue and Prevention of Vice*

Abdul Hakim Sharei, *Minister of Justice*
he remained in Saudi Arabia's prison (2010–19) for running a Taliban fundraising campaign in the Kingdom that collected over 6 million Saudi Rials[39]

Chart 2. Other important cabinet members[40]

fistfights broke out because of it![41] The men once renowned for their distaste toward sports were now breaking bones over it! A most interesting account dates to when the Taliban's relations with Pakistan were at their best, just before 9/11. A moment marked forever in Pakistani media was when the Pakistan soccer team had traveled to Afghanistan for a game—only to be deported almost immediately. Their crime was wearing shorts! When the Taliban noticed their "inappropriate apparel," they not only kicked them out of the country but shaved their heads (considered a sign of humiliation) before doing so—and this was when relations were considered good! The drastic contrast between then and now speaks greatly to the changes over time. Moreover, the sacred nature of cricket in the region cannot be overstated; it is loved beyond description. When the young Afghan cricket team started to make great strides, the Taliban knew they could not ambush them and lose public favor. The time had come for them to start conceding to the public, not the other way around.

The only leadership positions for which women were deemed suitable happened to be in the healthcare sector. Dr. Malalai Faizi was picked as the physician-in-chief of the Malalai Zizhanton maternity hospital in February 2022; Dr. Arian was appointed director of the Shahra teaching hospital (for gynecology), operating under the ministry of higher education in Kabul, also in February 2022; and Dr. Simin Mushkin Mohmand was appointed as the chief of staff of the Rabia Balkhi maternity hospital in October 2022. By Taliban standards these are unprecedented appointments but the fact remains that the overall health system in Afghanistan is on the brink of collapse according to the World Health Organization. Afghanistan continues to have one of the highest mortality rates in the world. With many international aid agencies suspending their operations (reacting to the December 2022 Taliban ban on NGO women workers), the situation is only worsening, raising questions also about the effectiveness of prevailing approaches to dealing with the Taliban.

Returning to cabinet formation and those calling the shots in the new Taliban government, most of the members have well-established credentials behind them. There were hardly any charges of nepotism or favoritism, except of course the view that the Haqqanis got the lion's share in the cabinet. This is a debatable point. According to Giustozzi,[42] the proportion of Haqqanis in the cabinet is fair, reflecting their influence, power and military contributions. Overall, Kandahar, the heartland of the Taliban, where the supreme leader resides, remains very powerful and dominant.

Many cabinet members had formerly worked alongside Mullah Omar and his close associates; among them, some served time in jails—from local Afghan prisons to Guantanamo. Others are those who lost immediate family members in US military raids and the Afghan military campaign, carrying that grief with them. There are also those who had moved to Pakistan with their families, bene-fitting from Pashtun tribal linkages and, in some cases, connections with Pakistani intelligence, who were always welcoming Taliban, keeping in view their strategic security interests in Afghanistan. And last but not least is the group that is smallest in number but one that contributed toward the Taliban return to Kabul in a big way: the group that moved to Doha to establish a political office and ultimately to conduct negotiations with the US. In some ways, they're the lucky ones, having to deal only with the Qatari government as their sponsor, without immediate interests in Afghanistan, and free of the strings that come attached to alignment with Pakistan. Without any ethnic or regional ties, Qataris were only investing in a new relationship for the long term, and for this group of Taliban it meant safety from being blackmailed into doing things they were not interested in. In addition, their families could live safely and comfortably on Doha soil. Meanwhile, those who went the Pakistan route would often live with one eye on the door, fearing a midnight knock, and remaining at the mercy of the ISI.

Even though most Taliban cabinet members are seen as allies of Pakistan or are linked to the relatively independent Kandahari network, a few positions in the cabinet went to pro-Iran elements. Most important among them is the position of deputy interior minister, which initially went to none other than Ibrahim Sadr. Interestingly, but at this point unsurprisingly, he too is engaged in a rivalry with Siraj Haqqani. The hierarchical command system among the Taliban today is complex, to say the least. It is a combination of many commanders and, in addition to the old Taliban guard and some newcomers, it's soaked in rivalries and competition. The power-sharing operates in more of a horizontal system than a clear vertical pyramid. The disorganization implied by that is quite clear.

To probe into the Taliban cabinet formation process, I had a chance to interview a senior Pakistani general involved in the Afghanistan situation, who shared with me some fascinating insights. First, he mentioned how Pakistan tried to convince the Taliban to give some symbolic position to former Afghan President Hamid Karzai and former chief executive Abdullah Abdullah, but the Taliban had their own ideas.

I then asked him my golden question: are these guys really the new Taliban? His answer did not surprise me. He said this is a new generation of Taliban, many of whom have traveled abroad, and are better educated than the older generation. Not only do they have this international exposure, they *like* it. And, they do not want to go back to old times—yes, the overarching worldview may be old—but they do not want to be isolated from the world. Now that they have it, they will not lose the engagement and connection so cherished by them; they will try their best to have both.

If this is accurate, then how this will play out with the hardliner elders—mostly holding top executive positions and cabinet portfolios, is a mystery as of now, though it does beg the question: are the Taliban having an identity crisis?

With the new cabinet firmly in place, the Taliban faced the biggest challenge of all. How does one turn a field commander into a government minister? Those who once acted as shadow governors, tasked with creating terror, were now meant to be the *real* governors, building bridges instead of burning them. In the blink of an eye, they had to learn to do the exact opposite of what they always did—instead of resisting the government, they had to run it.

In parallel to the government machinery in Kabul, governors of provinces are also very important. Since August

2021, Hibatullah has at least twice changed governors—randomly moving them from one province to another. The interpretation is that Hibatullah doesn't want any of them to develop political patronage networks for their own selfish benefits—rather, they should stay focused on their administrative responsibilities.

It is interesting that the person seen as the most influential player in relations with Hibatullah is the governor of Kandahar, Yousaf Wafaa. In some ways one can liken him to acting as Hibatullah's *pasha*, as one of the figures who is closest to the top man and whose voice is listened to. His importance also derives from the fact that he controls border check posts in the area and through that money; he provides funds directly to Hibatullah.

One of the first decisions that the new government had to take was about the flag of Afghanistan.[43] They wasted no time replacing the black, red and green Afghan national flag with the Taliban official white flag bearing the *Shahada*, the Islamic profession of faith: there is no god but God and Muhammad is his prophet. The color white is the color of purity and peace. After all, the Taliban view themselves as nothing short of divinely appointed heroes bringing reform to their land.

For the Hibatullah-led Rahbari Shura (leadership council), I was told in an interview, the new task of governing was seen as the most daunting challenge. There was a sense of isolation they felt, as many Western nations had packed up their embassies while the Taliban were taking over Kabul. They were committed to the ideal they waged their battle for, but they knew that a lot of work had to be done to achieve the vision of an Islamic Emirate they had spent decades building up. The challenge was that apparently hardly anyone knew the script in terms of a well-defined governance model and how to establish it. Or maybe it was a closely held secret! For ordinary observers, all that was apparent was chaos.

The Taliban's Theory of Governance

To try and put in place a method for governance, the Taliban's newly appointed head of the Supreme Court, Abdul Hakim Haqqani, also known as Abdul Hakim Ishaqzai (introduced earlier), published a book in June 2022 titled *Al-Imarah Al-Islamiah wa Nithamaha* or *The Islamic Emirate and Its System*.[44] Taliban supreme leader Mullah Hibatullah wrote the preface for this 312-page book and highly recommends it to scholars. It summarizes the essentials of the Taliban worldview and discusses important aspects of their philosophy and public policy approach based on his religious opinions, and their vision for a post-America Afghanistan. The book is not an official policy document per se, but certainly reflects the opinions and policy prescriptions supported by the Taliban leadership circles in Kandahar.

As one delves deeper into the contents of the book, many themes and explanations appear to be quite contradictory. It begins with an emphasis on the need to promote Islamic culture as seen through its highly dogmatic interpretations of Islamic values.

The opening chapter argues that the central goal of the Islamic Emirate, following their victory and the defeat and departure of the Americans and their allies, is to implement God's rule in Afghanistan by establishing an Islamic state based on Islamic law and Hanafi jurisprudence (one of the four school of Sunni Islam). It is interesting here again to note the implications contained in this statement: primarily, that the Taliban are chosen by God to implement his law on Earth and, further, their understanding of Islamic law is the only correct one.

Regarding governance, before delving into the details of the type of government to be implemented, the author voices concern for the poor of his country—referencing wrongful exploitation of the vulnerable for the gain of those in power. So far so good.

The level of intolerance in the book for those belonging to different religions, and even Islamic sects, is instructive as to the author's mindset. It strongly discourages Hanafi school followers to drift away from the core principles of the school, while acknowledging that those belonging to other schools of jurisprudence can follow their own path. It is baffling, though, that the author considers privileges conferred on minorities as a threat to the Islamic system—claiming these minorities could literally defeat the purpose of the Taliban government. Are the enemies who are so often referred to as weak and inferior really so dangerous that they can bring down the great, mighty and invincible Taliban? The language here brims with fear and insecurity.

The head of state is to be referred to as *Ameer-ul-Momineen*—literally meaning leader of the faithful; absolutely everybody must obey him, and anyone who does not deserves a death sentence. Being a judge, the author really means it. The way this leader will be elected should follow the historical precedent set by the four rightly guided caliphs (who succeeded the Prophet of Islam fourteen centuries ago)—which, according to the author, was through "allegiance, domination, and the formation of a council of the influential and prominent people in the country." He fails to point out that all four caliphs of Islam after the Prophet were picked through different mechanisms. There is absolutely nothing in the book that can be seen as supportive of any representative system, which stops just short of saying that democracy is forbidden.

A critical section of the book details the duties of the *Ameer-ul-Momineen* drawn from and inspired by the examples of the four rightly guided caliphs. What sources and historical works have been used to study the caliphs and their policies is a mystery as the author conveniently attributes to these important figures his personal interpretations.

The educational system is also discussed—specifically, what it can and cannot consist of. Since "modern" non-religious education has apparently caused most of the problems in Afghanistan, and weakens Islam and Muslims, the education system must be inherently religious, his argument goes. Of all the things they could have blamed for the troubles in their country, the choice of education is truly ironic.

According to the author, women have no use other than being wives and raising children—so certainly they have no place in the government! *Ameer-ul-Momineen* cannot be a woman, because, according to some mysterious narratives quoted, it is said that women should not engage in politics, otherwise the work will be ruined. He emphasizes that women are intellectually deficient in comparison to men. The only possible interpretation of his arguments on the subject appears to be that women should vanish from sight to raise the country's future generations in silence and invisibility, while the men spend another twenty years getting the "work" done!

The author also devotes a chapter to women's education —or the lack of it. According to the book, women are not banned from receiving an education, as long as it meets certain criteria—because how can women have anything without strict rules attached? They must be taught at home by family members—not leaving their homes unnecessarily, and absolutely no education alongside men. If they must leave the house for education, then their teacher must also be a woman. The study of chemistry and physics is considered totally unnecessary for women, without any explanation being offered.[45] Perhaps it was this "guidance" that inspired the Taliban, in October 2022, to block women from taking college entrance exams in subjects deemed "too difficult," including economics, engineering, agriculture, geology and even journalism.[46]

Mullah Hibatullah is surely impressed by this controversial treatise and author Mullah Abdul Hakim's interpretations, especially the emphasis on the implementation of the Taliban's convoluted version of Sharia fully and completely across all layers of state and society. With these two men in control of crafting the ideological component of the Taliban narrative, any Taliban reformers and moderates face an uphill task to change things around.

3

Taliban.gov

Policies, Politics and Internal Rivalries

The differences in circumstances and loyalty to various networks during the insurgency years naturally created rivalries among the Taliban. Now, in the corridors of power, these have turned into sharp contests to increase influence over policy decisions. With these rivalries becoming more obvious, the Taliban quickly realized that just because the ball is in the net does not mean the game is over. One crucial goal may have been scored, but to win, they must score more goals and defend well. Taliban teamwork has been put to a real test. They have a common agenda and one vision, especially in a religious sense, but it is also true that they had grown apart from each other during the insurgency, which makes sense as they were all over the place during that time. Some are more loyal to Kandahari roots than anything else, some are Pakistan-sponsored, some Doha-affiliated, and many are new and young warriors who were born after the fall of the first Taliban government in December 2001. These differences were further accentuated by personality clashes and different political preferences. Despite all this, though, it is remarkable that they are still able to hold the fort. Of course, huge differences in policy and approach continue to exist, some of which are worth probing further. This chapter is about the Taliban's policy choices and the dynamics driving them.

An early insight into Taliban policies came through a media interview with the new minister for prisons, Mullah Nooruddin Turabi. He is known for his harsh conservatism and strict enforcement of laws. In this exchange, he made it categorically clear that, "No one will tell us what our laws should be. We will follow Islam and we will make our laws on the Qur'an."[1] He went on to make a case for strong punishments to create a deterrent effect while stating that the cabinet was studying whether to carry out punishments in public or otherwise, indicating that some change of policy from that of the previous Taliban government was conceivable. However, he did say something else in the conversation that at least reflected an awareness of changes that were impossible to reverse. While insisting that the Taliban today are different, he mentioned that they would permit the use of television, mobile phones, photos and videos as, in his words, "this is the necessity of the people, and we are serious about it."[2]

The most important task of a government is to be a service provider and that's the arena which is not much talked about in Kabul yet. To project some progress in international forums, the Taliban are trying to take the credit for creating a 100,000-strong army and a 140,000-strong police force, as well as restarting work on several large infrastructure projects, including the Kajaki Dam's hydro-electric plant.[3] They inherited most of these initiatives and infrastructure projects, and sustaining them will be a crucial test of their administrative capabilities. Unfortunately, many of the skilled experts running various ministries left Afghanistan after the Taliban takeover. The Taliban had announced "amnesty" for all who had worked for the previous government, but their initial statements started to lose credibility as many instances of violations of the said commitment were reported.[4]

The First Test: Issues around Women and Girls' Education

One of the first things that people recalled after seeing the Taliban takeover were the blue *burqas* and portraits of women with sad eyes of the early Taliban era. There was a genuine concern about what would happen to the new generation of women in Afghanistan, who had experienced relative freedoms, and received educational and job opportunities, especially those living in urban settings. As feared but, alas, expected, the Taliban soon made public policy announcements regarding women's obligatory hijab, or modesty wear. This comes down to a fundamental series of issues they have always had with modernity and the concept of a mixed-gender society. So they started off by very casually declaring the rules: there would be no free mixing in public between men and women, girls above the age of puberty and women below very old age must wear a hijab—but this hijab must adhere to a strict dress code; it could not be too tight nor too thin. But in only a few months, these restrictions were tightened further. By May 2022, the Taliban would recommended that the best form of hijab would be the *burqa*, a head-to-toe covering with only a net for the eyes.[5] To be clear these statements were advisory in nature and not strictly enforced.

As is the tragic pattern of history, when disaster strikes, women are wounded the most. The Taliban's August 2021 takeover of Afghanistan is no exception, and for anyone who has paid attention over the last 30 years, the heartbreak accompanying these reopened wounds is far too deep. More than a year and a half after the US and NATO withdrawal from Afghanistan, it has become abundantly clear to all worldwide that this war never ended for the Afghan people, and the trauma of turmoil is ongoing as the Taliban begin to assert more power.

When the Taliban began making promises upon their victory post-August 2021, voices everywhere echoed the same sentiment—it was too good to be true. And so it was: the older generation of leaders guaranteed they would not be forgotten so soon, nor go down without a fight.

It was a pleasant surprise to hear from the Taliban that women would be able to continue working and girls could continue schooling from March 22, 2022.[6] This was in line with commitments made in Doha during the negotiations. But if history has shown us anything, it is that we cannot trust the Taliban's words. First, a shock came in December 2021, when the Taliban decreed that women seeking to travel long distances (more than 45 miles) should not be allowed on road transport unless a close male relative accompanied them.[7] The ministry for the "promotion of virtue and prevention of vice" also directed vehicle owners to refuse rides to women not wearing headscarves. Given the cultural norms and general practice no official policy directive was needed in the second case anyhow. The Taliban clearly were becoming more intrusive as time went by. One noteworthy exception was that government secondary schools for girls remained open in ten of Afghanistan's 34 provinces "either because of supportive local Taliban leadership or strong pressure by parents or teachers," as reported by the credible Afghanistan Analysts Network.[8]

Then came the bigger surprise as the decision to open girls' schools for grade 6 (age 11) and above was reversed.[9] When announcing this decision, the reasons cited included difficulty in segregating genders and lack of funds. Girls in primary school, fifth grade and under, would be able to continue, but girls who were older would have to stay at home. This was followed by more stringent restrictions in December 2022. The trauma and horror of the dangerous ideology underlying these decisions is still fresh for Afghans; people's worst fears were once again becoming a reality.

While it would be presumptuous to assume that there is a sizable percentage of the Taliban that did not in fact wish to stop girls' education—it is not too wild an assumption. The confusion and chaos that unfolded after the announcement signaled to everyone that the decision was, at the very least, not well planned. Clearly, there is not just one mind operating here but rather two—at war with each other. There is an invisible war within the Taliban between the old and the new, representative of the fragility, chaos and confusion that plagues this new government and era for the country. The problem is that we do not know who is going to win.

When the Taliban announced that girls would no longer be able to resume their education, it became widely known that this was in fact the wish of a hardline faction, comprising three influential clerics from the south, who have influence over Mullah Hibatullah.[10] These are chief justice Abdul Hakim Haqqani, minister for religious affairs Noor Mohammad Saqib (introduced in an earlier chapter) and minister for the promotion of virtue and prevention of vice Mohammad Khalid Hanafi.[11] The "outsized influence of this out-of-touch minority," in the words of Ashley Jackson, prevented the return of girls to school (grades 6 to 12), disappointing a vast majority of Afghans—including the majority of Taliban leaders.[12] It is these rigid hardliners, mostly based in Kandahar, who continue to promote bigotry. The three clerics had approached the supreme leader in Kandahar to confront him on the matter, which led to this ruling. Later there was pushback about this reversal from within Taliban ranks as well.[13] The glimmer of hope people had, tiny as it may have been, disappeared almost as soon as it arrived. Still, the battle of ideas among the Taliban is by no means over.

Another tragedy of this crisis is the reemergence of inaccurate, dangerous and bigoted misrepresentations of Islam. Not just by the Taliban themselves—but by some elements in international media, who, it appears, require a lesson on both cultural sensitivity and religious education. To describe what the Taliban are doing specifically with the restrictions on girls' education as "traditional Islam" is not only completely wrong but harmful as well.

The tragedy lies also in the fact that the Taliban routinely mix up their tribal norms with Islam. There is a famous saying by the Prophet Muhammad in which he exclaims, "Education is incumbent on every boy and girl," and goes further, saying that even if one must go as far as China for knowledge it is worth it. The greatest thing a Muslim can do is seek and acquire knowledge—not just male Muslims, but both men and women as per mainstream Muslim jurists. There is no sermon of the Prophet nor any verse in the Quran that claims women are to be prohibited from schooling: calls for education never come with a gender specification. The contrast between the truth of actual Islamic teachings and the Taliban's actions could not be more extreme. Women are the life force of society and community—without them and without the education of girls no society can truly thrive or prosper.

And so the battle between the old and the young highlighted once again the tragedy of women's place in war. They have become the bargaining chip, their liberties the sacrifice. The hardliners had chosen this battle and won, but no blood would stain the younger men in Kabul's presidential palace. Only the women would have to suffer.

This web of unfulfilled promises regarding women forces us to ask why the Taliban ever made such contradictory promises in the first place. Why claim girls' education would be allowed to continue only to reverse the decision soon after? Was this some sort of sadistic attempt to cause further stress? Or was it merely an issue of governance? Here lies the root of the issue—if there is one thing we know about the new Taliban it is this: there are two hands directing the show, only with different scripts.

To be fair, a few things have changed in comparison to the Taliban's earlier stint in power. Even with severely restricted access to workplaces and schools, women are more visible on the streets and are surviving wearing their headscarves (which Afghan women generally prefer) rather than wearing *burqas* (veils that cover whole body and face with a small screen in front of eyes to see). In December 2021, Taliban supreme leader Mullah Hibatullah issued an important decree (see Appendix III) banning forced marriage of women, categorically saying that "no one can force women to marry by coercion or pressure" and simultaneously directing courts to "to treat women fairly, especially widows seeking inheritance as next of kin."[14] These decisions defy some deplorable tribal norms and practices in the country and deserve credit.

The Second Test: Policy toward Muslim Minorities

Perhaps one of the groups most targeted by the Taliban—if not *the* most targeted group—is the minority ethnic group known as the Hazara. A predominantly Shia Muslim group, they have borne the brunt of persecution and abuse by the Taliban for decades. The award-winning novel by Khaled Hosseini, *The Kite Runner*, beautifully relays the story of suffering in Afghanistan through the drastically different experiences of two boys under Taliban rule—one a native Pashtun, and the other a Hazara. What Hazaras have experienced must not be understated: of all the atrocities committed by the Taliban, the Hazaras have experienced every single one. They are specifically targeted not only for tribal and ethnic reasons but because of anti-Shia sectarianism as well.

Continuously since the Taliban's inception, Hazaras have been victims of unbelievable human rights violations.[15] Mosques and religious processions bombed, normalized social discrimination, torture, killings, etc.—all have been regularly experienced. Heartbreakingly, mass graves of Hazaras have been discovered by the UN—their suffering at the hands of the Taliban has been nothing less than a genocide.[16] It is hard then to believe that today's Taliban, with such intense genocidal hatred in their past, could be capable of reform, of undoing such trauma and terror, particularly for the group that has faced their worst.

Hazara support for democracy and historical opposition to the Taliban created a violent, intense prejudice against them from the group and its supporters. This meant exclusion not only from the system but from society as a whole. Discriminatory beliefs surrounding their ethnic and religious identity have defined their position in Afghan society over the past few decades, as they have found themselves at the bottom of the pile. Even worse today is the threat they also face from ISK, whose extremist ideology also targets them. The misfortunes that follow Hazaras cannot be ignored in the story of Taliban brutality—and how the new Taliban will treat them will be a true test of their identity. There were some early signs that the Taliban would offer protection to Shia religious gatherings and processions against ISK and, despite mutual mistrust, the Taliban made efforts to live up to their commitment.[17]

According to some reports, the Taliban in some locations are forcibly displacing Hazaras from their ancestral lands, giving them instead to Taliban loyalists.[18] As if this was not enough, when Hazaras are displaced and in dire need of help, they are on many occasions excluded by the Taliban from receiving any humanitarian aid that comes in. They are the silent sufferers, largely both at home and in the media, vulnerable to the worst of the worst. An October 2021 *Al Jazeera* article by Sitarah Mohammadi and Sajjad Askary reports: "a clear pattern of Taliban atrocities being committed across Afghanistan, which could mean that the Hazaras may be facing imminent ethnic cleansing."[19] This is hardly a sign of any improvement in the lives of the Hazara.

Certainly, then, it is Hazara women who live with a constant target on their back, fitting into the two foremost categories of the Taliban's "most wanted." It does not help that they also have an incredibly successful track record in making strides forward[20]—their triumphs have only made them more of a target. As activists and organizers, Hazara women have regularly been abducted, imprisoned and murdered, losing their lives to the very struggle they fought so tirelessly to end. Despite the tragedies that have plagued them, though, Hazara people live on in their resistance— they are everyday heroes, triumphant in their existence. As they continue to face threat after threat, their inspiration and hope fail to dwindle, turning the landscape of sorrow into one hopeful of salvation.

Around mid-2022, I spoke in detail with a philanthropist leading an international charity organization who had recently traveled to various parts of Afghanistan. He generously shared with me fascinating and important insights about the reality of life on the ground.[21] Hailing from the Middle East, this Shia Muslim is involved in charity work, and his aim was to figure out ways to support the marginalized Hazara community, among others. His story provides crucial insights about the plight of Shias in Afghanistan today, and offers a more accessible glimpse into the lives of the ordinary.

Arranging a visa to travel to Afghanistan was complicated, but even with the stamp on his passport he was not sure if it would actually be accepted in Afghanistan. He was wary because he had already received feedback from people on the ground—that to be known as a Shia was not something likely to add to his safety. In fact, it could be dangerous: many government institutions have already kicked out Shias, he was told. On his arrival in Kabul, everything seemed normal in terms of immigration and customs, though the man scanning his passport at the immigration desk did not even bother looking at his visa, and instead asked him if he wanted a stamp or not—meaning he could essentially conceal his trip from his passport record. There was also one area at the airport with armed Taliban who were clearly overseeing the whole process, followed by an uncountable number of checkpoints outside, where his local team awaited him. Each check post was surrounded by young Taliban members—practically kids, he said—acting as watchdogs.

One of the first things he was told by friends on the ground, when mentioning the helpful airport officer, was that the Taliban are very strict when it comes to bribery—they regularly keep an eye out for it, even on government officials. He also observed that the airport had a proper system of biometrics in place, but for some reason there was an issue causing it not to work. The general impression was that all the data collected through biometrics was for Pakistani intelligence—whether this was true or not, either way the system was not working. The other story he heard on his journey from the airport to his destination was that the Taliban were now very actively conducting a tax review process. That meant that if you had not been paying a special extortion fee during the last government, you were now obliged to pay more, and all visitors had to show their accounting records.

The gentleman took it upon himself to observe as much as he could and ask as many questions as possible to capture the reality. For instance, when he asked his local hosts out of curiosity why people view Pakistan as controversial, he was told that currently coal prices have risen drastically because Pakistan is buying it all up. When he asked his charity network colleagues about the struggle of Shias, a local employee of his organization told him, "we are feeling more secure than before." When he reacted with surprise, the man continued: "The Taliban are not in the mountains any more—they're in the streets now. They are difficult people, but approachable." As the trend seems to show, their new positions of power have also meant new behavior—and accordingly, a new reputation in the making.

Soon after their victory some Taliban visited Mazar-e-Sharif, asking the Shias of the city why they did not "resist against the enemy" (meaning the US and NATO forces). They responded by saying that they did, by criticizing international intervention through Friday mosque sermons. The Taliban leader did not seem fully convinced, but it satisfied him for the time being. On the more sensitive issue of Muharram gatherings, mostly arranged by Shias to commemorate the tragic martyrdom of the Prophet's grandson Husayn at the hands of brutal caliph Yazid ibn Muawiya, the visiting philanthropist said almost every pole in the streets of Kabul hoisted a black flag signifying the days of mourning. The public display of some Shia symbols such as this was allowed without much interference; however, there are other changes the Taliban are introducing, like removing Ashura and Nowruz holidays (commemorated by various Muslim denominations) from the calendar. Additionally, the major Ashura procession in Mazar-e-Sharif was dropped—but for an interesting reason. The Taliban had told Shias there that a big procession would attract ISK's attention, and advised them to divide the community into four small groups across the city so the Taliban could provide better security—a great contrast from the days when such processions were either completely banned or targeted by the Taliban themselves! Another important insight about Taliban attitudes is as regards ethnic identity: Hazara are viewed more negatively in comparison to Tajik Shias.

When it became known what my interviewee was doing, the Taliban started asking questions. First, they asked him about the source of his funds—to which he responded, these came mostly as donations from Muslim communities in the West, and were meant for Hazara Shias. They asked him straightaway: "What about Sunnis?" To which he responded that many of their events regularly offer free food during Ramadan and other religious holidays for everyone, regardless of sect or religious affiliation.

During preparations for his trip, he had an opportunity to meet some Iranian diplomats stationed in Europe. He asked one of them about the inspiration behind their active engagement with the Taliban. They responded that there are actually growing concerns about Talibanization among Sunni Iranians, because of Afghan refugees and what Iranians believe to be Saudi funding of Iranian Sunnis and some Sunni Arab tribes that live in Iran. It is fascinating to note just how far these things can bleed.

On my query about any observations regarding girls' education, he shared that in actuality many private schools for girls were still operating, but for most families, sadly, this is not an option because of the dire financial situation. On another note, he also came to know that many Afghans think that ISK or Daesh is a group affiliated with the Taliban. These perceptions are incredibly important and telling. The picture is complex but also instructive. Perhaps one of the most insightful aspects of his journey came right at its end. When leaving the Kabul airport, a banner read, "*We want to present good Islam to the world.*" While the Taliban attitude to this guest may not have been entirely welcoming, no hostility was shown.

Whether Afghanistan is to truly see a new future as regards its treatment of minorities, who knows—but the intentions among some Taliban to do so are there. An indication of this is a response that the Taliban's Doha spokesman, Suhail Shaheen, gave to *The New Yorker* magazine's Jon Lee Anderson:

> The Hazara Shia for us are also Muslim. We believe we are one, like flowers in a garden. The more flowers, the more beautiful. We have started a new page. We do not want to be entangled with the past.[22]

The Third Test: Financial Crisis

The economic collapse after the Taliban's official entry into Kabul has spared nobody in its devastating consequences. Struck by a severe drought and the Covid-19 pandemic, the economy was already struggling even before the fall of Kabul. Until the Ghani government's collapse, around 80 percent of the national budget of Afghanistan was provided by the US, its partners and international organizations. That support vanished overnight and beyond that, the Biden administration froze all Afghan government funds in US banks—a little over $7 billion. The United Kingdom, Germany, the UAE and a few others followed suit, blocking access to an additional $2 billion. The Afghan banking system could not function without access to these foreign exchange reserves. Cash withdrawal limits from banks were sharply reduced to prevent a banking collapse increasing public distress. Human and capital flight, and massive internal human displacement, has shocked the economy further.

While imports have sharply declined, exports doubled toward the end of 2022 largely due to increased coal output and exports to Pakistan. The Taliban raised coal prices from

$90 to $200 per tonne in 2022, leading to a sharp rise in customs duties.[23] With high inflation and rising global food and energy prices, the impact of this is minimal. One other bright spot in this gloomy scenario is a significant reduction in corruption at customs and checkpoints, and through the dismantling of smuggling routes. They have choked off the informal rent collection rackets that were earlier run by provincial powerbrokers.[24] In fact the Taliban themselves were a major driver of such corruption as insurgents so they know well how to close the loopholes and fix the problem. The major beneficiary of this new trade pattern under the Taliban, according to a UK aid-funded research program, is Pakistan, while it is proving to be disadvantageous for Iran and Central Asia (partly due to a dramatic decline in fuel imports from Iran and Uzbekistan).[25]

The overall economy has shrunk by 20–30 percent since August 2021.[26] Hundreds of thousands of government employees are still without salaries and, with the collapse of the social service sector, ordinary Afghans have nowhere to turn to for help. This is fast emerging as one of the world's worst humanitarian crises, and there seems to be no end in sight for people's suffering as the international community limits its aid. Twenty million people are currently short of food, according to UN figures, and that number is expected to grow as international resources are limited as a result of the Russia–Ukraine war.[27] According to *The Economist*, families "that were middle-class a year ago are surviving on a single meal a day," and tragically some of them "have taken to selling organs or children."[28] In many locations, families with women and small children from rural areas have had to move to temporary makeshift camps near provincial capitals, waiting in long lines patrolled by the Taliban, hoping to receive a family ration of basic food commodities like beans, oil, flour and salt.

The faces in these lines represent the magnitude of the crisis: even formerly wealthy families wait somberly, not spared by the crisis. The issue only intensifies as food prices increase, making it even harder to afford food for all those who need it. Soon enough, more programs will be cut as the international community remains hesitant about lending aid out of fear of "helping" the Taliban. The anti-women policies in particular deter international governments from wanting to contribute to the cause, leading them to depend on non-governmental organizations. The severity of the crisis demands more than that, though. The question is not who will concede, but if, for the sake of preventing more human suffering, anyone will at all. If not, the scarcity this will exacerbate will only worsen the situation on the ground, where understaffed and undersupplied hospitals are filled with children suffering from severe malnutrition. A harrowing statistic captures this tragedy in a way only numbers can: at least 3.2 million children suffered from malnutrition in Afghanistan in 2022 alone.[29] The worst type of tragedy is the preventable one—if the international community should choose to act, this does not have to happen. But in the words of Palestinian poet Mahmoud Darwish:

The war will end/ The leaders will shake hands/ The old woman will keep waiting for her martyred son/ And those children will keep waiting for their hero father/ I don't know who sold our homeland/ But I saw who paid the price.[30]

An interesting development impacting Afghanistan's economic policy is the appointment of Mullah Baradar as the chief of economic policy. He now has oversight of the finance ministry as well as all matters pertaining to revenue generation. He was specifically put in that role not for his knowledge of economics but because the Taliban know they desperately need aid and financial support to run the country. Baradar fares well on the global stage—he is a good face for the Taliban making requests. The Taliban are not lacking in that sense; they do not want him or his moderation to bleed into their domestic policy choices, but they would not throw him out of the corridors of power when he can be of good use. They know they can utilize his relatively better reputation abroad for the financial support they cannot move forward without.

The Taliban have also been marketing some of their economic progress via social media and YouTube quite actively. One of the younger spokesmen representing Afghanistan's ministry of foreign affairs is Abdul Qahar Balki, who grew up in New Zealand and speaks fluent English. He is often at the forefront of Taliban image-building. A former Afghan minister in the Ghani government told me that Balki is the son-in-law of late Taliban leader Mullah Akhtar Mansour. Through his Twitter account he has been emphasizing the resumption of commercial flights to and from Kabul, the initiation of some road construction projects and the accommodation of about a thousand foreign journalists who have traveled to report from the country since the Taliban takeover.[31] These are small but important developments and few were expecting the Taliban to be focusing on any of these things.

However, current statistics offer a very challenging picture. According to Afghanistan's ministry of finance, it is daily collecting roughly 400 million Afghanis ($4.4 million) as tax, which potentially comes to around $1.6 billion per year. In May 2022, the Taliban had announced their first annual budget figures—$2.6 billion with a $500 million projected deficit—which was seen by experts as adequate for running the government.[32] Under the distressing circumstances, this was a decent effort, inspiring even *The Economist* to run a story with a headline: "The Taliban government has proved surprisingly good at raising money."[33] Deputy Prime Minister Abdul Salam Hanafi, while sharing the budget details proudly claimed that the "entire budget, including spending on education, health, development, defense or other sectors, will be funded by our national revenue sources without any foreign contributions."[34] Yet for millions of ordinary Afghans, destitution and death are what stare them in the face, and this budget cannot change things. The Ghani government was functioning with roughly $8 billion a year—and still failed to create sufficient economic growth, or offer security and a hopeful future. It is an extremely challenging situation for the Taliban to manage. The World Bank puts all of this is in perspective while arguing that:

The economy is now re-adjusting from the "aid bubble," and the international community's ongoing humanitarian and off-budget basic service support is expected to mitigate some negative impacts of the contraction. Still, it will not be sufficient to bring the economy back on a sustainable recovery path.[35]

One step that could give some breathing space to the economy of Afghanistan is what over seventy economists, including the Nobel laureate Joseph Stiglitz, strongly recommended to US President Joe Biden in a letter dated August 10, 2022: to allow the central bank of Afghanistan, Da Afghanistan Bank, to reclaim its international reserves frozen by the US. The letter argued:

> without access to its foreign reserves, the central bank of Afghanistan cannot carry out its normal, essential functions. Without a functioning central bank, the economy of Afghanistan has, predictably, collapsed . . . . it is both morally condemnable and politically and economically reckless to impose collective punishment on an entire people for the actions of a government they did not choose.[36]

As powerful as the line of reasoning is, there are some serious constraints imposed by the US legal and judicial framework on pursuing this path.[37] The Biden administration, along with some international partners, meanwhile, has established a foundation based in Switzerland to release half of the amount—$ 3.5 billion—to help address humanitarian and critical Afghan needs, including paying for electricity imports. It is a step forward, offering some hope for ordinary Afghans as well as an opportunity for the Taliban to positively engage with the international community.

The Challenge of Internal Cohesion: Jealousies and Fractures

The Taliban are a fractious bunch, as most politically intense groups tend to be. Just how serious their divisions are, though, requires a deeper look. There are ethnic, geographic and tribal divisions that we know of—but there are also network divisions that can become quite serious at the upper level. Not to the point of provoking fractures (at least yet), but more so rivalries that in turn create conflicts. Pulling out guns during arguments is a minor example, ratting each other out to the enemy during a raid, a major one.

There is an interesting and growing sense of jealousy and competition within the Taliban's inner circle, especially following their return to Kabul. Less so on the Haqqani side, but hierarchies exist nevertheless. Their dynamics are reminiscent of the Italian Mafia, with rivalries seeping all the way to the topmost echelons. However, it stops there—these are not divisions that can become anything bigger than attitudes of pettiness and childlike jealousy. They would not risk separation because they know there's far greater benefit in being in the group than being separate, and thus vulnerable, with no critical access. During the weekend, they may send spies to monitor each other's every move, but when Monday comes with a threat, they are united again, hand in hand. At the end of the day, their sense of brotherhood acts as a veil—thin as it may be—of protection from any true animosity.

The relationships the Taliban have with each other blow hot and cold, but despite the cold days they overwhelmingly bind themselves together when facing a threat, and even do favors for each other. These internal power struggles are still massively important though, especially post the 2021 take-over. When Hibatullah came to power as the top Taliban leader in 2016, he established a fresh slate, and got rid of his predecessor Mullah Mansour's entire team.[38]

Hibatullah is indeed a very interesting figure, a cleric lacking charisma with nothing to make up for it—very different from Mullah Omar, who was famous for his cult of charismatic personality. One US intelligence official I spoke to, who knows Afghanistan very well, compared Hibatullah's position to when influential Iranian politician Akbar Hashemi Rafsanjani (who later became president) paved the way for Ayatollah Ali Khamenei to become the supreme leader in 1989 (at the time of Ayatollah Ruhollah Khomeini's death). Thinking he was easy to manage and manipulate if need be—someone they could control—but it turns out, he's tough as nails. Khamenei quickly established himself and was always his own man. Similarly, the Haqqanis and Yaqoob viewed Hibatullah the same way, and so offered their full support to him for the golden seat in August 2021. Hibatullah, as we now know, is far more authoritarian and controlling than was generally believed. The word "supreme" in his job title (used in the Western media) had not escaped his notice after all.

There have been too many men in history like Yaqoob, assuming that because their father sat on the throne, they own it. His youth is prominent enough to keep him off it for a while, but his eyes stay glued to the spot of successor. So much so, that when acting prime minister Mohammad Hassan Akhund, in a crucial small meeting with the most influential cabinet members, made the case for putting Mullah Baradar up as a top Taliban executive leader (practically as his own replacement), even temporarily, arguing that he was better suited to the international stage, Yaqoob vehemently rejected the idea.[39] If it could not be him, it could not be anyone. This dynastic mentality is not new to the region, but to everyone's surprise, Sirajuddin Haqqani offered his support to Yaqoob, despite their on-again, off-again relationship. According to one source, their standing up to Mohammad Hassan Akhund made for quite an awkward moment. Time will tell, though, how long Siraj and Yaqoob's current dynamic will last.

A Taliban insider shared with me that initially Mullah Baradar was angry and disappointed at being left out of the core leadership team, and as a protest he stayed away from cabinet meetings for the first three to four months after the government's formation.[40] Some rumors of a physical fight between Baradar and Khalil Haqqani appeared in social media but those are exaggerated. They did indeed exchange heated words as regards who deserved more credit for the Taliban victory and it was their respective followers who brawled with each other at a different location.[41] Mullah Baradar has in fact politically recovered since assuming his additional role as chief economic strategist for the Taliban, as mentioned above. He is believed to be working very diligently and his decisions on economic policy are deemed as final by all. While many Western dignitaries who visit Kabul for meetings believe he does not hold much influence in the corridors of power, this is only partially true. As to his future, a senior Pakistani diplomat who regularly interacts with Taliban leaders told me that Baradar believes that he will most likely be Hibatullah's successor as top Taliban leader. All reports indicate that Hibatullah is in fact in better health than Baradar, so the chances of Baradar emerging as supreme Taliban leader in the future are mixed at best. Both the Haqqanis and Pakistan are unlikely to support such an eventuality—but given increasing anti-Pakistan feelings among the Taliban, that can only be helpful for Baradar.

The difference between Yaqoob and Siraj is not an ideological one but a political one, soaked in the sweat of a desperate power grab. The very reason they stand behind Hibatullah, even though they disagree with his intense, rigid religious outlook, is that it suits them politically. He has the clerical support base they would need for their own survival. Siraj is relatively more open than the others and coordinates well with his cabinet colleagues. For instance, Siraj wanted the girls' schools to open in March 2022 as promised. However, the chances of him taking sides in an ideological tussle are next to zero—he would not waste his capital in such debates, so as to remain relevant to all sides. The sacrificing of ideological leaning for the sake of power is clear here—they both operate on purely political lines. As long as they are in the control room, to hell with all else.

Another person with inside knowledge of Taliban workings in Kabul told me something quite fascinating in an interview. He believes that while the two new string-pullers, Siraj and Yaqoob, seem to be hand in hand with each other, behind the scenes their trust in each other is diminishing as they both hope to succeed Hibatullah. They have even resorted to spying on each other, he further disclosed. This shows not only their ambition but also the kind of cut-throat competition going on within the Taliban's cabinet. At every corner of the group lies an intense power struggle that could have more than deadly consequences—and threaten everything they have fought for. Siraj Haqqani, meanwhile, has successfully grabbed critical posts in various departments under his ministry, as that is where the money is: taxes, smuggled goods, drugs, and so on.

While these political rivalries are brewing, the messaging to the outside world seems consistent. Yaqoob, for instance, in an interview to National Public Radio (NPR) clearly expressed his wish to have better relations with the US and even called the need for establishing constitutional law in Afghanistan a "necessity."[42] Similarly, Siraj, in a conversation with CNN's Christiane Amanpour, declared that for the Taliban, the US is an enemy no more (even if they have reservations about the US's intentions); they would like to have good relations with the US and the international community, he said, "based on rules and principles that exist in the rest of the world."[43] This signifies that a Taliban foreign affairs strategy is in place.

Andrew Watkins, a leading expert on Afghanistan, believes that before August 2021 Hibatullah had increasingly deferred to rule by committee, a style in line with the group's traditionally consultative decision-making process while solidifying the horizontal network of its leadership.[44] A Taliban leader I talked to confirms that the Rahbari Shura largely retains an important role and in most cases critical issues are thoroughly discussed and debated in the Shura meetings led by Hibatullah. Members of the Shura can propose agenda items and Hibatullah has allowed that tradition to become stronger over time.[45] Some administrative adjustments were introduced recently though, given that now a large cabinet is in place in Kabul (with many members holding Shura membership as well). Some social media reports suggesting that the Shura is becoming dormant sound exaggerated.

Prime Minister Hassan Akhund is believed to be quite ill, prompting conversations about potential successors. The top contender so far seems to be Abdul Hakim Haqqani, the top Taliban ideologue. Were this to become the case, the conservative factions of the group would only be strengthened, altering the power balance even more.

The political climate in Kabul today is surprisingly not very different from that during the previous government in Kabul. Then it seemed Ghani and Abdullah Abdullah were running parallel governments. According to an insider I interviewed, today the Afghan presidential palace is operating in essentially four adjacent buildings—where staff from one part cannot go to another without a body search. One part of the palace is under the control of Prime Minister Hassan Akhund, another is shared between mullahs Baradar and Yaqoob, a third is under Deputy Prime Minister Maulvi Kabir, and the final quarter under Siraj Haqqani.

So the splintering between the hardliners and pragmatists —with promises made and betrayed—lies at the root of the Taliban today. The pragmatists do have the capacity to come out on top, if their attempts to convey to their counterparts that their vision is a necessary one are successful. Their use of international relations and building of connections with foreign states, and the subsequent benefits of that for the country as a whole could potentially dilute the stance of the hardliners. The international community can engage and promote this moderation, and perhaps bridge the gaps that are dangerously growing. But, at the same time, the dilemma is that the schism's ideological basis is strengthened by accusations of disloyalty to the group and moderates' reputation as internationally acceptable. The stubborn foolishness of the hardliners, choosing isolation and starvation over co-operation or "submission," will have disastrous consequences for all. Effectively, moving forward, the policies of the group are dependent on reconciliation between these factions.

The disorderly nature of the actual decision-making body within the Taliban puts at risk everything they have fought for and, effectively, the livelihood of all Afghans. Hardliners and ultra-conservatives have established a rigid monopoly undermining the work and ideals of the moderates who put them back on the throne. In reality, influence over decision-making comes from different sources at different times, with no real structure. The autocratic hardliners have little interest in developing institutions that are representative and accountable. All hope is not lost though, as the group's former representatives in Doha (many of whom are now cabinet members in Kabul), for instance, are likely to continue to push for better governance in order to seek international recognition and needed sources of aid and investment.

The trap Afghanistan is in right now due to the hard-liners' tight grip is a tragic one for the millions of people seeking basic aid, rights and a livelihood. Only when these internal divisions are resolved, be it through internal work or external dialogue and support, can the Taliban prove themselves to be something different this time. Otherwise, they are the same as we have always known them.

An insightful example of the internal divisions is what transpired in early August 2022—a targeted attack in Kabul killing Taliban ideologue Rahimullah Haqqani. He was known as a leading anti-Salafi figure who had issued fatwas against ISK. Accordingly, then, the first suspect for his murder was ISK. However, when I spoke to a journalist who was in Kabul investigating this, he shared some interesting insights with me. Locals had told him that although it's true Haqqani was on a target list because of those fatwas, he was also vocally campaigning for the reopening of girls' schools, as mentioned in a BBC report. He had categorically maintained that, "There is no justification in the sharia [law] to say female education is not allowed. No justification at all."[46] My source went on to say that it's entirely possible that he was actually killed from *within* the Taliban ranks by those opposed to that position. It was an easy strike for them, because everyone knew the suspicion would fall on ISK. Even more, ISK would happily claim responsibility because that suits their narrative: to build fear, and show up the Taliban as incompetent. This then, is the nature of the challenge regarding the internal divisions of the Taliban—brutal and bloody when it comes down to it. The bigotry of the group's hardliners is alive and kicking, unsurprisingly. Only this time around the threat they pose also targets the vision of the more open-minded elements among them.

Certainly the Taliban take their unity and cohesion very seriously. Those who challenge Taliban policies from within are dealt with particularly severely. For instance, former Taliban ambassador Abdul Salam Zaeef, ex-foreign minister Abdul Wakeel Muttawakil and an important member of the Quetta Shura, Agha Jan Motassim, were all demoted and sidelined within the group for showing dissent.[47] With regard to local resistance, the Taliban believe they can effectively contain the threat from the National Resistance Front (NRF) based in Dushanbe, Tajikistan. The initial challenge to their return to power from the Mazar-e-Sharif area was quickly and effectively tackled.

Looking for Legitimacy: Hibatullah Speaks in Kabul[48]

As the Taliban approach the second anniversary of their victory and the American withdrawal, they remain mired in confusion with parallel power centers contesting for control and influence. So the decision-making process is still chaotic. However, they are fully cognizant of this fact. Just as they were serious about reentering Kabul after two decades of struggle, they are serious about forming a solid government recognized by the world. Accordingly, they have begun strategizing and ticking off the checklist to bring their vision to life once and for all. On June 30, 2022, they initiated a mass gathering of 3,500 to 4,000 members organized at Kabul Polytechnic University, made up of religious scholars and tribal elders, all brought together to sanctify the Taliban government and solidify their national policies and formalize their government. Each district sent two religious representatives and one tribal elder in addition to provincial representatives. The goal was to foster unity and stability, and mainly to discuss the agenda of economic and social issues and how their Islamic government will address them. Aside from its large audience, this conference was special for another reason: its guest of honor. For the first time, supreme leader Mullah Hibatullah left his ordinary residence of Kandahar and stepped into Kabul for the special occasion. Despite being the supreme leader and belonging to the important Durrani tribe, Hibatullah himself is from the Noorzai sub-clan, which was seldom represented in the power structure within Afghanistan ever before, so this was an extremely important moment for him. Even the Taliban movement's founder, Mullah Omar, had never addressed a public meeting in Kabul.

The world has grown used to the generalized ideas of who the Taliban are and how they work. In contrast to what most believe though, they do in fact strategize and analyze—they have hierarchies and structures that they adhere to. Like any other group, they hear each other out and make plans with the intention of following through with them. Exhibit A—this gathering. And, this was only one step toward fulfilling their goal, which is seeking internal legitimacy and gaining acceptance from the international community. Whether or not they have respect for the international community, they are not so daft as to view it as unnecessary. If anything, they are only too aware of how desperately necessary external validation is to their regime—or at least open ears. So, they are putting on the costumes, playing the role that needs to be played and making a concerted effort. This is not to say, however, that their internal work is admirable in any way at all. They are simply overwhelmed in the face of a massive looming economic and humanitarian crisis.

As expected, this gathering was an all-male event. However, they claimed that women's input was being considered as well, but out of respect for them it would be their sons or spouses who would convey their messages to the meeting. It sounds ridiculous in this day and age but they believe in it. Notably, among many other important conversations, they discussed the place of women and their future in Afghan society. They reiterated that women must abide by rules of dress in wearing the obligatory chadors, and cannot travel certain distances without a male relative. Perhaps the most internationally recognized issue of girls' education was only briefly brought up by a handful of attendees, without a conclusive consensus. If legitimacy is what they are seeking, the first attempt was lacking in many ways.

Emir Hibatullah Akhundzada spoke in Pashto mainly (aside from reciting many Quranic verses in Arabic) for a little less than an hour.[49] He avoided calling the meeting a *jirga* and instead referred to it as a "great gathering of *ulema*," eliciting religious consensus in support of the government. He started off by calling the Taliban victory a moment of pride not only for the Afghan but also the larger global Muslim community. Some radical and militant Islamist groups across the world indeed congratulated the Taliban on their return to power in Afghanistan but the hard fact he failed to acknowledge is that not a single Muslim-majority country has recognized the regime at the latest time of writing (January 2023).

He made no mention of the continued closure of girls' schools and did not touch on the economic problems staring the country in the face. Surprisingly, he offered no direct critique of ISK even when some ISK militants tried to target this very gathering. His primary message was that the Taliban will not compromise on their interpretation of Islamic law and that ideology, rather than pragmatism, would define and drive Taliban policies. He admonished the international community for not recognizing the legitimacy of the Islamic Emirate but sounded more accommodating to political opponents in exile and within Afghanistan, emphasizing that the Taliban amnesty announced earlier would hold.[50] On the economy, he sounded skeptical about international and development aid and emphasized reliance on internal sources. This is contrary to what Taliban ministers dealing with the economy are trying to project. Either he was not briefed well on the topic or he does not care much. Nevertheless, the gathering concluded with a pledge of allegiance to Mullah Hibatullah. A few direct quotes from his speech offer an important insight about his long-term and broader goals:

> The Taliban do not know how to apply Sharia but the ulema have that knowledge. Everyone should obey them in this regard. . . . Afghanistan's ulema not only makes an Islamic regime successful but will also assume a leadership role for the global Muslim community.

The executive branch should enforce Sharia Law all over the country and people should obey and implement those rules in their daily lives. [The] Judiciary should dispense justice based on Islamic principles. No sentences or punishments shall be executed outside of the court's order.

While I do not have much knowledge of governance, we should govern ourselves rather than let others govern us. Other countries do not want us to be independent and have always intervened in our internal matters. Now is the time for us to take complete control.[51]

What are Pragmatic Taliban Elements Up To?

In a conversation with journalist Kathy Gannon, whose time in and expertise of Afghanistan spans over three decades, she shared with me a number of fascinating insights about the internal politics of the Taliban.[52] No other Western journalist understands the Taliban better than she does. As Gannon emphasizes, "the Taliban are not a monolith." Indeed, they have a variety of viewpoints and backgrounds that have shaped them, as discussed throughout this work. "The Taliban have many pragmatists in their ranks," Gannon argues, "but in a way the West doesn't understand." Gannon went on to discuss the divisions within the Taliban leadership circle that continue to haunt their decision-making. The pragmatists of the group, including Mullah Yaqoob, Mullah Baradar, Sirajuddin Haqqani and Khairullah Khairkhwa, harbor a growing discontent with the series of directives issuing from Kandahar, Gannon maintains. Disloyalty is not an option for this group, but they have developed a strategy of sorts on the fly: "ignoring some edicts coming from Kandahar," as Gannon puts it. Some decisions are simply not being implemented. She acknowledged that "this is no sustainable way to run a government," and with "such obvious leadership divisions, the Taliban will struggle to create a stable future for themselves." So it is not that the Taliban are not aware of their shortcomings. They simply can't afford to have their leadership hierarchy disintegrate.

Another aspect of the reality in Afghanistan that Gannon talked about passionately was the deeply held view among the Taliban and their supporters that Western ways are opposed to Afghan culture and norms. Of course there is a long history behind this notion. A series of interventions and invasions from all directions over the course of centuries have entrenched this perception. Such a mindset requires careful handling. Gannon is perplexed, however, at the West's continued lack of understanding of Afghanistan, Afghans and the Taliban. She is certainly not alone in this assessment.

The Taliban are surely struggling to maintain unity and cracks are visible at many levels beyond ideological issues. According to an influential Taliban cabinet member, Mullah Nooruddin Turabi, five major issues are keeping the Taliban leaders up at night: a) from where can enough economic resources to run the country be generated? b) will a majority of Afghans accept the new Taliban government? c) will the international community recognize the Taliban government? d) how can qualified people who are also loyal to the Taliban be attracted to run the government? e) how can the many Taliban members who are waiting to be appointed to important government positions be accommodated, and how will those who don't get what they want react?[53]

Turabi shared these concerns with Pakistani journalist Habib Akram, who published them in an informative book on the Taliban in late 2022. Turabi told him that the Taliban are far from harmonious among themselves but, irrespective of the seriousness of the differences, internal conflict is very unlikely. He also dismissed the option of seeking Pakistan's help to run the government, fearful of the perception that Pakistan has taken over Afghanistan via the Taliban.[54] In fact, relations with Pakistan are yet another major issue that divides the Taliban. Pakistan has a terrible reputation among Afghans, including many—if not most—Taliban. One of the first official requests from the Taliban government to Pakistan was to not send Pakistani journalists to cover the developments in Kabul. Kabul's lackluster support in pushing Pakistani Taliban to come to terms with Islamabad and regular clashes and firefights on the Pakistan–Afghanistan border crossings are a reflection of this distrust. This is not to deny that Pakistan helped the Afghan Taliban significantly during the insurgency years—but it is also true that almost simultaneously it mishandled the Taliban magnificently.

Lastly, the debate around what an inclusive government really means also haunts the Taliban. This is what had led to an early confrontation between Mullah Baradar and the "Helmand group", also known as Kandahari Taliban, led by finance minister Gul Agha Ishaqzai. Helmand is seen as part of the larger Kandahar area (even though it is now a separate province adjacent to Kandahar). Being a childhood friend of Mullah Omar and having lived with him in the same house during the first Taliban government (1996–2001), Ishaqzai has significant influence over Mullah Hibatullah also. This "Helmand group" claims to be the "real" Taliban and believes that only the old guard and loyal Taliban members deserve to be included in the government. Baradar was making a case for a broad-based government, keeping in view the recognition challenge that the Taliban were bound to face. Contrary to many media reports, the dispute was a verbal clash and Baradar walked out, complaining to Mullah Hibatullah, who intervened to keep the two sides apart.[55]

The rumor that continues to make rounds among the "Helmand group" is that Mullah Baradar is among the very few who is privy to the three secret annexures of the 2020 Taliban–US deal. Besides providing for the sharing of information on global terrorist groups, the annexures are believed to include guidelines on an inclusive government model as well as the Taliban's relations with its neighbors.[56]

As discussed in a later chapter, Taliban relations with the immediate neighborhood as well as the Gulf countries are also leading to some sharp differences among the Taliban. It should come as no surprise that the Kandahari Taliban are leaning more towards the east and influential Muslim-majority states for its relationship building. While Turkey and Qatar seem to be combining their outreach efforts to gain economic advantage in Afghanistan, the UAE, Iran and Pakistan have their strong lobbies at work too. China can outsmart all others but as always it is keeping its cards close to its chest. The relatively new entrant in this regional power play is Uzbekistan. It views the Taliban "as a reality that must be accepted," and sees Afghanistan as an integral part of Central Asia.[57] It is hard to quantify, but many Uzbeks view the Taliban positively. The Taliban foreign minister Muttaqi's visit to the Samarkand grand mosque in July 2022 and the warm public reception he received there—with many Uzbeks trying hard to get a photograph with him— was something that Uzbek security had not anticipated.[58] What is worth noting here is that any leverage that countries like Uzbekistan may acquire can ultimately be employed to nudge the Taliban in a positive direction.

The Way Ahead

The international community has made it clear that women's rights must be prioritized before the Taliban are ever deemed legitimate or worthy of the validation they seek—with no inclusivity, it seems nothing has changed, so why pretend it has? Well, the Taliban are proving to be an optimistic bunch, and certainly a committed one. Perhaps the truth is that they will never earn the legitimacy they feel they deserve. After all, they have decades of bad reputation to their name. For them to change would basically necessitate a complete identity overhaul—and it seems this reality is becoming frighteningly more obvious to them each day. The question is—will they make the sacrifices they need to in exchange for recognition? Have they learned from their past mistakes? Is there a chance they could abandon the entire endeavor of diplomacy and conversations, letting the country sink deeper into economic crisis?

In his speech at the Kabul Polytechnic gathering, Hibatullah expressed a view that the Taliban will likely "double down" on the policies that bar them from receiving domestic and international legitimacy. Many Taliban cabinet ministers were surprised as well as disappointed with this approach, but they would avoid saying so in public. With billions of their assets frozen by the US as a humanitarian and economic disaster sweeps throughout the country, some Taliban leaders in Kabul recognize that it is time to loosen the strings a little. Contrary to that, Hibatullah emphasized that they would carry out their mission despite any external criticism. So differences within the Taliban are becoming increasingly obvious (e.g. Siraj's critical speech in February 2023). The hardliners among them, following Hibatullah's lead, wish to remain loyal to their fundamentalist cause and face the consequences of global isolation.

While the West remains committed to its demands, the Taliban are reassessing their options. They are perhaps trying: they are creating committees to improve governance and reprimanding nepotism and corruption, discussing differing viewpoints and even directly saying that the issues the world is most concerned about are not being ignored but rather being carefully discussed. Moreover—arguably one of the most important facets of their current reality—they continue to tell both Afghan citizens and their neighboring states that they want peace and security. They offer consolation—albeit, many times hypocritically and contradicting themselves—emphasizing that they are not here to wage war but to create a new life for their country, one created by Afghan people for Afghan people.

Ultimately, they are not content with just getting off the bench—they are in the game, and want to be treated as such. Their work did not end in August 2021—it had just begun.

A conversation I had with a former senior US official is relevant here. This is a story about a coffee-table conversation between the US official and Abbas Stanikzai, Salam Hanafi (now deputy prime minister), Mullah Zaeef (former Taliban ambassador to Islamabad) and Suhail Shaheen (Taliban spokesman in the Doha office), around the time the Doha negotiations started. The impression the US official got was that all four of the guys, despite their doing well on the ground, knew they could not defeat the US. It was a stalemate. But the pragmatic elements of the Taliban were not crying over that; they knew there could be a power-sharing formula in Afghanistan that worked for all. The official remembered how the personalities of the men shone through the conversation, particularly how Stanikzai had a great sense of humor. He was an "unguided missile," which was perhaps why he was not given any position of note later on—also, his reputation as an alleged drinker (rightly or wrongly) had persisted and was not doing him any favors. Hanafi, also present, was almost the opposite: reserved, skinny and very serious in his remarks. Then there was Shaheen, who spoke excellent English, hence his role as spokesperson.

The conversation offered insights into the future. The US official talked about the heavy US investments in building military bases and explained to them the job they were aspiring to—emphasizing that once the Taliban came into power, they would have to deal with criminal groups and all sorts of troublemakers, including ISK. So, the US official tested the waters by saying hypothetically: "Consider that even if we leave, you may need to ask the US to come back for counterterrorism help, and those bases can be in use for our common cause." The brilliant Stanikzai caught on quickly, retorting: "Ah, you want to keep an eye on China, well, it will also help us keep an eye on Pakistan." He continued, neither agreeing nor disagreeing to the use of military bases, saying once the Taliban are back, "we would like to have technical support and help with education." Another in the group agreed—"you are better than the Russians, and we would like to benefit from that." The Taliban can indeed be engaged on issues of mutual interest if these are framed well.

With all this change, the Biden administration has been thinking hard about how best to engage with the Taliban without recognizing them officially. The reality is that the Taliban are the de facto government of Afghanistan, and the Biden government is directly communicating with them on financial and humanitarian issues, and there is some intelligence sharing going on as well; but it does not *recognize* or *accept* them—and will surely want to be the last to do so officially. The US special representative for Afghanistan, Thomas West, a thoughtful diplomat, has met with many Taliban officials, including defense minister Mullah Yaqoob Anas Haqqani, Shahabuddin Delavar and cabinet members dealing with economic affairs; some of these engagements were reported on the US Department of State's website.[59] While the US reluctantly considers further options, others are stepping up: the Turks, Russians, Pakistanis and Chinese have thriving "embassies" in Kabul. The conversations have not stopped, but have become more intense and broader in focus.

For the US and its allies, the most important thing is to ensure that extremist groups like ISK and Al-Qaeda will not be able to thrive—and it seems, at least through some statements, that the Taliban want to live up to the promises they made on this issue. The CIA drone strike in Kabul on July 31, 2022 which took out Al-Qaeda chief Al-Zawahiri, and the muted Taliban response, shows that the Taliban are embarrassed. Media reports indicated that only a handful of people besides Siraj Haqqani, who was hosting him, had any clue that Zawahiri was moving about Kabul, but others find it inconceivable that the Taliban leadership were unaware of his presence. One view is that Pakistan shared the critical intelligence leading to the strike in order to resurrect its deteriorating relationship with the US.[60] Nonetheless, US counterterrorism officials believe that Al-Qaeda "has not reconstituted its presence in Afghanistan since the US withdrawal," and the terror group still "does not have the ability to launch attacks from the country against the United States."[61] That assessment supports the Taliban's contention that they will not allow any terrorist group to use their soil for terror activities abroad.

Afghanistan's foreign minister Amir Khan Muttaqi, while making a case for international recognition of the new government at an international conference in Tashkent in July 2022, gave voice to his government's oft-repeated commitment that they would not allow the security of neighboring countries to be compromised.[62] Taliban policy appears to be unchanged on this point as far as Kabul is concerned.

It is also important, however, to continue to follow the current direction of Taliban policy through what Hibatullah has to say. His speech in Kabul discussed earlier in this chapter proved to be startling, giving insight about his views. He indicated that Muslim countries should be looking up to the Taliban since their victory. After all, the Taliban see themselves as divinely gifted victors, with the one and only perfect model for an Islamic government, their own form of Manifest Destiny. The international audience, understandably and expectedly, are at a loss as to how to interpret this. One US intelligence official, however, gave me some insight, saying that all we can tell, based on that speech, is that Hibatullah is healthy and his leadership is not threatened in his assessment—basically, he is sticking around.

This chapter offered pieces of evidence that may appear to contradict each other, though my purpose is to present all the credible information I could glean from different sources. More importantly, the truth is that the Taliban are inherently a contradictory bunch of people, muddled in complexity. The following chapters investigate what to make of these contradictions and where to go from there.

Deobandism, Islam and the Religious Narratives of the Taliban

Throughout the history of the Muslim world, the way Islam has manifested and operated within various societies has taken many forms. Religious scholars and clergy have enjoyed positions of great influence across various regions through the rule of different dynasties, while the mystical appeal of Sufism or Irfan (spiritual knowledge) has made a lasting impression on the cultural landscapes of multiple Muslim nations. The case of South Asia is a particularly fascinating one, with these two currents penetrating deeply within society, meshing together intricately and, sometimes, quite disagreeably. To this day, the spectrum on which Islam exists within the region is a vast one, marked by ends more opposite than can be simply expressed. Unfortunately, this diversity has not been spared the bloody footprints of decades-long conflict sunken in chaos and violence, threatening the integrity of the broader region and replacing the once glorious legacy of religion with one of turmoil and terror. Worse yet, this conflict rages on today in a manner that risks preventing tolerance and peaceful coexistence in a truly disastrous manner. To better understand the complexity that lies beneath this multifaceted story, it is worth examining and analyzing the historical context that has helped create the Afghanistan of today.

Some would say the Taliban are, at root, more a religious organization than anything else. Is that correct, though? They could just as accurately be described as a political group, or a militant one. French scholar Olivier Roy suggests that while the Taliban were not prone to manipulation on certain issues such as in relation to women, they were profoundly expedient when it came to securing a power base.[1] The Taliban's use of, and relationship with religion has long been a deeply complex one, littered with controversies. Certainly, however, one cannot begin to understand the group's past, present, or future without first acknowledging the religious ideology that fuels their activities. Let us look now at the primary basis of their religious mindset, before delving into how it came to be and what is challenged in the process. We must first understand the Islamic roots of the group to comprehend how they achieved their supposed spiritual legitimacy and built their base. This is part of a larger issue—the degeneration of Islamic theological study within the Muslim world, as well as the politicization of Islamic principles.

The Taliban are adherents of the Sunni sect of Islam, and specifically the Hanafi school of thought, one of four sub-sects within Sunnism. Within that, they also belong to a political brand in South Asia known as the Deobandi school of thought—a relatively new incarnation of the religious ideology of South Asian politics from the nineteenth century.[2] It is critical to look at and understand the dynamics of the Taliban beginning from their ideology—therein lies their soul. While the group is seen as radical, with people often disregarding their Islamic label, it is their hardline interpretation of religion that underlies all they do, like the air they breathe. Within the region and South Asian context especially, this religious grounding is vital.

Deobandism and Revivalist Islam[3]

What is Deobandism? This little-known ideology and its adherents are not often mentioned on our TV screens, but that does not make them any less important. First, we cannot understand Deobandism if we separate it from its South Asian context, otherwise one of the biggest and most essential pieces of the puzzle is missing. Deobandism as a religious ideology originated in South Asia, where most of its adherents are concentrated. This strain of Islamic political thought was born around a hundred miles from the Indian capital in a seminary known as Darul Uloom Deoband in 1866. At the peak of British colonialism in India, Islamic revivalists found the path to their sovereignty through religion. The seminary's two founders had participated in a failed rebellion against the British a few years earlier.[4] The group has undoubtedly experienced many changes since then, and ultimately, as it became increasingly dependent on sponsors in Saudi Arabia and the Gulf region, factions of it also fell victim to more fundamentalist thoughts and behaviors.

The stains of the footprints of colonialism have not yet faded globally. Today the linkage between religious fundamentalism and imperialist activity serves as a vital junction in the study of the origins of such groups and their motivation. Colonialism had an especially deep impact on South Asian ulema (scholars) and religious thinking that would ultimately define over a century of action by "Islamist" socio-political actors. The idea that colonialism had corrupted Islam led to the creation of an anti-imperialist Islamic revivalist ideology that eventually took the shape of a nationalist, and then Islamist, development. This brings us to the birth of *revivalist* movements. Growing out of discontentment with the political state of the time, these groups turned to religion to heal the wounds caused by society, believing that new interpretations of religion could be the cure. Deobandism was a product of Indian frustration with British colonialism in the late nineteenth century. Fast-forward to the twentieth century and in the rise of the Taliban we see a product of political, cultural and economic imperialism—Soviet invaders, Saudi petrodollars, Pakistani madrassa education and American weapons.

Within South Asia, it is an accepted fact that Islam came to the region by way of the Sufis, who did not belong to any one school of jurisprudence, but who shared a gentle, mystical approach to faith.

Deobandis are a sub group of Sunnis, but it is more complicated than that. Within Sunnism, there is a wide spectrum ranging from the more rigid Salafis to the less rigid Deobandis, all the way to Barelvis, a Sufi-oriented, relatively more progressive group. Deobandis eventually developed an intensely anti-innovation stance that, in turn, manifested in a deep rivalry with their Barelvi counterparts.

Both had roots in religious institutions in British India. That historical relationship has now led to the widely accepted idea that Deobandis are thus anti-Sufi. In reality, the claim that Deobandis are inherently anti-Sufi bears little weight. The complexity beneath identities warrants further examination of each individually and when in confrontation with each other. The root of the discussion lies in how the Taliban identify themselves—and essentially, despite their Deobandi roots, their stances often fall more into a realm of their own.

In simple and direct terms, the Taliban are Hanafi Sunnis with borrowed aspects of Salafism and influences of Wahhabism, thanks to Saudi infiltration into Deobandi madrassas—but they are still Hanafi.[5] Their ideological lines began to blur when they were exposed to foreign terrorist groups like Al-Qaeda.[6] The Taliban, as we have witnessed, take what they can when it is convenient. This points us to the reality that their ideological basis can be interpreted in ambiguous ways. Both religion and culture are molded to their ever-changing desire. The only real consistency is their end goal. Professor Barbara Metcalf, a leading scholar of the Deobandi school of thought, aptly says:

> What is perhaps most striking about the Deoband-type movements is the extent to which politics is an empty "box," filled expediently and pragmatically depending on what seems to work best in any given situation.[7]

Here it is important to note that there are significant theological differences among the Afghan and Pakistani brands of Taliban. Based on my interviews with scholars in

Pakistan, the Pakistani Taliban today feel they no longer identify with the scholarship or discipline of Deobandis. In terms of religious practice, they simply do not live up to what might have been expected of them as Deobandis. The Pakistani Taliban are fundamentalists with very independent thinking, unique in the way their religious attitudes mesh with tribal culture. Even though they receive religious education in seminaries associated with Deobandis, they do not represent them, nor do they practically align with them. Thus Deobandism is no longer relevant for the Pakistani Taliban, but is still very useful for understanding the Afghan Taliban and their history. Essentially, the Taliban increasingly have their own fusion of fundamentalist beliefs—combining the rigidity of Salafism and militant Deobandis with the tribalism and elements of Pashtunwali.[8]

It is important to note that Deobandis historically spearheaded a lot of scholarship—their contributions to South Asian intellectual discourse are significant.[9] However, unfortunately today this ideology, and the way it is practiced in parts of Pakistan and Afghanistan, represents something deeply opposed to how Islam has usually been practiced in South Asia—in fact they are a stain on the legacy of tolerance and mysticism that defined the religion's presence in the region, replacing it with one of terror and trauma. On all levels, this model of strict adherence the Taliban cling to was never the norm, and perhaps that is exactly why they are so attached to it—as a desperate mechanism to sustain what they have.

Yes, they already adhered to a tribalism that was restrictive and oppressive, but the issues began when they fell under the toxic influence of Al-Qaeda's political adventurism and militancy. Shias in Iran establishing an Islamic system also influenced them, despite the sectarian differences. The 1979 Iranian revolution was inspiring to many radical and political Muslim movements—it was a world-shaking moment, evoking awe even among those who had sectarian differences with the revolutionaries. Abul Ala Maududi, a leading Deobandi thinker and politician from Pakistan, even went to Iran after the revolution to see Ayatollah Khomeini and praised the new Islamic system.[10] It was a shared desire among them, this notion of the rule of clerics. Although Iran follows the notion of the "supremacy of the jurist" while remaining partially democratic, the Taliban have no inclination to follow that model.

Modern interpretations of Deobandism can be aggressive and militaristic, as exemplified by the Afghan Taliban—a product of a combination of dogmatic tribalism with a rigid version of Islam, especially when coupled with the geopolitics of the Afghan resistance to the Soviets and later the Americans. The Mujahideen or Islamic warriors that the US empowered and equipped, hand in hand with Saudi Arabia and Pakistan, ultimately turned out to be a monster. From Al-Qaeda to the Taliban, the Afghan "Jihad" played a vital role in offering space and facilitation for militant groups. The ideas of armed jihad for Afghans and Pakistanis were largely drawn from the Deobandi school.

When the Taliban emerged in the early 1990s, they were ideologically influenced by the Saudis, armed by the Americans, and educated by Pakistani Deobandi madrassas that had conveniently changed their curriculum to fit the needs of the hour. They are the legacy of Reagan's Holy Warriors, the Mujahideen—surrounded by Western resources and regional Islamist inspiration.

Ultimately, though, it would be truly unfortunate if, once again, we fell into the trap of mislabeling an entire group of people (such as Deobandis) based on the twisted interpretations and actions of a few extremists claiming their identity. As mentioned earlier in the chapter, Deobandism has a deep and rich history of scholarly contributions to Islamic studies, in South Asia and beyond. There are many, many people who identify with the Deobandi school of thought and are vehemently against the Taliban. In fact, they are adamant opponents of their actions. The Taliban are not monolithic: we must recognize the multiple subsections within them. This allows us to gain a better grasp on how the Taliban view themselves—their organization and structural tiers, and, further, how local communities view them.

Traditionally those we refer to as "Islamists" are politically motivated actors, rather than clerics or scholars. However, in South Asia, these actors are guided by the traditional clerics and their students.

Interestingly, Saudi Wahhabism and Deobandism were cut from the same cloth, with their historical roots intertwining through the paths of their founders.[11] Today as well, they echo each other in their respective arenas of belonging. The original goal of the founders of Deobandism was to break the chains of British colonialism—it was a resistance movement with a religious support system beneath it. Similarly, when the Soviets invaded, once again the Mujahideen's resistance to the imperialists was grounded in religious fundamentalism. Deobandism almost naturally assumed a position at the forefront of that campaign and found willing state sponsors in Pakistan, Saudi Arabia and the US.

The Historical Context of Deoband

Deobandism began as a religious revivalist endeavor, born from the idea that sovereignty could be achieved through religious education and development, where the clergy/ulema are the leaders of the land. Eventually, it moved beyond its humble beginnings to transform into a transnational movement that is more politically ambitious and regionally connected. The group's actions are essentially a series of efforts to re-Islamize Afghan society. Clerics act as the brain of the group, and Islamism is the life force pumping blood through the body. This revivalist idea of bringing back true, original Islam, and of viewing problems as a result of man's drift away from true faith, ensures that the only ones who can resolve the problem are the religious scholars—the clerics. This ideology guarantees them the authority they so desperately seek. We could delve deeper into the conversation about the general psychological and sociological aspects of clergy—from all faiths—demonstrating such, but that would be a whole other book.

The idea at the core of the group's movement was that Islam, and thus Muslim religious participation, had diminished in India, and lost its purity due to meshing its ideologies and practices with the coexisting majority Hindu faith.

The aim was to re-purify it, return it to its original reality, and therefore create the sovereign society they sought. It was the avenue to all their problems' solutions. However, they were not a divisive movement. In fact, they were pro-Muslim–Hindu unity, with the main enemy being the British colonialists. Over time, as new ideologies arose in the subcontinent, the Deobandis gained more competition and opponents. The attitudes of all these groups were impacted by the others' stances and popularity. It is hard to reduce the differences between such groups to mere sectarian lines or ideological differences; it was all deeply political and rapidly changing as well. Anyhow, the Deobandis continued to gain ground and expand their network of schools and thus students. They did not, however, stay confined to the classroom. Slowly but surely, they found their way back to armed resistance to the British. Even when facing losses on that front, they would not surrender to British rule, and so began a long and complex journey of the expansion of Deobandism's religious and political arms. It was not until the final lead-up to the India–Pakistan partition that Deobandism experienced an internal schism, with one faction falling deeper into puritanical thought and inching closer to fundamentalism. Later, in the 1980s, Pakistan's military dictator Zia-ul-Haq shifted the scene even further, empowering the militant Deobandis who soon found themselves at the forefront of Islamism in the region.[12] Years went by, and the group only grew more motivated and violent, leading us up to today. It turned ultimately into a divisive ideology, both internally, driving Sunni–Shia sectarianism, and externally, creating anti-Hindu narratives to recruit militants to fight in Indian-controlled Kashmir against Indian security forces.

The Afghan resistance to the Soviet invasion was spear-headed by Deobandi leaders, and the event was the perfect catalyst for them to finally obtain their Islamic-governed state. With Saudi Arabia funding them and strengthening their ideological base, this would be the beginning of the Taliban's story—the sparks leading to a wildfire.

The Islamic Revolution in next-door Iran, while inspiring for some Deobandi segments, like Maududi of Jamaat-e-Islami in Pakistan, also increased anti-Shia sentiments among other, more Wahhabi-influenced, Deobandis. That deeply sectarian mindset would further transform the nature of the extremist factions, heightening their divisive-ness and intolerance. This level of sectarianism would become a staple identifier of the Taliban, whose attacks on the Shia minority in both Afghanistan and Pakistan have been ongoing for decades.

Perhaps from a sociological point of view, we can acknowledge the Deobandi school's life so far as a long journey of expanding political ambitions and failures, only to recoup, try again, and eventually to meet the same fate. The series of failures only energized and intensified the sense of devotion and militancy, when the easiest and apparently last remaining option was to turn to violent means to acquire power. Thus today we have an armed group far removed from the humble origins of a people seeking sovereignty. Today, they are the face of a dogmatic and authoritarian regime in a land that is uncomfortable with what they are up to.

Placing the Taliban in the Deobandi Framework

Professor Brannon Ingram, in his insightful book *Revival from Below: The Deoband Movement and Global Islam*, makes valid points when discussing the unfair generalizations surrounding Deobandism.[13] However, it is critical to note that the extremist factions associated with the Deobandi school of thought that have emerged over the past few decades project only their political goals in their manifestos while avoiding discussions on theological issues. This does not diminish their existence and significance within the broader Deobandi movement; indeed, their sectarian narratives often expose their leanings. For instance, terrorist outfits in Pakistan such as Jaish-e-Mohammed (JeM) and Lashkar-e-Jhangvi (LeJ) may not publicly say that they are associated with the Deobandi school but most of their stalwarts graduated from madrassas aligned closely with Jamaat e Ulema e Islam, which is a product of Deobandi thinking. These are profiled by intelligence organizations in various countries as being of Deobandi orientation.[14]

So yes, while we must make distinctions between mainstream Deobandis and hardliners like the Taliban, it is still important to note the roots of the groups' religious beliefs. Deobandis' original problem was with Barelvis who, as mentioned previously, are pro-Sufism falling at the more progressive end of the spectrum. The real problems arise when discussing ISIS—when they came on the scene, they had a major impact on how the Taliban viewed their own beliefs. Here was a group that was actually worse than them—in reality and reputation—consequently forcing them to push themselves to the middle. Thus they moderated themselves slightly so as to make a distinction between them. As noted, the two groups have vocally expressed disdain for each other—with ISIS insulting the Taliban's founding father Mullah Omar, and the battle between them continuing in the present through the actions of the Islamic State in Khorasan (ISK). We are long past the days of pushing all such groups together under one umbrella term such as "jihadists" or Islamic fundamentalists. The reality is far more complex. There are many reasons behind Deobandism's gradual descent into radicalism and violence, as explained, however it's important to note that this affected only a fraction of the Deobandis, not all of them. In the same way, certain Christian groups have, in recent years especially, fallen into the traps of militant action and ideology, though they do not represent the entirety of their church.

Ultimately, in attempting to build a religion-led state, the Taliban are now attempting to co-opt Afghan nationalism and the fight for a better future by lacing it with their own sense of extreme religious nationalism. Javid Ahmad aptly frames it as "Talibanism"—a concept that moves "away from traditional Deobandism and toward a more tailored and unwritten mixture of puritanical beliefs wrapped in Islamic sharia."[15] Whether their task seems impossible or not, we have to remember that the Taliban rose from the ashes of much that has gone before—clerics, fighters, governments, imperialists, wars. Today, they have risen again from very similar ashes, only this time it seems the fire they are recreating will burn a lot brighter.

The most insightful story for understanding how the Taliban think they derived their legitimacy is a fascinating account involving their original figurehead, Mullah Omar. In 1994–95, Omar walked into a museum in Kandahar that was renowned for having in its possession the cloak of the Prophet Muhammad. Some people believe this was the cloak the Prophet wore upon his ascension to heaven known as Miraj, gifted to him by God. This very cloak used to be in a museum in Uzbekistan, until King Durrani, the founder of Afghanistan who ruled from 1747 to 1772, went to Bukhara and brought it to Kandahar. Since then, only three people have ever dared to open the box and see it for themselves. The first was Durrani, followed by King Zahir Shah—who was actually too afraid—then the leader of the Qadiriyya, a political figure with Sufi leanings, Gilani Shah. And finally, but most notably, Mullah Omar. What differentiated him from the rest though is what defines the essence of the Taliban and their mentality. He wasn't content with only his sight touching the cloak—he had to wear it as well. Not only that, he had to do this *publicly*, standing on a rooftop for all to see. And when everyone did witness the fact, and he claimed to be "*Amir ul-Momineen*"—that is "commander of the faithful," a title reserved only for the holiest of personalities—his supporters genuinely looked at him as such. They truly believed him to be a leader destined for such power, fully worthy of the cloak and title. None of them had gasped in shock, nor had their jaws dropped at the audacity of his doing what others would never think of. Instead, they cheered him jubilantly, filled with praise. If there is anything that differentiates these men from Muslims worldwide, it was this reaction. This would be the beginning of their battle.

While a love of the Prophet is ingrained in people's minds, this sort of behavior is something beyond that—it can't be explained only by that. This psychological phenomenon is often seen in leaders of such zealous groups—a burning desire to not only possess great power but be heralded as a one-of-a-kind hero, a savior. Mullah Omar wearing the cloak publicly reflects the mindset and behavior he displayed compared to those who preceded him. This was a critical moment for his supporters. A glaring light had been shone on their mentality, displaying just how seriously they took their divine inspiration. Only a few months after Omar's rooftop performance in 1996, the Taliban had taken over Afghanistan.

Sufism in Afghanistan

What compounds the tragedy of the Taliban's mindset is just how vastly opposite it is to the legacy of faith so deeply embedded in the fabric of Afghanistan: a country and history soaked in the soft melodies of mysticism, and reverence for saints known for their gentleness. All this sacred space has been declared profane by the Taliban, who earlier tried to erase any trace of Afghanistan's Sufis and sanctity. An iconic relic of these memories lies in Mazar-e-Sharif (the name literally translates as "tomb of the saint"). In the center of this city lies a magnificent blue mosque supposedly housing the grave of Imam Ali ibn Abi Talib, the fourth caliph of Islam and a great Islamic hero. Although it is widely accepted that Ali is actually buried in Najaf, Iraq, for centuries Afghans have held this site as a beloved sanctuary and sacred landmark. Its turquoise hues are reminiscent of holiness and have always been a symbol of the tranquility that should come with faith. What is so significant about this place is that it is truly representative of the country in which it stands. Its serene landscape and devoted pilgrims carry a light with them that the Wahhabi-inspired elements including some Taliban desperately want to get rid of. This shrine is not just a special site for Shia Muslims though, it stands as a holy landmark for all Muslims. Another unique aspect of this being arguably the most significant shrine in Afghanistan is the relevance of Ali's personality. Ali, the cousin and son-in-law of the Prophet, is remembered not only for being the original mystical master but also as a figure renowned for his religious wisdom, just governance, and tolerance in the face of authoritarianism. His life and perseverance were a testament to the ultimate victory of gentleness and knowledge over ignorance and power-obsession. The fact that this shrine associated with him stays standing today, after the destruction of so much around it, perhaps can be read as a sign of hope and optimism, that minds and hearts like his will experience victory once again—and it is they, not their opponents, who will be remembered gloriously in song and memory.

This is truly the mystic heartland: some of history's greatest Sufi saints originate from here, including the iconic poet Rumi. Entire Sufi orders have been born here, and the region carries in its soil the melodies of poetry and art lovingly crafted by such mystics. The very veins of Afghanistan are made up of such gentle, yet powerful, vibrations. Because of this, there's a rich legacy of Pashto poetry illuminating messages of tolerance and love that has now sadly not only been discarded but completely betrayed.[16] Afghanistan, famously the land of poets, has now seen the Taliban utilize the country's beloved art of language to further their own cause. The medium has remained, but the message has been so drastically altered that it is now unrecognizable as such. While today people often heartbreakingly refer to Afghanistan as "the graveyard of empires"—on a sweeter note, it has also lovingly been known as "the Home of Saints." And while those saints and their songs may appear to be silenced by ISK right now, they linger still and have the power to resurface.

It cannot be overstated how deeply the influence of Sufism penetrates into the history and reality of Afghanistan. The country's history is soaked in thousands and thousands of pages of Sufi writings and intellectual advancements that spanned far beyond the borders of just Afghanistan. These orders and writings solidified the land as the cradle of Sufism, where knowledge was the king, and mysticism was the heart and soul. These were Sufis who made prized developments in all arenas and thrived in their sense of tolerance and inclusivity—honoring the spirit of Islam. In these orders, women Sufis traveled and fought in battle alongside men; they were respected and listened to. They were encouraged as students and teachers and highlighted as essential parts of society, reflecting the harmony that defined the land and people.

There is a long and rich list of Afghan Sufis who passionately condemned imperialism and colonialism, rallied against the tyranny of oppressors and advocated for peace over the evils of war. This is the beautiful fabric of Afghanistan—people with bravery, beauty and brilliance. Here, Islam was not practiced in the same way it was in other lands. It was the "abode of Sufi saints" with intellectual links stretching far and wide.[17] The founder of modern Afghanistan, Ahmad Shah Durrani, himself was linked to the prominent Naqshbandi Sufi order. Sufis have been so integral to the foundation of Afghanistan that all leaders of the country held them in high regard. That makes what the Taliban are doing even more of a horrendous break in tradition, a crime against the truth and reality of the people's history. It was at Sufi shrines that kings were crowned, it was dervishes who legitimized their rule.[18] What once burned as the brightest light has now been dimmed to a dying flame.

A long-standing belief at the heart of the country's history is that what flows from the heart is often superior to what flows from the mind, as many spiritual people have believed across borders and time. The conflict between the Taliban's way of thinking and Afghanistan's history makes sense when analyzing the Deobandi background of their education. While Deobandism has for much of its history been inherently legalistic and political, it's natural that the flexibility—the heart—of Sufism could pose an issue for the Taliban. Inconveniently for them, Afghanistan's history has been defined purely by its Sufi identity. It has lived and breathed Sufism's light for much of its history—so the Taliban's war against that is only logical in this regard.

Dawood Azami brilliantly explains how it was not until the Soviet invasion and the influx of foreign ideologies, such as Wahhabism and Salafism—typically disparaging of

1. Taliban representative Mullah Baradar (right) and US representative Zalmay Khalilzad (left) are photographed signing the February 2020 US–Taliban peace agreement in Doha, Qatar. A moment nobody thought possible had become a reality—a deal not only being signed, but one also largely seen to be favoring the Taliban.

2. In a truly remarkable moment, US Secretary of State Mike Pompeo meets with Mullah Baradar and the Taliban delegation in Doha, 2020. Nobody could have imagined the two standing side by side after twenty years of war—but that's exactly where they found themselves.

3. Taliban members sit at the opening session of peace talks with the Afghan government in Doha. The group surprised everyone with their detailed preparation, organization, discipline and efficient negotiating skills. They strategized their moves in an effective fashion—proving to the world they were more sophisticated than anticipated.

4. A September 2021 glimpse of the Pakistan–Afghanistan border crossing at Spin Boldak with a local Taliban governor standing on the far left. Contrary to Pakistani expectations that the border would be safe with the Taliban in control, tensions remain high after many gun battles.

5. In an interesting move, Pakistan sent its minister of state for foreign affairs Hina Rabbani Khar to meet with Taliban foreign minister Amir Khan Muttaqi in November 2022. Whether the hosts were comfortable with the choice or not, they were nevertheless all smiles. Times have changed, certainly.

6. US representative Zalmay Khalilzad greets the Taliban delegation during the negotiations in November 2020. Members include the Taliban spokesman in Doha Suhail Shaheen, Taliban leader Abbas Stanikzai, and Abdul Hakim Ishaqzai, who later emerged as the chief justice of the supreme court. A few smiles in sight—a cordial atmosphere, apparently.

7. On the streets of Kabul, Taliban members are pictured enjoying their return to power in August 2021, casually seated on a Humvee once belonging to US-funded Afghan security forces.

8. Young members of the Taliban remind everyone who's in charge: soon after their victorious return to Kabul in August 2021, the Taliban took to patrolling the streets, weapons in hand. The message was simple: the city was theirs.

9. In what would become one of the most historic, memorable and heartbreaking photos of the US departure from Afghanistan, over 600 Afghan citizens are pictured cramped together on a US military plane departing Kabul. Faces of uncertainty, fear and trauma capture the hard reality of America's chaotic farewell.

10. Taliban spokesman Zabihullah Mujahid smiles for the camera at the first official press conference in Kabul following the Taliban's return to power in August 2021. It came as quite a surprise to onlookers who heard the group's confident answers. It was clear that they knew what they were doing.

11. In the Taliban heartland of Kandahar lies a shrine housing a cloak that once belonged to the Prophet Muhammad. In an unprecedented move, in the mid-1990s Taliban founder Mullah Omar famously stood on the rooftop wearing the garment. Today, the Taliban have ensured their huge flag is hoisted above the city, flying high.

12. Taliban interior minister Siraj Haqqani—who remains on the FBI's most wanted list with a $10 million reward for information leading to his arrest—walks with an aura of authority as he receives a salute from freshly graduated Afghan police recruits.

13. Defense minister Mullah Yaqoob, son of Mullah Omar, is flanked by Mullah Baradar on the left and, on the right, Bashir Noorzai, a drug smuggler and a senior Taliban leader, Kabul, September 2022. Detained by the US for nearly two decades, Noorzai had recently been released by the US in exchange for US citizen Mark Frerichs.

14. Courageous young women chant for their rights at a protest against the genocide of the ethnic minority Shia Hazaras, just one day after a suicide bomb attack at a Kabul school in October 2022. Afghan women and girls have felt more empowered in recent years, displaying immense bravery—often at the cost of their safety.

15. Taliban members stand guard outside a Kabul shrine frequented by Shia and Sufis, where *Nowruz* (the Persian New Year) is being celebrated, March 21, 2022. ISK's ongoing spree of terrorist attacks targeting minorities poses a threat to the space—and interestingly, propels the Taliban to secure it.

"innovation"—that the antagonism toward Sufism began. From that point forward, that antagonism only grew stronger, spewing hatred, division and intolerance—the opposite of what the country had embraced for centuries. Upon the Taliban's introductory reign in the mid-1990s, pilgrimages to Sufi shrines, a staple of culture and devotion, came under threat, though Sufis remained defiant and have not allowed their legacies to be lost. It is also vital here to acknowledge the difference between the Taliban and ISK in this regard. While the Taliban are clearly not supportive of ideologies besides their own, their attitudes toward Sufis and the Shia minority have not been as extreme as those of ISK, who have declared both groups non-believers. Additionally, it is important to note that Shias and Sufis maintain a small but powerful presence—their status as minorities doesn't mean they're actually that small in numbers, or small enough that they can be ignored. In fact, they're a significant part of Afghanistan's makeup and history and incredibly relevant beyond their persecution. The religious disagreements between ISK and the Taliban will be elaborated on in a later chapter, but it is important to mention briefly that they are not identical in the religious sphere, despite surface-level commonalities.

The Taliban as a New Religious Movement

Another vital key to understanding all the intricacies and ironies of the Taliban's intense religious history is an examination of their sociology, especially through the lens of new religious movements. Sometimes imperfectly defined as a "cult," the term is applied to all new faiths or those operating on the margins of wider religions, founded often by charismatic or highly authoritarian figures to address specific modern needs not catered to by traditional religions and as a reaction to modernity, pluralism and the scientific worldview.[19] Almost everything we see happening with the Taliban today can be explained precisely through this framework— more importantly, its application can help us better comprehend not only how they recruit, but how they're so successful with it. Roel Meijer argued that Salafism is Islam's "new religious movement."[20] However, I argue that we can take the Taliban as a more specific instance of the phenomenon. Most notably, the framework of "new religious movements" —that is, movements offering alternative spirituality or that are peripheral to dominant religious culture—provides us with the opportunity to understand how religious groups evolve based on different societal factors. In the case of the Taliban, this serves as the premise of this chapter. Using this model, we can potentially understand how to predict the Taliban's future—even if not as a new religious movement but as a political movement with a heavily religious identity, these aspects still hold relevance.

Sociologists of religion have offered multiple components shared across new religious movements that offer a solid understanding of what exactly goes into changing them, and thus their future. What defines the success or failure of such movements comes down to a few criteria that we can identify quite readily with the Taliban. First is the analysis of socio-demographic changes within the group's makeup. As the members change, so too does the heart of the group, impacting their political goals, religious thinking, approaches to policy and governance, etc. Especially as the age demographics of the group changed, and the members increasingly belonged to the younger generation, their identity, and thus perspectives and actions, changed too. Likewise, as the world around them advanced and their leadership changed, their growth was pulled in different directions. In many new religious movements, the arrival of the second generation is notable in altering the group's fundamental essence and future. As the socio-demographics of the members change, challenges mount. The Taliban today have huge numbers of young men born after 9/11 and the US invasion—they have grown up in a different world than their seniors. Accordingly, they pose challenges to the group's survival. Eventually, as we see now in this identity crisis, members can potentially begin to reconsider ideology and commitments. When the senior hardliners start to die out, the question is whether the younger men of today, who adore their mobile phones and desire a relationship with the outside world—when they grow fatigued of the famine and global isolation—will slowly end the Taliban as we know it.

Second, changes in leadership pose a huge threat to new religious movements—be it in the individual, the structures or mediating networks. The face of the movement acts as a substantial component of adherents' belief and dedication to the cause. Without the leader, members lose sight of the goal—they require not just motivation, but encouragement from someone with bold, worthy authority. After Mullah Omar died, the gap could never be quite filled—his cult of personality and status as founder trumped whatever successors could offer. Today, the focus on the supreme leader's decision furthers the dependency of the group on such a figure for its continued survival. Moreover, the issue of succession that arises following the death of a leader creates confusion and chaos, and thus an opening for the group to be weakened. That is manifested in the current situation through the rivalry brewing between Siraj and Yaqoob. However, as long as the supreme leader is solid, with strong support, the risk of the group collapsing due to the leadership is incredibly minimal. This is merely a path through which new religious movements can face struggle, though with the Taliban there are other paths that seem far more plausible in terms of causing issues endangering their survival.

Such groups must have legitimate leaders with adequate authority to be effective—and not only that, these authorities require clear doctrinal justifications for effective and legitimate leadership—like Mullah Omar's rooftop performance or Mullah Hibatullah's clerical and scholarly status. Added to that, this authority is regarded as more legitimate and increases in effectiveness as the members begin to perceive themselves as participants in said system of power—their self-confidence amplifies. Also, the group must be able to produce a highly inspired volunteer, religious force that is motivated to proselytize. This, the Taliban clearly have in great quantity. Thus far, the checklist items are ticked, with the Taliban displaying all the essential elements for a new religious movement's future success. Finally, though, and arguably most relevant in the discussion of the group's future today, is the ability of the group to socialize its young well enough to avoid the chance of them defecting. As the younger generation of the Taliban today are products of the digital age, their attraction to social media and thus global interaction poses a severe threat to the older, more hardline, traditional members' dependency on isolation. For context, the internet was banned during the Taliban's first stint in power but now there are 7 million internet users in Afghanistan (57 percent using Twitter, 39 percent using Facebook, and 2 percent YouTube).[21] Again, here is a problem the group confronts when looking to its survival and future—will they be able to manage the generational differences? How will these play out over the next ten years? This is a key point, if not *the* key point, for understanding their future success.

There is a significant sense of cognitive dissonance at the heart of the group—one intense enough to upend their entire future. In essence; the beliefs and actions of the group are having a hard time aligning. Even when it seems cohesive, there's evidence pointing to an aura of disagreement. Furthermore, changes in the social environment are hugely important for new religious movements. In the case of the Taliban, the importance of globalization should not be understated. While it poses opportunities for growth and expansion, this is a constraint for the group. With the growing digital socialization of the young, there is no longer the comfort blanket of isolation, and thus dependency on and loyalty to the group alone. The boundaries that sustain these groups' isolation and devotion pit the members against the rest of the world—it becomes "us versus them." The issue begins when these boundaries start to interfere with the necessities of life. As Afghanistan undergoes a massive famine due to economic constraints and global sanctions, eventually people's faith in the Taliban will begin to dwindle, and the members' priorities to change. Here lies the first stage of failure for such groups, according to sociologists. When the Taliban first came into power in the 1990s, they were challenged not long after, in 2001. This time around, after running a successful twenty-year insurgency, they are confident in assuming that nobody will challenge them again—at least on such a massive scale. That brings us to the added pressure of political changes, which can pose advantages or disadvantages for groups. As mentioned, the regional players here are of monumental importance. What affects them, affects all—whether they choose to support the Taliban financially and politically alters their livelihood completely. Most relevant here is Pakistan—historically, their lifeline. Other players, like Iran and China, also now play a larger role in a similar capacity.

Sociologist Brian Wilson explains how new religious movements "offer surer, swifter ways to salvation." The Taliban's obsession with paradise, much like other religious fundamentalist groups, and their urgency in building a model to obtain it, can best be described as such a desperate attempt to attain salvation.[22] This aspect can, however, perhaps be better ascribed to ISIS and Al-Qaeda, which have demonstrated that desperation very clearly in the last few years. The Taliban, on the other hand, are now more focused on their national governance—though the concept of salvation helps in understanding the roots of their radicalization and armed jihad more generally. What these groups have in common, though, is their sense of a universal religiously defined identity—one that is both global and locally rooted—which then enables political action based on that. This is seen across new religious movements, and particularly Salafism. The Taliban of course fit perfectly within this mold—their vision is not limited to themselves, but extends to the whole world, and can only be fulfilled through a political movement. Religious reform as the solution to political and social problems is a classic trope within new religious movements sociology—it is what feeds the group's recruitment, motivation and continued survival. The Taliban's uniqueness and their drift away from the traditional aspects of the ideologies they are borrowing, as well as their individualism in that regard, contributes to the theory that they can be classified as a new religious movement. Moreover, analyzing the relationship between religion and identity helps in gaining a clearer image of what creates these movements' personal appeal. Religion serves as the ultimate justification and legitimation of social and political action, based on ideas of divinely sanctioned attributes. Also, on an interpersonal level, it is the ultimate source of how we judge others. It provides a pristine source of selfhood that empowers people, and thus fuels the idea of religion as a transformative force. These movements redefine identity—they enable, motivate and constrain adherents. In mobilizing they view themselves as a group force, which motivates them further in their actions and commitment to belief. Finally, it constrains them in establishing an us-versus-them dynamic that eventually isolates them. We can easily identify how the Taliban fit into these spheres; with this generation, however, the last constraining point does not stand as well as it did with the earlier 1990s group.

Ultimately, whether or not the Taliban can be sufficiently classified as a new religious movement, looking at different sociological perspectives regarding religion can be of great benefit to studying them, particularly as we move forward into uncharted territory.

Taliban Narratives and the Contemporary Muslim World

The various categories Taliban members fall into span quite a range, from the ideologically schooled Taliban to inactive members, from forced participants to local fighters, front-line insurgents to the totally disaffected and, finally, those considered either cruel thieves or clean, pure, "real Taliban." This categorization covers a vast range, certainly, but does a great job at giving us a glimpse into the nuanced reality of the makeup of the Taliban, as opposed to viewing them as a massive crowd all one and the same. Also, regarding catego-rization and the dangers associated with clear-cut labels, we can acknowledge that the rigidity they adhere to and espouse is a shift away from traditional Deobandism, one major factor enough to demonstrate how their labeling as such in the current realm is fairly inaccurate. There comes a point with all groups who give rise to extremist sub-sects where questions and arguments come up over whether their major differences are enough to deprive them of the identifying label completely.

It is heartbreaking to acknowledge the irony in the very self-assigned label of the group. "*Talib*" translates to student or seeker of knowledge in Arabic—and yet the Taliban work desperately to erase any trace of knowledge so beautifully entrenched in the fabric of Afghanistan's history and culture, while also depriving women and girls of the opportunity of an education.

Of great importance, as well, is the need to look at the Taliban as a religious institution in the environment they are trying to fit into. The contemporary Muslim world is constantly undergoing socio-religious transformations as education and media expand and older hierarchies are replaced by reformed attitudes. If there is any opening in the Taliban's way of thinking, as this book proposes there may be, with the differences they have and are showing compared to their forefathers in the 1990s, the future may include their own reform and efforts to work alongside contemporary trends, and in the process distinguish themselves again from more extremist groups like ISIS/ISK. Their new reality of governing will surely have an impact on how they apply their theocratic model, and so the lines of their religious ideology thus far are arguably up in the air—or at least they have the potential to be. Modern Muslim intellectualism, which includes ulema, is itself experiencing a shift—could the Taliban be impacted by that? If we see them removing themselves from their traditional isolation, the idea that they can be impacted by (and thus also impact) trends in the Muslim world—in a positive rather than negative manner—is hopefully not that far-fetched. There is a tradition across the Islamic world of scholars

creating a religious establishment where ulema have historically been viewed as reformers. The Taliban probably aspire
to follow that tradition but have not shown much potential
of spearheading any progressive reforms through their
power so far.

To address contemporary realities without considering the
historical complexities that created modern phenomena can
be misleading. Religion and its place in history is a deeply
compound thing. We cannot, however, limit these issues to
the classroom. The notion of radicalized students sitting in
madrassas and suddenly engaging in extreme violence and
"armed jihad" is a very dangerous one; one that leads into the
trap of reductionism and Islamophobia. The most important
thing to remember is the social and political circumstances
of the time these students were in the classroom. In the 1980s,
it was the war with the Soviets, fighting a foreign invader—
and, with the US having fully supplied the Mujahideen
movement, it is hard to claim their resistance was not an
acceptable reaction. And not that long after, the US invasion
again promoted this idea of resistance against a foreign
power. Though one might perhaps wonder if the political
circumstances had been different, what would have come
out of these madrassas? Would anything have come out at
all? And one might ask not what Afghanistan would be
without Islamists and the Taliban, but what Afghanistan
would be had it never been invaded—by either the Soviets or
the US?

Notably, it was not just in madrassas where these ideologies were being espoused. It was in refugee camps, too:

people living in the poorest of circumstances, without a home, in a foreign land with only memories of what once was, exhausted and traumatized, searching for answers. Enter: the voice of preachers. The Taliban today are not a product solely of some larger evil ideology—but of a people's pain, desperation and lack of options. Half of the analyses we have seen over the past twenty-plus years have been so empty precisely because of the willful ignorance of this fact. To deny the human element of it all is where we start to lose our way. To attribute anything to theology alone is a problematic notion too often espoused in our era. Religion has become associated with global issues as an overarching cause of destruction when in reality it is far too vast and complex a structure to be reduced to that aspect so ignorantly and easily. Religion, politics and society interact in ways we are still trying to understand—it has often been religion itself that has cured our social ailments and eased the world's suffering. When we take a nuanced global perspective, one that accounts for the realities of power dynamics, imperialism, economic inequalities and discrimination, we can begin to better understand how it is that such groups come to view their religious backdrop as something to be altered and applied as a solution to such legacies.

While Afghanistan remains steeped in division, both ethnically and in terms of urban–rural distinctions, it is plausible that people may look to religious ideals as a uniting force to save them from the morass—and, in the process, force the Taliban to be more accommodating and inclusive in their thinking and pursue needed reforms. Hopefully, then, the strong Sufi heritage Afghanistan is known for can also become more potent and relevant in such an eventuality. It may be a less likely scenario, but it is one with enough potential to be considered seriously, and would be an outcome that is well-deserved.

5

Allies and Enemies of the Taliban

The Pakistani Taliban and the Islamic State in Khorasan (ISK)

The return of the Taliban in Afghanistan has rippled across the Durand Line to Pakistan already, where its emboldened sister organization, the Pakistani Taliban (Tehrik-i-Taliban Pakistan—TTP), has reasserted itself. Pakistan witnessed an increase of over 50 percent in terrorist activity in a single year after the Taliban's return to Kabul.[1] This is the group that shot the defiant Malala Yousafzai in October 2012, hounding her from her homeland Pakistan, and later murdered 141 schoolchildren at the Army Public School in Peshawar in 2014. A terrorist conglomerate comprising various shades of extremism—ranging from anti-Shia sectarian thugs to Kashmir-focused militants—the group is now reorganizing and repositioning itself after years of being tackled and confronted by the Pakistan military. Pakistan tried to engage the group through negotiations sponsored by the Afghan Taliban (since August 2021) but to little avail. It publicly announced resumption of its terrorist campaign across Pakistan in late November 2022. The Afghan Taliban so far have only helped Pakistan half-heartedly in pursing the TTP, as the two groups have enjoyed a mutually beneficial relationship for a long time. This has created tensions between Afghanistan and Pakistan. Pakistan's premier English newspaper *Dawn* in an editorial on November 30, 2022 aptly says:

> . . . the state needs to realise that where we are now is the result of decades of flawed, security-centric policies, particularly the notion of "strategic depth" that, with the second coming of the Afghan Taliban, has boomeranged —and raised the spectre of a nightmare revisited.[2]

In parallel, while the Taliban's return is undoubtedly a disruptive reality for the region, they might not be the worst force on the scene anymore. ISK, the Islamic State in Khorasan province, is the newest terrorist group to use Afghanistan as a playground. Except they are not so new after all. They first raised their ugly head in Afghanistan in 2015, and have gradually upped their number of members, and consequently, terrorist attacks. As an offshoot of the atrocious group we know as Daesh or ISIS, from their name alone it is clear that they are a dangerous problem. ISK attracted global attention when they attacked the Kabul airport during the Taliban takeover of the city in August 2021. While the group has targeted civilian populations in Afghanistan and Pakistan dozens of times over the years, killing hundreds, their primary target is actually the Afghan Taliban—especially since their return to Kabul. One may rightly wonder why that is so when everything we have been told about such groups would imply they are two sides of the same coin. However, with the slow changes unfolding within the Taliban, they are developing a strategy to counter them. A war between the extreme and the ultra-extreme is brewing, making the Taliban's new job all the more difficult, and the peace for the Afghan people even more tentative.

The Pakistani Taliban

Background

In the immediate aftermath of the 9/11 attacks, while the Afghan Taliban were initially subdued under the US military presence in the country, right next door an ugly and dangerous reality had started to emerge in Pakistan. Many Taliban and Al-Qaeda members had escaped to the mountainous and hard-to-reach Federally Administered Areas (FATA) of Pakistan. Operating as a semi-autonomous region at that time, the area was cut off from mainstream Pakistan and had long been utilized as a sanctuary by criminals and militants, both local and foreign. The area was used as a platform and staging ground for Afghan Mujahideen—religious warriors—and militants invited from dozens of Muslim countries during the 1980s to confront the Soviet invasion of Afghanistan. Saudi money, Pakistani territory and management, and American weapons had combined to turn the tables on the Soviets by 1989. That was then; but for the "soldiers of God" who reclaimed Afghanistan successfully, the taste of victory became an addiction.

While the US washed its hands of Afghanistan to deal with other pressing matters, such as the breakup of the Soviet Union and its consequences, especially in Eastern

Europe, the now jobless and homeless militant cadres gave birth to a new generation of radicals and holy warriors. Al-Qaeda, the Taliban and Lashkar-i-Taiba were the offspring of that era. Pakistan employed some of them to turn their guns toward India, especially in the disputed and restive Jammu and Kashmir, while others either returned to their homelands to establish militant start-ups, such as the Islamic Movement of Uzbekistan and Jemaah Islamiyah in Indonesia, or ambitiously launched independent terrorist franchises—such as Al-Qaeda—from Afghanistan.[3]

Since the anti-Soviet "Jihad" era (1980s), FATA had served as a hub for militants of all stripes—those favored by Pakistan as well as those with a grudge against it. The War on Terror after 9/11 further attracted militants to this sanctuary. Pakistan's army moved into the area in 2002–3 to quell the resistance posed by tribal gangs that were fast turning into sophisticated terrorist outfits, but it was in for a rude surprise. The militants were ready for a fight and Pakistan made a poor choice at first: negotiated peace deals that only empowered the militants as they were in the ascendant. The tribal institutions, which historically served as partners of the Pakistani state, were sacrificed in the process and that only exacerbated the situation. I have heard from so many Pashtun friends in the region that the power shifted from local tribesmen—known as *Maliks*—to militants the day a Pakistani general directly signed a peace deal—known as Shakai agreement—with 27-year-old freelance militant Nek Mohammad in 2004. Local tribal leaders were not involved in the process, which was a blow to their status and influence. They had previously served as a cushion between the state of Pakistan and local tribes. The deal also made militants richer (by at least $540,000) as they demanded this amount from the general on the pretext that they had to return the financial favors of Al-Qaeda before they could cut ties and direct them to leave the area.[4] In the process the militants negotiated the release of many of their comrades from Pakistani custody as well. Close to both the Taliban and Al-Qaeda, Nek Mohammad had no intention of abiding by the agreement and only intended to gain time to expand the tentacles of these organizations in the area.[5] He had to be eliminated and this was accomplished in a matter of two months by a US–Pakistan coordinated drone strike. The damage was already done though.

Failing to learn any lessons, Pakistan opted to cut a few more deals with various militant groups in the area during the 2004–6 timeframe, thinking that they had meanwhile developed a better understanding of the militant landscape. They even sponsored a few militias in the area to fight with irreconcilable militants, but all of this only created more Frankenstein monsters. Brigadier Asad Munir, a conscientious officer in Pakistan's ISI who followed the group closely, explained it best:

A focused strategy to deal with terrorists was never followed. In September 2006 the government concluded another peace deal with the Taliban of North Waziristan. Because of this deal, foreign militants started operating openly. The only option for the locals was to accept Taliban rule.[6]

181

Enter the Pakistani Taliban as a consequence of Islamabad's self-defeating policies—locked, loaded and lethal. The group known as the TTP emerged in 2007 as a violent band of extremists, causing havoc all over Pakistan. It had declared Mullah Mohammad Omar, the leader of the Taliban, as its spiritual leader, and had committed to support the Afghan Taliban in its war against the US. While the group has roots dating back to the anti-Soviet "Jihad," as explained earlier, following 9/11 and the subsequent war in Afghanistan their organization grew and gradually expanded in terms of its capabilities and viciousness. In the years following 2007, their horrific series of suicide bombings, and targeted attacks on the Pakistani military and government as well as on civilians, tragically displayed the emergence of devastating militancy in Pakistan.[7]

While their declared aims of enforcing their particularly virulent version of Islamic law in the country, establishing "sovereignty," particularly in the tribal regions of Pakistan, and waging a war against Pakistani security forces were reminiscent of the Afghan Taliban—who they considered a friend and inspiration—their differences, too, were prominent. The Haqqani network, led by Jalal-ud-din Haqqani, a legendary figure in the Pakistan–Afghanistan tribal areas given his role during the Afghan Jihad of the 1980s, served as the bridge between the two groups. While historically close and loyal to Pakistan's ISI, the Haqqani group needed to sustain their network in Pakistan's tribal areas and the TTP were one of their important local allies. Divided loyalties helped these groups survive in the treacherous environment.

The regularity of suicide bombings and intense violence in Pakistan between 2007 and 2014 showed just how powerful the Pakistani Taliban had become. Motivated by tribalism and massive amounts of money, they rose further through a chaotic blend of religious, political and socio-economic factors, gaining power in Pakistan's tribal regions. The tragic result was the merciless killings of thousands of people, and a looming sense of fear and distress across the country. Pakistan, in part due to the incredibly poor counterterrorism strategy in the early phase, had found itself in a pit of despair—and a self-made one at that. As the military fought tirelessly to end their brutality, the TTP's network had grown so widely across the country—courtesy of alliances with militants in Swat and Punjab—that such campaigns encountered great difficulties.[8] They were not easy to defeat in the at all—even those of them in jail often managed to escape and immediately return to their heinous attacks. The group committed the vilest of human rights abuses, creating hell on earth for the victims who fell in their path. To make matters worse, not only did they lack the religious credentials to implement the theocracy they desired, but investigations into their inner workings proved just how little they knew of Islam at all—they worshipped only themselves. Furthermore, they became notorious for exacerbating ferocious sectarianism in the country.

A group of thugs seeking riches and the power to abuse took advantage of the gaps created by Pakistan's indecisiveness—attempting to deal with the TTP on the one hand while supporting the Afghan Taliban on the other.

This was not helped by the fact that drone strikes, a regular occurrence in those years, were a massive motivator for the TTP. They were an infected wound taking over an already weakened body. While Pakistan just barely managed to get it bandaged up one last time, since the Afghan Taliban staged their comeback the question arises: is Pakistan ready for round two? The Pakistani Taliban, after being degraded and dispersed, are now surely staging their own comeback. The success of their mentors and heroes in Afghanistan was bound to inspire them to reactivate and return to action.

The Pakistani Taliban Regains a Foothold in the Pakistan–Afghanistan Border Areas[9]

Pakistan's security forces had indeed effectively terminated the TTP reign of terror (roughly 2007–15) through their Operation Zarb-e-Azb launched in June 2014. The US drone campaign's success in decapitating the TTP leadership had facilitated it in no small way.[10] Consequently, the TTP splintered and many of its surviving leaders escaped to Afghanistan. However, some of its splinter factions either merged into ISK or pledged allegiance to it. The TTP's most lethal splinter Jamaat ul Ahrar, in collaboration with the TTP's Tariq Gidar group, which was responsible for major terrorist attacks, including on the Army Public School in Peshawar in December 2014, had survived the Pakistani counterterrorism operations and continued its terror operations from its new base in Afghanistan's Nangarhar area.[11] This was one of Pakistan's complaints against the former Ghani government: that they had not effectively pursued the TTP factions that had found sanctuary in Afghanistan.

It's entirely possible that Afghan intelligence perhaps wanted to respond to Pakistan in the same coin for its support for the Afghan Taliban. A former TTP spokesperson, notorious terrorist Ehsanullah Ehsan disclosed in 2017 (while in Pakistan army custody) that both Afghan and Indian intelligence funded and assisted the Pakistani Taliban.[12] After a mysterious escape from an intelligence safe house in early 2020 he retracted his "forced confession." Hard to trust anything such characterless people say but the episode is reflective of layers of deceit and deception at play in this unholy arena.

Feeling empowered after the February 2020 US–Taliban peace deal, many of these splinter groups, including Jamaat ul Ahrar and Hizb ul-Ahrar, decided to come together again in August 2020 and renewed their pledge of allegiance to the current TTP leader, Noor Wali Mehsud, alias Abu Mansour Asim. Hizb ul-Ahrar, especially, have an agile terror network in and around the Peshawar region, and the return of a Mehsud as the TTP leader also persuaded many disgruntled Mehsud tribesmen to return to the TTP fold. Even the Punjabi Taliban's Amjad Farouqi group, closely aligned with Al-Qaeda, and the Usman Saifullah group, a Lashkar-e-Jhangvi (LeJ) splinter, also returned to the TTP platform. All of these groups had remained deeply involved in the reign of terror in Pakistan during the 2007–15 timeframe. The latest to rejoin this notorious gang of terrorists in late November 2020 was influential Ustad Aleem Khan (from the Gul Bahadur TTP faction) and Umar Azzam. The TTP proudly marketed the video of this allegiance through their media outlet Umar Media. All of this should have been enough to ring some emergency alarm bells in Pakistan, but it did not.[13] The pattern of TTP consolidation gained further momentum after the Afghan Taliban's return to Kabul in August 2021.

The earlier assessments about the presence of a high number of the Pakistani Taliban in Afghanistan was substantiated in July 2022, by a UN Security Council report noting that the TTP constitutes the largest component of foreign terrorist fighters in Afghanistan.[14] The report further added that various terrorist groups were enjoying greater freedom inside Afghanistan than before. Many TTP militants are now drifting back into Pakistan, in an attempt to regain control in parts of the Pashtun tribal belt sandwiched between Pakistan and Afghanistan. This area—FATA— has been legally incorporated into Khyber Pukhtunkhwa (KPK) province, one of Pakistan's four provinces bordering Afghanistan, since 2018. The TTP were responsible for more than a hundred cross-border attacks from Afghanistan into Pakistan between July and October 2020, indicating that TTP cadres had started returning to the Pakistan side.

A significant increase in targeted killings in the Pakistani tribal areas during 2020–23 carried out by terrorist groups indicates that something is amiss. Those targeted lately are tribal elders (senior leaders), reminiscent of when the TTP emerged in 2007 and eliminated hundreds of them. Analyst Daud Khattak maintains that increased targeted killings in Waziristan and Bajaur tribal districts are caused by the TTP's "involvement in resolving local disputes, forcing people to pay protection money, and targeting those believed to be their opponents."[15] This was how they gained space in the tribal belt more than a decade ago. The TTP attacks on security forces in South and North Waziristan, and in Bajaur and Mohmand areas—an old stronghold of the TTP—increased significantly in 2022–23. One of the reasons behind this resurgence has been the release of TTP leaders from Afghan jails since August 2021, including the most notorious, Maulvi Faqir Mohammad. This move sent shudders across Pakistan's security services when they observed the TTP celebrating the freedom of its members through a massive caravan of vehicles in eastern Afghanistan, soon after the Afghan Taliban's return to Kabul.[16]

The return of suicide bombings, targeting Quetta, Peshawar and Islamabad in late 2022 and early 2023, added further urgency to the security crisis. Former ISI chief Faiz Hameed, who also served as corps commander in Peshawar (November 2021–August 2022), had led negotiations with the TTP (supported by Afghan Taliban) that offered a safe passage to the TTP to return to Pakistan in exchange for agreeing to a long-term ceasefire.[17] Hundreds of TTP militants returned to Pakistan around mid-2022 and dozens were released from Pakistani prisons under this arrangement, but as before, the TTP used this as an opportunity to gain time to prepare for the next terror campaign. It was a very poorly conceived "peace" deal. The late December 2022 siege of the counterterrorism center in Bannu (bordering North Waziristan district) by thirty-three TTP prisoners who had overpowered security officials is a case in point. After being surrounded by the army, the terrorists tried to negotiate a way out by demanding a safe passage to Afghanistan. Though an army commando unit eliminated the terrorists after a pitched battle (in which it lost its three well-trained soldiers), the TTP made clear its dangerous intentions. Various TTP extortion rackets are now also very active across the Khyber Pukhtunkhwa province.

One of the major reasons behind the TTP's resurgence as a serious threat, however, is Islamabad's lackluster effort in bringing FATA into the mainstream, as envisioned by the 2018 FATA Reforms Bill, a major constitutional initiative. FATA was merged into Khyber Pakhtunkhwa province through this belated but commendable legal initiative which, on paper, abolished the draconian colonial-era regulations governing the frontier area. The legal, administrative and financial measures needed to facilitate this process, however, are absent, or seriously lacking, in turn provoking a rise in public frustrations.[18] A pertinent example is the recent rise of the Pashtun Tahafuz (Protection) Movement (PTM) led by Manzoor Pashteen, a revolutionary but non-violent protest movement demanding an end to extrajudicial killings in the area by security forces and the elimination of military check-points that restrict the free movement of people. PTM pleads for Pashtun rights, maintaining that the lives of ordinary Pashtuns have been disrupted over the last two decades on a massive scale and that they are victims of both the Taliban and the security forces. The TTP used similar criticism of security forces to gain public sympathy, but PTM emphasizes a non-violent approach, distinguishing it from militant organizations.

PTM's genuine but provocative slogans condemning the role of the Pakistan army, however, resulted in Pakistani governing authorities publicly presenting it as a threat. PTM should have been welcomed by Islamabad as an ally against the extremist and radical ideologies propagated in the tribal areas, but the authorities' short-sightedness served as an obstacle to such an understanding. PTM's popularity across Pashtun communities, from Peshawar to Karachi, increased, despite the military's effort to contain the group's reach. A few of the PTM's leading lights made it into the parliament, but that did not prevent them from being depicted as "Indian agents" or "enemies of the state," charges that are unfortunate and unfounded.[19] In fact, Pakistani security forces hired criminal and extremist elements to confront PTM on the ground, as explained by imprisoned Ali Wazir, currently an elected member of Pakistan's National Assembly and one of the co-founders of the movement:

> It is ironic that the institutions responsible for protecting Pakistan's territorial integrity and protecting it from dangerous threats are bankrolling thugs to launch a Pakistan Zindabad Movement (Urdu for Long Live Pakistan Movement). . . . It is telling that former Taliban commanders have addressed their gatherings. We also have indications that efforts are underway to mobilize sectarian terrorists and other fanatics to "counter" our peaceful campaign.[20]

Trends in Pakistan's Policy toward the Afghan Taliban and the Implications for the TTP

The trends presented here are based on my interpretations of conversations with many diplomats and security officials in Islamabad, Washington DC, London and the Gulf that mostly took place in 2022.

In the early days of the Taliban takeover of Kabul, the former chief of Pakistan's ISI, Lieutenant General Faiz Hameed, had requested Taliban high command to offer both Abdullah Abdullah and Hamid Karzai some high-sounding positions, even if they would have no authority, for the purpose of Taliban international image-building and to be seen as inclusive. The Taliban simply looked the other way. Nonetheless, they remained respectful to both of them and even allowed Abdullah to travel abroad—he returned afterward as promised. Interestingly, Karzai was refused this privilege (until early December 2022) and he continues to live in his palatial mansion next to Afghanistan's seat of power in Kabul.

Siraj Haqqani, the Taliban's interior minister, obviously remains the all-time favorite of Pakistan's security establishment. He basically filled the shoes once worn by Gulbadin Hikmatyar, during the Afghan Jihad of the 1980s against the Soviets. He was the recipient of most weapons received from the West then, through Pakistan. On a side note, Hikmatyar returned to Kabul after agreeing a peace settlement with Ashraf Ghani in 2016 and was known to have adversarial relations with the Taliban. He continues to live in Kabul today.

Back to Siraj Haqqani, a senior Pakistani military official with whom I had a candid conversation genuinely views him as a brilliant statesman worthy of great respect! I was also briefed about his excellent linguistic skills and graceful manners. The attempts to build his profile are certainly evident—however, what's interesting to point out here is that Siraj's Pashto dialect is actually not one widely spoken or understood in the Afghan Pashtun belt. More so, his popularity is restricted to Haqqani strongholds even though his role as interior minister is helping him expand his network. I was also told that many Europeans and important Western visitors who get an audience with Siraj Haqqani (often arranged by the ISI) come out singing his praises. Clearly, the ISI's strategy is heavy on the use of exaggeration. One fact worth mentioning, however, and reiterated in multiple interviews, is that Siraj Haqqani is seen as one of the most pragmatic Taliban leaders. He is among the very few cabinet ministers who are keen to arrange for better training of officials working in his ministry and especially for members of border security forces. Siraj has made this request to many foreign diplomats and officials who met him. Like his father, he continues to build relations with Gulf leaders as well as his group's old benefactor Saudi Arabia. He does not keep all his eggs in Pakistan's basket. The big question is about his wisdom in moving Al-Qaeda leader Al-Zawahiri to a Haqqani safe house in Kabul. As mentioned earlier, it could very well be Pakistan that spilled the beans about Zawahiri's location. Zawahiri was always very vocal against Pakistani security forces and bashing Pakistan was a regular feature of his narrative.

The Taliban are as concerned about local legitimacy as about international recognition but were frightened at the thought of calling a *loya jirga* (major tribal consultative body) to seek support. As we know, they instead opted for a different route—a gathering of religious leaders whose support and sanction they were more confident about. The frequent use of the word "interim" for both the government and its functionaries was deliberate—to gain time in which to choreograph a mechanism that could grant legitimacy to the Taliban. A *loya jirga* could offer such a platform but at the time of writing (January 2023) Mullah Hibatullah and his coterie in Kandahar are not yet convinced it is necessary.

Of significant note is that for the Taliban, the priority is to obtain counterterrorism capability to fight ISK. When asked what kind of capability, I was told, "drones, signal intelligence and other high-tech equipment." Pakistan is lobbying on behalf of the Taliban to receive such support even from the US. I received an elusive reply to my question on why China is not offering such support.

In the midst of all this, the Afghan Taliban are now increasingly conscious of their reputation as closely aligned with Pakistan's army and intelligence services—and they know that the relationship is not particularly popular in Afghanistan. Consequently, when the Taliban requested Pakistani military and intelligence leaders to publicly keep their distance from them, it still came as a surprise. Islamabad was initially unclear if it was Taliban diplomacy or hypocrisy. Relations even started deteriorating once Kabul expressed its inability to pursue Pakistani Taliban roaming around in Afghanistan the way Pakistan wanted. After a few reminders that fell on deaf ears, Pakistan decided to take things into its own hands in April 2022 and ordered its air force to strike TTP targets inside Afghanistan. This turned out to be a fiasco as poor intelligence led to the death of 45 Afghan civilians, including 20 children.[21] Zabihullah Mujahid, the Taliban spokesman, wasted no time in jumping on to his Twitter account (currently he has well over 750,000 followers) calling on Pakistan, "not to test the patience of Afghans on such issues and not repeat the same mistake again otherwise it will have bad consequences."[22] Pakistan's foreign office shot back, reminding Kabul about its warnings to secure the Pakistan–Afghan border region and indirectly defending its actions, saying, "Terrorists are using Afghan soil with impunity to carry out activities inside Pakistan."[23] The reason the Afghan Taliban are hesitant to take strong action against the TTP is due to their considered opinion that TTP cadres currently hiding in Afghanistan could easily drift toward joining ISK ranks in the event that the Afghan Taliban are seen to be ditching them. Disgruntled TTP members, after all, had initially formed the core of ISK. USIP scholar Asfandyar Mir further pinpoints factors that form the roots of the relationship:

> There are strong interpersonal, war-time bonds between the influential Haqqani family and the TTP and between some southern Taliban leaders and TTP's political leadership. There is abundant ethnic amity, built around tribal ties and disdain of the Pakistani state—at least in the rank-and-file and middle tier of the Taliban.[24]

Pakistan, reversing its earlier policy pattern, systematically started to reach out to non-Taliban Afghan leaders meanwhile. It had helped many of them to leave Kabul safely and continues to assist many to settle in Pakistan for the time being. Pakistan also arranged for the transportation of many senior officials who served in previous governments to Turkey. They believe this is a way to correct a past mistake that had allowed India to extend its influence in Kabul. A senior Pakistan official shared that, besides the former Afghan vice president Amrullah Saleh (known for his very critical stance toward Pakistan), the ISI is in touch with all major political players of Afghanistan who are now in exile. He said that they are even ready to engage with Saleh. It seems Pakistan's strategy is to keep the Taliban under pressure, in order to keep them in line.

As discussed earlier in the book, various factions of the Taliban are indeed struggling to get along with each other. Pakistani intelligence believes that the hardliners who they call "traditionalists" are still the strongest within the group, but the younger generation has more motivation and a desire for better lives with more connectivity, regionally as well as globally. For the time being, Pakistan is not willing to upset the apple cart and wants to go along with the ways the Taliban top leaders pursue their ideological goals. They often offer them strategic advice for attracting financial resources but avoid discussing matters of religion and even controversial issues such as girls' education. However, a group of senior Pakistani clerics—led by a prominent Deobandi scholar Mufti Taqi Usmani—visited Afghanistan in July 2022 to meet Taliban leaders. The Taliban were hospitable to them and asked them for support in projecting Islamic values more effectively. The visiting delegation was not expecting an invitation to join the Taliban in proselytization. They were hardly given an opportunity to share their thoughts as the Taliban could guess that they were visiting to offer some unsolicited recommendations. Taqi Usmani had written a letter to top Taliban leader Mullah Hibatullah a few months earlier that was shared with the media, emphasizing the need for girls' education in an overly cautious manner:

> Girls' education is currently an important issue which the enemy of the Islamic Emirate has used as a propaganda tool. We value the wise and wholehearted measures which the Islamic Emirate has taken so far. But we are of the view that it is necessary to make appropriate arrangements for girls' education in accordance with Sharia.[25]

The delegation also met TTP members, who basically snubbed them by handing them a list of impossible demands, including the reversal of FATA's integration into mainstream Pakistan.[26] The TTP's audacity shows that the Afghan Taliban likely told them that they would stand by them, come what may.

As regards Pakistan's regional competitors trying to engage with the Taliban, a Pakistani general contended that, "Qatar can't deliver what Pakistan can." They, of course, want the US and Europeans to engage with the Taliban exclusively via Pakistan. On Iran, he argued that Iranian influence over the Taliban is limited and they are still investing in non-Taliban Afghans. Iran, he shared, has appointed a new special representative for Afghanistan, namely Hassan Kazemi-Qomi, who fought alongside the Fatimiyoun brigade comprising Afghan Hazara/Shia in Syria and has excellent relations with them. He further shared that Iranians have lately been trying to be friendly with Pakistan intelligence, but the ISI remains skeptical of them, given Iran's links with India. He also shared that they are fully in the picture as to how India attempted to access Anas Haqqani, the younger brother of Siraj Haqqani, via the Iranian IRCG (International Revolutionary Guard Corps).

Pakistan further believes that the TTP has sharpened its teeth in part due to the fact that it managed to get its hands on a large consignment of weapons left by the US for Afghan security forces, especially night vision equipment. Further, the TTP's sniping capabilities have improved significantly—posing a major terrorism threat for Pakistan. The Pakistan military's first response has been to purchase as much military equipment—available on the open market in Afghanistan—as possible, to ensure that groups like ISK and the TTP won't have access to it.

Another official I talked to reiterated that the West needs to understand that it will have to lower its expectations about the things it regularly brings up with the Taliban, namely inclusivity, human rights and women's rights. With the same vigor he employed, I pushed back to make a case for girls' education, explaining that aside from it being a good idea and a basic human right it would be a good PR and trust-building opportunity for the Taliban. He looked unconvinced and a bit surprised, arguing that the Taliban first need stability and control.

During a conversation with a seasoned Pakistani diplomat still engaged with the Taliban, I asked if we are witnessing the "new Taliban." His response was in the negative, maintaining that most Taliban cabinet ministers today also served in the old cabinet of 1990s and their ideological outlook had not transformed—but, with advancing age, they are less ambitious and even less rigid. "Years of war and fatigue has made them more pragmatic," he went on. "Their kids are educated, have exposure to the West—and have a huge impact on them," he maintained, after having met many of them in Doha and the UAE. "They have learned their lessons," he emphasized. Young Taliban radicals, in comparison, are more loyal to their field commanders, according to him, and that is more frightening for the top hierarchy, he disclosed. The last point he made was new to me when I talked to him around mid-2022. I raised this with many other Afghans, including a former Ghani cabinet member who knows the Taliban well, and he strongly agreed with this assessment. If true, then there might be more hope from the older generation of Taliban than the younger generation, especially those who actively participated in the battlefield.

In all of this, the hard fact at play is that 75 years on from partition, the India–Pakistan rivalry continues to haunt South Asia's security dynamics. Even though Pakistan came out victorious in terms of getting their favorites on top and getting India kicked out of Afghanistan, they feel the challenge isn't over for them. Pakistan remains totally convinced that India was using its access to Kabul during the previous government's reign to restrict Pakistan's influence in Afghanistan as well as lending its support to some anti-Pakistan groups, such as Baluch insurgents. With this background, it is nothing short of a big surprise that Pakistan signed off on the Taliban's diplomatic relationship with India. Afghan foreign minister Muttaqi had a detailed meeting with Pakistan's army chief Bajwa before he could request that India send back its diplomats and technical staff to the Indian embassy in Afghanistan. Understandable, as almost every other regional country has a presence in Kabul, and India would never want to be an outsider in this sphere. Regardless, it couldn't have happened without Pakistan—and Pakistan acted this way because it just might open up prospects of some aid for the Taliban in Afghanistan. Pakistan is as desperate as the Taliban themselves about getting financial support to run the country. Indian intelligence services, RAW, had been working overtime in 2021–22 to get access to the Haqqani group to open some doors. Some Taliban leaders, such as Abbas Stanikzai, the Taliban's deputy foreign minister, are believed by Pakistan to have a soft spot for India.

The Islamic State in Khorasan

Background

ISIS had shocked the world when they savagely destroyed parts of Iraq and Syria from 2014 on, carrying out some of the worst violence enacted by modern terrorists. While they have diminished in force to some extent, unfortunately they live on across the wider region, carrying on their sick legacy of brutality and extreme, hate-fueled fundamentalism. With their growing ideological expansion and base of experienced militants (drawing from various regional militant groups, including from the Taliban), ISK is becoming more lethal in Afghanistan, making the Taliban look moderate in comparison. The ISK attack at the Kabul airport during the US evacuation was not targeting only the Americans though; it was equally an attack on the Taliban. Their anger with the

Taliban and thus motives for attack stem from a few central points of disagreement.

First, ISK's extremely intolerant attitudes toward Sufis and Shias (and other minorities) mean the Taliban's recent lukewarm approach to the historically marginalized is seen as a betrayal of ideology. For instance, on Ashura, a religious holiday marking the martyrdom of the Prophet's grandson Imam Husayn commemorated annually by Muslims, especially Shias and Sufis, the Taliban (in 2021 and 2022) broke from their reputation of anti-Shiism by avoiding any extremist action aimed at the minority. Ashura has long been a target for extremists motivated by sectarian hatred, and 2022 was no exception. However, the violence that occurred was not initiated by the Taliban, but rather ISK, who have quickly claimed responsibility for multiple attacks on Shia neighborhoods and mosques in recent years. According to Human Rights Watch, between August 2021 and September 2022, 13 major terrorist attacks targeting Hazaras have led to over 700 deaths.[27] Richard Bennett, the UN special rapporteur on human rights in Afghanistan, argues that:

> attacks specifically targeting members of the Hazara, Shia, and Sufi communities are becoming increasingly systematic in nature and reflect elements of an organizational policy, thus bearing hallmarks of crimes against humanity.[28]

For ISK, the Taliban's presumed leniency toward minorities makes them strayers from belief, guilty of incomplete faith. They see their efforts to attack them as divinely guided, a purifying endeavor meant to establish Afghanistan—and the greater region—under the righteous umbrella of their caliphate.

Beyond the issues of religious interpretation, though, they have other bones to pick. The Taliban's deal with the US acts as a delegitimizing force in terms of their identity in the eyes of ISK—working with the ultimate enemy is a grave no-no. Luckily for them, they have a massive network of isolated like-minded actors desperately seeking such an avenue. For the extremists who have spent decades devoting their life to intense anti-West violence—those who once belonged to the TTP, Al-Qaeda and the Taliban—ISK offers a new home and lifeline.

As they have made their way into the political landscape through bombs and bloodshed, ISK have dethroned the Taliban as the ultimate villain of the region. They represent a most serious threat and, with the continuing regional instability and inconsistent counterterrorism policies of Pakistan and Afghanistan, the road ahead is littered with obstacles.

The Genesis and Growth of ISK

A few basic facts about the origins of the group are instructive. The foundation stone of Islamic State in Khorasan was laid in October 2014 when Hafiz Saeed Khan, a TTP commander from FATA's Orakzai agency, who had worked for the Afghan Taliban, pledged allegiance to ISIS.[29] When the establishment of ISK was officially announced a few months later, in January 2015, Hafiz Saeed Khan was designated as its first chief (*Ameer*). The first wave of recruitment was made from the disgruntled elements of the Pakistani Taliban as the new chief had access to the group's network database.[30] The second layer of recruits came from mostly non-Pashtuns hailing from Pakistan's Punjab province, who were mainly members of defunct militant groups focused on Kashmir and anti-Shia sectarian terrorists such as LeJ. These were also known as the Punjabi Taliban for easy identification of their roots.[31] Nine former members of Al-Qaeda too had joined the bandwagon.[32] A simultaneous recruitment campaign was targeting members of the Islamic Movement of Uzbekistan and the Turkestan Islamic Party, a Uyghur militant group, which provided ISK with new expertise and wider geographical knowledge of Afghanistan's neighborhood.[33] This strategy, according to noted expert Abdul Sayed, attracted militants from various ethnicities to switch allegiances for both practical and ideological reasons.[34]

The group's early base was a set of small hubs in southern Nangarhar, with its de facto headquarters in the valleys of Achin district. ISK couldn't sustain its early growth pattern once Afghan and US security forces began to zoom in on the group. From 2016 to 2019, according to scholar Amira Jadoon, "state-led operations captured, killed, or forced the surrender of over 10,000 of the group's affiliated members in Afghanistan and Pakistan combined, including hundreds of upper- and lower-level leadership," unsettling the group to a significant extent.[35] The surviving cadres of ISK moved to the neighboring Kunar province and urban centers to lie low. Interestingly, Kunar had also emerged as the TTP's command center in Afghanistan. The weakened ISK started to resurrect itself in 2020–21, after the news of US–Taliban negotiations in Doha. This is reflected through data that speaks for itself: from June 2020, ISK attacks in Afghanistan gradually started to rise, month on month to June 2021, surging from just three attacks in June 2020 to 41 in June 2021.[36]

ISK Strategy in Afghanistan

There is no doubt that the Taliban today face serious competition in Afghanistan, unlike during their earlier stint in government in Kabul. ISK, the new disruptive militant force, appears to be more aggressive and ambitious than the Taliban—or even Al-Qaeda—in some ways. Unlike the Taliban, who primarily recruited Pashtuns from rural southern and eastern provinces in the country, ISK continues to take advantage of a large pool of militants with battlefield experience, especially among disgruntled Taliban elements and decommissioned Afghan security forces who are on the wrong side of the Taliban. As an ideological extension of ISIS, ISK draw from the most extremist cadres of the Afghan and Pakistani Taliban, especially those with Wahhabi and Salafi orientation. New ISK recruitment campaigns in Central Asia have also gained momentum in recent months. Given its regional and global network—at least in the ideological realm—it has sufficient space to forge new alliances and strategize terror activity. ISK is also being depicted by some observers as the new Taliban today and as an insurgent group. This comparison may not be very apt as ISK lacks a solid ethnic constituency.

It is instructive that, in the first five months following the Taliban's return to power, ISK claimed responsibility for

127 attacks in Afghanistan, nearly 80 percent of which targeted the Taliban, specifically their new checkpoints, security convoys and Taliban personnel besides those who have spoken out against ISK.[37] Overall, from August 2021 to August 2022, the first year of Taliban rule, ISK claimed 262 attacks across Afghanistan. This dangerous trend was an important agenda item in the conversation between Pakistan's ISI chief, Lieutenant General Nadeem Anjum, and CIA Director William Burns in early May 2022 in Washington DC. The Pakistani delegation included former ISI chief Faiz Hameed as well. Burns told them that at this rate of growth ISK could gain control of 20 percent of Afghanistan by mid-2023. In response, Anjum stressed the need for targeting the top leadership of ISK and for this he recommended the US share relevant intelligence with the Afghan Taliban. Both sides also reached an interesting conclusion—if the Pakistani version of the conversation is to be believed: the Afghan Taliban are no longer a primary threat to the national security of the US and Afghanistan's neighboring countries.[38]

Professor Ali Jalali, a former interior minister of Afghanistan and a respected Afghan-American scholar, alerted me to two other aspects that are not widely discussed.[39] First, the Taliban are likely exaggerating the ISK threat in his view, as it suits them perfectly to gain sympathy and support in the name of fighting this notorious group. He argued, "for Taliban, ISK is a blessing." Second, the Taliban are targeting and eliminating many of their opponents and critics by calling them ISK terrorists. They are by no means the first to do so as many South Asian and Middle Eastern states adopted this strategy during the "war on terror" years. The most convenient and efficient way to curb dissent and silence critics and enemies was to declare them terrorists.

For ISK, the early months of Taliban rule in Kabul served as a boon to exploit distracted and preoccupied Taliban "to bolster its own recruiting, fundraising, and territorial control within Afghanistan."[40] According to a US treasury department report, "ISIS-K primarily raises funds through local donations, taxation, extortion, and some financial support from ISIS-core."[41] Empowered by prison breaks during the chaotic collapse of the Ghani government, ISK had quickly reorganized its ranks. Its hardened and experienced hands could strategize better than the foot soldiers. It is intriguing why the Taliban were not closely following the whereabouts of prominent ISK prisoners. They were their established arch-enemy, unlike Al-Qaeda, with whom the Taliban, especially the Haqqani faction, had good and functional relations.

Another strategy that ISK has employed since the Taliban returned to Kabul is to conduct major attacks against the government to raise its profile, in turn presumably attracting more funds from global and regional Salafi sources. It is hard to decipher, at this point, how ISK might balance its domestic agenda with its regional and international aspirations, but it is likely that it would first focus on establishing safe havens in Afghanistan and would then start to target regional hubs where it can find traction: such as Pakistan's Karachi and, on the Indian side, Kashmir. This could be followed by a focus on Western targets. All of this could be pursued in parallel and simultaneously as well, but currently

ISK lacks the resources and expertise to operate in multiple directions. The first and immediate mission will continue to be fully established in Afghanistan and aim to keep the Taliban on the defensive.

ISK is likely to concentrate its energies on targeting and assassinating Taliban leaders, thereby disrupting the entire Taliban project. To confront ISK, the Taliban will have to be cognizant of their ideological base, and may return to their more radical activities to dampen the attraction of ISK. By extension, if Taliban leaders start sounding too "moderate" in their approach, it is the hardcore fighters who will start defecting and boosting ISK cadres. That is the dilemma the Taliban face today.

The Taliban's Dilemma and Options

In a conversation with an adviser of the Afghan Taliban, I learned that one of the major questions now being openly and regularly discussed within Taliban circles deals with what constitutes the nature of an "Islamic state." When they came onto the scene, ISIS had raised this question loudly and violently, forcing everyone to consider how a government claiming the "Islamic state" label would work. What are the criteria for such a state and, more importantly, how do we engage with one? Aside from that, the other major topic of discussion, he said, is hierarchy within an Islamic government. Such debates, if not handled by experts who understand the ISIS narratives, could lead to more support for the ISIS—and by extension ISK—worldview within the ranks of the Taliban. That is a new intellectual challenge of sorts for the Taliban clerics.

The challenge posed by ISK to the Taliban in ideological terms hence is significant. The test this poses is expressed best through an anecdote. A conversation between the late religious leader and head of Darul Uloom Haqqania, Sami ul Haq—known also as the father of the Taliban—and Yunus Khalis—seen as one of the founders of the Mujahideen movement and someone who inspired the Taliban—in Akora Khattak, went like this: while addressing Haq, Khalis asked him how they should deal with extremists like those who joined Daesh and/or the Pakistani Taliban. Haq responded by comparing those men to "*aag ki shalwar*"—translated as "burning pants." What he meant was, if you wear them, they burn you—if you take them off, you are naked. Essentially, you are stuck. It does not matter if moderate members are angered, what causes trouble is upsetting the extreme elements. Such was the intensity of the extremist factions' pressure. The battle of polarization is not easy for anyone—and the Taliban are no exception. Meanwhile the Taliban have started targeting Salafi madrassas (seen as recruiting hubs for ISK) across Afghanistan and a few prominent Salafi clerics (including Shaikh Abu Obaidullah Mutawakil) have been abducted and eliminated, leading to protests even from various Salafi groups in Pakistan. The Taliban committed some excesses in these campaigns.

Still, the Taliban can draw confidence from the fact that ISK will not be able to borrow from the Taliban insurgency model toolkit as it lacks the critical elements that helped the Taliban, such as a significant rural Pashtun ethnic base and extensive madrassa networks across the country. ISK's Salafi ideology has a limited constituency in Afghanistan, and its repeated targeting of minority communities will increasingly alienate many Afghans.

As regards the Pakistani Taliban, Islamabad has repeatedly tried to use its influence with the Afghan Taliban to force their hand but the Afghan Taliban have only complied half-heartedly, mainly because they cannot give up their relationship with the Pakistani Taliban who had hosted them in Pakistan's tribal belt for years and might still be useful for them at some point in the future. On Islamabad's prodding in late 2022, Mullah Hibatullah declared TTP violence in Pakistan to be "unIslamic," but at the same time Afghan Taliban complained that Pakistan was not doing enough to stop ISK militants' movement from Pakistan to Afghanistan.[42] There exists this strange triangular dynamic on the border there, which may keep the area unsettled and, as before, allow criminals and militants to use the area as a sanctuary. This bodes ill for the prospects of peace in the region.

TTP, under its shrewd leader Noor Wali Mehsud, is attempting to convert itself from a terror outfit into an insurgency and a new narrative—both in ideological and political spheres—is being projected. Through delegitimizing the Pakistani state and voicing ordinary people's frustration with corruption and severe financial challenges (exacerbated by impact of climate change), it is trying to reinvent itself. Its targeting pattern has also changed accordingly, now avoiding civilian casualties, and focusing exclusively on police and army. This strategic shift has impressed Hibatullah of all the people, strengthening TTP's hand and further complicating regional security dynamics.

6

The International Relations of the Taliban

Afghanistan can play a great role in creating important corridors. We want to be connected to China through our Badakhshan province. .... The geostrategic position of Afghanistan could lead the country to play a positive role in linking neighboring countries in the region and beyond.

—Abdul Salam Hanafi, Taliban deputy prime minister[1]

August 2021 pulled the international community into a storm they never saw coming. One that perhaps they should have been able to predict, yes, but nevertheless one that came all too suddenly and far too intensely. Ever since, the moral and political dilemma has been a dark, looming shadow over the international arena. After two decades of being at war with US forces, the Taliban had ascended to power at a startling pace. In this whirlpool of geopolitical changes that panned out in Afghanistan, nations have found themselves at a crossroads: too hesitant to challenge the Taliban's authority, and too reluctant to support it.

While global powers implicitly acknowledged the Taliban's victory in Afghanistan, they underestimated the Taliban's communication and engagement with the international community. The Taliban had been conventionally viewed by nations as a non-cohesive group that lacked the bureaucratic support and financial means to run a country. However, their recently established formal communication channels with the foreign ministries of countries like Germany, China, Russia, India, etc. have surprised the international community. This pivot, given their stance from two decades ago, when leaders like Mullah Omar refused even to meet foreign delegates, is startling.

The Taliban's seamless international engagement, I argue, is not a new or recent phenomenon. Since 2012, Doha has actively hosted and harbored the group's interests in various bilateral and multilateral meetings at international forums. This can be traced back to the Taliban's engagement with world leaders like Russia's President Vladimir Putin in 2015 and China's Foreign Minister Wang Yi in 2014.

So, it comes as no surprise that years of formal conversations have prepared the Taliban to finesse their relations with the international community. In a span of a year and a half with extensive diplomatic engagements, the Taliban have demonstrated that they have the toolkit to do better than before.

Included among the Taliban's cabinet members are men who are still considered terrorists and are sanctioned by the UN. Such members have close ties with Al-Qaeda and other transnational militant organizations, which are an ongoing security threat for South Asia and its neighboring countries.

However, the engagements since August 2021 highlight the international community's mixed response toward the Taliban. Their dilemma in engaging with an insurgent group turned government has led to a cautious and calculated approach toward the Taliban.

From what we have seen so far, the Taliban are clearly not the easiest group of people to work with. Engagement with them therefore consists of multiple aspects, primarily communication regarding geopolitical developments and future relations. It is vital here to acknowledge the difference between *engagement* and *endorsement*. Engagement is a tactic which aids in providing a deeper understanding of the parties' interests and actions. This does not, however, imply mutual alignment of beliefs. Endorsement of the Taliban, on the other hand, entails believing in their ideas, and supporting and propagating them to the international community. The current debate surrounding nations' engagement with the group is being wrongly conflated with a recognition and endorsement of the Taliban's actions. If the Taliban are to move forward as an effective government, offering better prospects to the Afghan people, who are severely distressed, the international community has to seriously consider engaging with them—and this should not be seen as equivalent to endorsing them. The Taliban continue to pose very serious challenges to human rights, but only through creative engagement with corresponding incentives can they be influenced effectively.

While Russia, China, Turkey, India and several other nations have consistently assisted the Taliban in infrastructure and development projects, as well as offering humanitarian and financial aid, they still refuse to give any formal recognition to the group. While actively engaging with Taliban officials, they are steadfast in their refusal to endorse or legitimize them. It seems as if they are willing to have a relationship, but too shy to put a label on it. How long this will last, and how long the Taliban will tolerate it, remains unclear.

The Motivation behind the Taliban's Need for Recognition and Communication

The Taliban's quest for recognition can be better understood by looking at their economic, social, political and psychological needs. Once they are formally recognized as a government, multiple new avenues will open for them, making their task of governing easier. Wider diplomatic engagements, entrance into profitable trade deals, and the social acceptance of being included in the global community, as well as access to legal tools, are all benefits they will potentially attain. The Taliban are aware that without formal legitimacy, they will not be able to maneuver effectively to win over the support of the Afghan people, nor build legal cooperative agreements with other nations. Given their current economic crises, the recognition will also allow them to obtain financial aid from global banking institutions, which at this point is a desperately urgent need.

To spin a more positive, inclusive image of themselves across different countries, the Taliban have taken to the modern era's most beloved medium: social media, and in particular, Twitter. Every Taliban cabinet member since August 2021 has an official Twitter account with millions of followers. As an open, accessible platform, Twitter allows them to dominate and control the information environment displayed to the domestic and international audience. Their choice of imagery and tweets in both Pashto and English highlight their advancement in technology and media; they understand the different engagement channels required to communicate with the broader Western community, and are putting efforts in that direction.

Although the Taliban are not adhering to their initial promises of protecting women's rights and governance, their diplomatic engagements with the international community demonstrate their willingness to work with them. This willingness stems from two major concerns: security, and economics. Ultimately, nobody wants the Taliban's Afghanistan to become a breeding ground for terrorists, disturbing regional and international security. Whatever that requires of their neighbors, we are beginning to see—they will do.

The systematic expansion of their ties and efforts to expand their political offices beyond Qatar have allowed the Taliban to interact with leaders from all over the globe. Slowly but surely, the Taliban are proving that diplomacy is no longer their Achilles heel. However, the international community should not forget that while the Taliban are undergoing an organizational change, to claim an ideological one is under way is more complex. Their actions on the ground, like their broken promises over girls' education, have unfortunately—but unsurprisingly—been true to the tenets of their rigid ideology. While some ideological changes are certainly under way with the new generation, any overwhelming expectation of change from them is naïve—or at least, something for the future. However, it is indisputable that the group's foundation has historically been based on radicalism and blatant disregard for human rights. The picture of them we have all known and feared has been one painted with the blood of their victims. To forget that or to move beyond it into a rehabilitated image will not be easy—or perhaps even possible.

China

The Chinese Communist Party (CCP) are no strangers to the international arena; and as one of the most powerful global players, they were bound to be involved in Afghanistan at one point or another. The convenience of their proximity, however, makes their role all the more crucial. Consumed with the ideas of stability and security, territorial sovereignty, national security, and protection of its strategic investments through what is termed by some as debt trap diplomacy, the CCP are no easy friend—or foe—to have. A special Chinese envoy had met Mullah Omar in Kandahar in 2000, opening the channel of communications. Things then turned ugly and the link was broken. China's gradual building of a relationship with the Taliban since 2014, however, indicates the high level of China's security concerns regarding an unstable Afghanistan, and what any spillover effects could mean for China.[2] The CCP are of the firm belief that control and security come hand in hand—and with control over the Taliban's Afghanistan, their security will be a comfortable given.

Since 2014, Taliban leaders and Chinese officials have engaged in multilateral meetings[3] in Doha, Beijing and Kabul, which opened avenues for the Taliban to receive public recognition and acknowledgment by the international community. In 2015, to address its security concerns, China even facilitated negotiations between the Taliban and the previous Afghan government to curb the Taliban from aligning themselves with the East Turkestan Islamic Movement (ETIM).[4]

The CCP under President Xi Jinping also became pragmatic regarding Afghanistan's domestic politics and the future of the Afghan peace process, realizing its power in the future of Central Asia politics. Furthermore, in the fourth China–Pakistan–Afghanistan trilateral dialogue in June 2021, China's foreign minister, Wang Yi, applauded the Taliban's return to mainstream politics.[5] This signifies that the CCP was forward-looking and well prepared for the Taliban's takeover in Afghanistan in 2021. Furthermore, before the final takeover that summer, the Taliban's spokesperson, Suhail Shaheen, publicly announced the new friendship established between the two countries, and the promises exchanged.[6]

Analyzing these trends, it is evident that China knew that, in order to secure its economic interests and stability, consistent political engagement with the Taliban would have to be a requisite. At the same time, it also signifies the Taliban's finesse in letting China build communications and a relationship with them ignoring many differences.

China's interests in Afghanistan are transparent and fluid: to combat the threat of Uyghur militancy and separatism through the Wakhan Corridor—a strip of territory connecting Xinjiang to Afghanistan—and to secure its economic investments in development projects. China's biggest fear is any potential threat to domestic stability from the minority population of Uyghur Muslims in Xinjiang province, where the government has been accused of genocide.[7]

Coming to China's economic interests, Afghanistan's geostrategic location in Central Asia, the estimated $3 trillion mineral reserves of the Mes Aynak copper mines, and the railways and power plants built through the Belt and Road Initiative, serve China's wider interests in the region.[8] China's rocky history with the operations of the Mes Aynak copper mines, the world's second largest copper ore mine, can now be reset through its interactions with the Taliban. China also intends to pull Afghanistan into the China–Pakistan Economic Corridor (CPEC), which could be a training ground for an operational component of the Shanghai Cooperation Organization (SCO).

On the other hand, the Taliban's interests in China's engagement in Afghanistan are multifaceted. As a failed state suffering from economic and humanitarian catastrophes and global isolation, the Taliban's quest for recognition, legitimacy and economic assistance is its most urgent priority.

A cohesive and functional political economy is vital for Afghanistan to establish itself as a working country and to gain recognition in the international community. With unprecedented sanctions from the West and Russia's invasion of Ukraine, the Taliban are increasingly looking toward China for rebuilding Afghanistan. Since July 2021, the diplomatic energy exchanged between the CCP and Taliban is worth noting. From the statements of senior Col. Zhou Bo of the People's Liberation Army's (PLA) on China's readiness to fill the void left by the West, to foreign minister Wang Yi's bilateral meetings with the Taliban, to the Taliban's encouragement of Chinese investments—the budding relationship here is clearly mutual.[9]

So it came as no surprise, then, that China not only kept its embassy open but also welcomed the Taliban's new status. Moreover, it even urged the UN Security Council to unfreeze Afghanistan's funds and went a step further in providing them initially with $31 million in humanitarian assistance.[10] These strategic moves helped China create the narrative that it can succeed where the United States has failed. It also crystallizes its projection of the United States abandoning nations.

The Taliban are looking more than ever before toward China with hope. In October 2022, Taliban spokesman Zabihullah Mujahid, referring to a cabinet meeting, announced that:

> it was decided that the Silk Road, which will connect Afghanistan with China, must be built. This historic road can play a great role in the economy of the country. It is a great opportunity, we have good security and it is the time to start major economic projects.[11]

Beijing, for its part, still appears to be moving slowly and cautiously in its relationship with the Taliban. The targeting of Chinese nationals in Pakistan by ISK as well as Baluch insurgents has made it extra cautious in its regional engagements.[12] Chinese nationals in Kabul have also been targeted by ISK in recent months. The Taliban have high expectations of China and may get quickly disappointed if projects are left undelivered and resources exploited. With the current political and economic turmoil in South Asia, as well as consequences of Russia's war in Ukraine, the developing friendly relationship between China and the Taliban is yet to be tested. And China may opt to avoid taking any major risks in Afghanistan, preferring instead to safeguard its interests in the country via Pakistan.

Iran

Another next-door neighbor, Iran, is arguably the second most impacted nation by Afghanistan's continuous troubles. After Pakistan, Iran hosts the most Afghan refugees, and acts as Afghanistan's second largest trade partner—and with 572 miles of shared border, the two are connected in more ways than one, whether they like it or not. Following the Taliban's return to power in 2021, Iran was among those nations that kept their embassies in Kabul open, indirectly declaring its willingness to work with the new government. While this may come as a surprise based on the deep, conflicting attachment both nations have to their sectarian identity—this is the nature of politics. They view each other through a purely geopolitical lens, not a sectarian one—and arguably, they have no choice but to do so. The countries' shared cultural, financial and physical landscapes mean engagement is inescapable—though despite the ongoing dialogue, Iran has so far refused to formally recognize the Taliban's new government.

While Iran and Afghanistan today work in cooperation, and have done so for years now, this wasn't always the case. Their history extends far back; most notably the connection with the Taliban began in the 1990s. In particular, Iran and Afghanistan under Mullah Omar nearly went to war with each other in 1998, following the killings of Iranian diplomats in Mazar-e-Sharif by Taliban militants. Following the US invasion, though, the scene began to shift. Initially, Iran was supportive of US military action against the Taliban but its inclusion in the "axis of evil" category by President George W. Bush abruptly ended that phase. Only a decade later, in the mid-2000s, Tehran and the Taliban started talking to each other and in some instances collaborating as the Taliban began to regain control of certain territories during the insurgency phase. These parleys were mostly hidden from the public eye as Tehran had reasonably good connections with both the Karzai and Ghani governments in Kabul. Tehran in fact actively backed Taliban insurgents, believing that the US, a major foe of theirs, would eventually leave the region and the Taliban would likely make a return to Kabul. Thus a new relationship was nurtured—a complex one, sure, but useful for both sides. It is interesting to note as well that this marked the start of certain Taliban leaders' families moving to Iran, a trend we saw happen again in 2020–21. Today, not only is the Iranian embassy in Kabul still standing (and vibrant), but the Taliban actually have a consulate in Mashhad (to facilitate Afghan Shia pilgrims), and Iranian delegations regularly travel to Kabul and Mazar-e-Sharif.

There are multiple aspects that draw the nations together today and drive the communication between Tehran and the Taliban. Among them, most notably, is the massive Afghan refugee population in Iran—a source of great strain for both countries for different reasons. With the current humanitarian crisis in Afghanistan only worsening, and the already fraught refugee situation in Iran, Tehran would like to prevent this challenge from growing. Every year, as a matter of fact, Iran deports large numbers of refugees back to Afghanistan—fearing extremism and economic strain. Accordingly, dialogue with the Taliban, and ensuring development to prevent additional refugees and potential security concerns, is high on Tehran's to-do list. Additionally, while Afghanistan has a sizable Shia population, it is not the sectarian commonality between the two countries that inspires Iran's interest. While Iran has advocated for a more inclusive government under the Taliban, aiding persecuted Hazaras has not been a major consideration—in fact, Hazaras and other Afghans face severe xenophobic discrimination as refugees in Iran.

Today, the challenges faced by any one country are, in many instances, shared among neighbors. The threat posed by ISK, for instance, is just as serious for Afghanistan as it is for Iran. For Tehran to not engage with the Taliban to combat such a common enemy would be a serious, perhaps lethal mistake—and this they are fully aware of. Hence, Tehran has done its part to engage with the Taliban to ensure its own national security. In addition, regarding the climate crisis, issues of resource-sharing, and particularly water scarcity, necessitate urgent dialogue. As climate change intensifies and Afghanistan's resource crisis grows, the historical tensions with Iran over water-sharing are again in the spotlight. On another note, the issue of drug trafficking into Iran through Afghanistan places a major burden on the former—with no clear solution in sight. To say the least, the two nations have a lot to work through.

Understandably, Tehran has its own hesitations over offering formal recognition to its new neighbors. Ultimately, it is the convergence of interests that will overcome the differences between them. Of course they face issues, and the Taliban do have a notable sectarian bias—but the political repercussions of not enjoying diplomatic links are recognized by both countries. Iran also continues to exercise a sizable influence over the Taliban, as mentioned earlier in the chapter, regarding the finances and private lives of the top Taliban leaders—a perk to be exploited, no doubt. Working with the Taliban is both inevitable and necessary for Iran's security, but the ice hasn't fully thawed just yet. Where the two will go from here is not clear, but one thing is certain: whatever their differences, they're stuck with each other.

Qatar

The Taliban would not be where they are today without the help of arguably their most remarkable—and most surprising —sponsor and benefactor: Qatar. There are many views as to how exactly they found themselves in this position, but two things must be remembered. First, unlike the UAE and Saudi Arabia, Qatar—while being wealthy and resource-rich—lacks the international stature the others possess in terms of visibility and prestige. This all began to change, however, with the ascent of Sheikha Mozah, the mother of the young Amir of Qatar, Sheikh Tamim Bin Hamad Al Thani. She helped her husband, Sheikh Hamad Bin Khalifa Al Thani, to redefine and reform Qatar and continues to actively engage in activities ranging from efforts to modernize Qatar's public transportation to the reform of the higher education system, building non-Muslim public places of worship, and sponsoring public debates via the Doha Forum.[13]

With the resources to build modern infrastructure, Qatar wanted to compete with regional players—and they did this in their own style. Qatar had a history of mediating in Lebanon, Yemen and Sudan. It became more adventurous over time. With a strong Muslim Brotherhood affiliation, Qatar decided to take a stake in the Taliban as a future investment. In 1999, Qatar had sent Yusuf Al-Qaradawi, a famed television host in the Muslim world, to speak with Taliban founder Mullah Omar and other Taliban leaders to try to stop them from destroying the ancient Buddha statues at Bamiyan. The attempt was unsuccessful, but this instance indicated their developing interest in playing a role to resolve regional challenges.[14] Two decades later, their strategic thinking would finally pay off.

That leads us to the modern era, when Qatar (since 2012) became the host for Taliban's political negotiations with the US, culminating in the February 2020 deal that empowered the Taliban's return to Kabul.[15] Notably, as well, they helped significantly in the mass evacuations that took place immediately following the Taliban's takeover in August 2021, keeping Kabul airport open and transporting thousands of Afghans in what became one of the largest human evacuations in history. Today, they continue to provide humanitarian assistance in the form of emergency aid, and even scholarships for Afghan students.

Qatar generally aimed to stay aloof from the actual ideology of the Taliban, while rejoicing over the success of the negotiations. As Dubai became globally famous for its modernity and for its glorious vacation facilities, and as Oman became a revered neutral space—along the lines of Switzerland in Europe—Qatar offered its space for the building of universities and enhanced its international stature by successfully hosting the FIFA World Cup in 2022. The Taliban merely became another investment that paid off, and perhaps their most important geostrategic initiative. Even as early as 2015, Qatar's leaders were almost certain that the Taliban would ultimately return to Kabul.[16]

However, to play host to the Taliban was not without risks. It certainly added to regional rivalries. The UAE, for instance, was really annoyed, as they were vying to win over the Taliban as well and had offered them space for negotiations. In fact, they even attempted to undermine Qatar's effort by complaining to the US that Abu Dhabi was supposed to be America's first choice for the purpose—and its ambassador to the US even went on the media to condemn Qatar's closeness to Muslim extremist groups including Hamas, the Taliban and the Muslim Brotherhood.[17]

Despite all this though, and regardless of playing the role of mediator and essentially paving the way for the Taliban to achieve the deal they did, they are yet to formally recognize the Taliban's new government. Qatar is content to have the Taliban's permanent political office on its soil, acting as their political refuge, yet shies away from publicly embracing their new role. Qatar's close alliance with the US cannot be ignored in this case: it hosts the biggest US military base in the Middle East. It will likely wait for a green light from Washington DC before officially recognizing the Taliban government but, beyond that, Qatar is actively engaged with the Taliban, while urging the West to step up its engagement with Kabul to rescue Afghanistan from chaos and rising extremism.[18] Evidence of its continued critical role is its hosting of a crucial meeting between David Cohen, CIA deputy director, and Abdul Haq Wasiq, the head of Taliban intelligence, in October 2022, to discuss ongoing counterterrorism cooperation, especially against ISK.[19]

Russia

Pinpointing where historic messes began is never easy, or entirely accurate, but in the case of Afghanistan it's not far off to say it began with the Soviet Union's invasion in the 1980s. Prior to that, however, the Soviet Union was actually the first country to establish a diplomatic mission in Afghanistan in 1919.[20] Fast-forward six decades, and the failed invasion drastically changed the face of their relationship, setting off a storm still raging today. As history began to play out, the Kremlin eventually shifted its policy toward Afghanistan and extended its support to the United States in combat operations against the Taliban throughout the 2000s.

However, after 2015, Russia's Afghan calculus and strategy shifted significantly. The mutual desire of the Kremlin and the Taliban to combat ISK and its growing extremist footprint in Central Asia led them to join hands and work together. On the basis of their shared anti-US sentiment, Russia established active channels of communication with the Taliban in various international forums—a clean slate was established, it seemed.

Russia, which is an active member of the SCO, along with China, India and other Central Asian countries, has used the platform to address the impact of terror groups in Afghanistan. This led to the SCO forming the Afghanistan Contact Group (ACG) in 2005 to support Afghanistan in combating the spread of drugs and crime.[21] The SCO also played an important role in facilitating a conversation between the Afghan government and the Taliban, specifically during the withdrawal of NATO troops in 2016.

In fact, in March 2017, President Putin's special envoy for Afghanistan, Zamir Kabulov, commended the Taliban movement and requested the withdrawal of US troops.[22] Beginning in 2018, the Kremlin invited the Taliban for several rounds of peace talks in Moscow,[23] which helped officials understand the core interests of the Taliban. This also gave the Taliban an opportunity to gain some international exposure and reframe their narrative and communications in a better light.

Russia also hosted the Moscow regional peace consultations and informal inter-Afghan dialogues from 2017 to 2019 and regularly invited and hosted the Taliban as participants.[24] Evidently, these engagements prepared the Taliban in terms of understanding the nature of political leaders at both a tactical and strategic level.

Hence, it is safe to conclude that Russia was well prepared for a Taliban-ruled Afghanistan. It started building its bridges and ties a decade ago to mitigate the impact of Afghanistan's instability on Russia. Before the takeover, the Taliban delegation was also invited to Moscow in July 2021 to offer assurances that there would be no escalation of violence in Central Asia posing challenges for Russia.[25]

To understand the drivers of Russia's attitude toward the Taliban, Russia's major security concern must be acknowledged: regional instability in Central Asia, and the supply of opium—that is, drug trafficking. Afghanistan has long been the biggest producer and supplier of opium, which has caused havoc for Russia's domestic policies and national security.[26] Combating the spread of drugs in the region is crucial for Russia. Similarly, the threat of organized extremist groups targeting Central Asia would have spillover effects in Russia. Accordingly, the Russians began to deploy strategies to mitigate the risks associated with an unstable Afghanistan.

With the fall of the US-supported Afghan government in August 2021, Russia did not shy away from publicly sharing its anti-West position and the satisfaction it derived from the failure of the United States' state-building efforts.[27] It gave Russia an opportunity to step up its engagements with the Taliban for the protection of its own security needs.

Since then, Russian officials, foreign minister Sergey Lavrov and Taliban delegates have conducted eight rounds of bilateral and multilateral meetings on issues of humanitarian aid, human rights, and Afghanistan's future economic recovery. To strengthen Afghanistan's internal security, Putin has even proposed the Taliban's removal from the list of international terrorist organizations.[28]

Moscow's pragmatic and soft approach toward Afghanistan signals its acceptance of the new reality. From providing humanitarian and financial aid to urging the removal of the Taliban from the list of terrorist organizations, Moscow acknowledges that they can neither be ignored nor isolated. Furthermore, Russian officials also did not evacuate their Kabul embassy, exhibiting their reciprocity and trust in the Taliban's governance.[29] All in all, Russia seems optimistic about the Taliban and their future, citing them as a powerful force and people of sound mind.[30] However, Russia's real and tangible interests of safeguarding its own economic and security interests will always come first.

The Taliban, which have also moved beyond the historical relationship with Russia, have renewed interest in Moscow's engagement. The Taliban provide Russia with the economic benefits of investments in agriculture and energy projects, as well as the Belt and Road Initiative, which would improve supply chains in the region. The Russian export of LPG (liquefied petroleum gas) supplies through the gas processing plant in Afghanistan and the Trans-Afghan railway line[31] serve as major underpinnings for Russia's influence in the region. Regional security is essential for the smooth operation of these projects.

With the Russian invasion of Ukraine, Putin's misadventure makes the Taliban a bit cautious with regard to Russia being a trusted partner, thus limiting its influence in the region. Interestingly, the Taliban advised Russia to work toward a peaceful resolution and end its invasion of Ukraine. Currently, Russia has no resources to invest in Afghanistan's economic growth. With this dynamic shift in the geopolitical environment, the nature of the Taliban–Russia engagement will likely change as the Taliban grow wary of Russia's intentions.

As history reminds us, it was the Mujahideen, which then more or less became the Taliban, who kicked Russia out (with help from the Northern Alliance) and killed thousands of Soviet men. Some even argue that this was one of the breaking points of the USSR. Certainly this is not a fact lost to history, especially not to a leader like Putin. Russia, despite being involved in its own quagmire, more than anything might be interested in ensuring that the new Afghanistan doesn't fall under US influence ever again. The rivalry and competition between great powers is never-ending, after all.

India

Until August 2021, India and the Taliban shared a hostile relationship with each other, catalyzed by the hijacking of Indian Airlines flight IC-814 in 1999.[32] Throughout the 1990s, India's approach toward Afghanistan, and the Taliban in particular, was shaped by interests similar to those of Iran and Russia. The trilateral relationship provided support to the Northern Alliance to fight against the Taliban. Post-2001, India consistently provided support to Karzai and then Ghani government to bring a peaceful solution to the then Afghanistan conflict.

Abiding by its "Neighborhood First" policy,[33] the Indian government was one of the largest regional donors in South Asia during Afghanistan's reconstruction period from the

2000s on. New Delhi has invested close to $5 billion in Afghanistan's economy during 2002–21 by way of development and infrastructure projects.[34] From the construction of the $300 million Afghan–India Friendship dam, aka the Salma dam, to the $90 million Afghan parliament building in 2015, and its generous humanitarian aid during the Covid-19 pandemic, India has proved itself to be a trusted neighbor to Afghanistan.

Indian Prime Minister Narendra Modi also highlighted the support as "tribute to democracy in Afghanistan."[35] While India rooted for "an Afghan-led, Afghan-owned and Afghan-controlled process,"[36] New Delhi and the Taliban share a trust deficit, as India was excluded from both the 2020 Doha Agreement and the Moscow peace negotiations.[37]

Since August 2021, the moral and political dilemma faced by the Indian government is multifaceted. India's direct security concerns at their borders arise from Pakistan and China more than Afghanistan. However, Afghanistan during the Taliban's first stint in power had become a refuge of terrorist groups such as Pakistan's Jaish-e-Mohammed (JeM). Any return to that scenario could be very dangerous for India, whose ultimate aim is to protect its territorial sovereignty and combat terrorist organizations, such as Al-Qaeda in the Indian Subcontinent (AQIS)—who might target the Indian side of Kashmir.[38] Hence, India does not want the Taliban to nurture anti-India sentiments so as to mitigate any threat of terrorism in the country.

India's skepticism also stems from the Haqqani network, with its deep affiliation to Pakistan's intelligence services. The Haqqani network has previously launched repeated offensive attacks against India's interests in Afghanistan, including attacks on India's diplomatic missions in Kabul in 2008 and Herat in 2014.[39]

India also acknowledges the strategic position of Afghanistan in the region for its own economic interests. Its previous investments, along with trade exports and imports through the 218-kilometer Zaranj–Delaram highway, and the laying of 202 kilometers of electricity transmission lines from Uzbekistan are crucial for maintaining its economic influence in the region.[40]

Unlike Russia and China, India had cut off its diplomatic ties with Afghanistan and closed its embassies during the takeover. Its strategic partnership with the United States, and close association with the previous Ghani government, were the major reasons for its initial diplomatic absence. However, India is now seriously reassessing its position and moving toward a "balancing act" in its effort to engage with the Taliban and help stabilize Afghanistan.

With Russia and China's over-enthusiastic engagements with the Taliban, and China's growing offensive posture at the Line of Actual Control (LAC) between itself and India, India opened its first formal bilateral lines of communication with the Taliban in June 2022.[41] The long haul to establish a dialogue over a span of one year is indicative of New Delhi's extreme apprehension with regard to any engagement with the Taliban.

The Taliban's desire is simple—international legitimacy and recognition. Huge external investments are essential to reconstruct and revive the country. The Taliban understand that India's economic relationship with Afghanistan in the past could pave the way for long-term investments in the future, aiding in their quest for legitimacy. With India's growing significance in South Asia and the Indo-Pacific, it is imperative for the Taliban to have a strong neighbor in them.

The Indian embassy in Kabul was unaffected during the takeover, indicating the Taliban's firm intention to re-engage with the Indian government. Similarly, the Taliban also placed pressure on Pakistan to allow free passage for Indian wheat to enter Afghanistan through Pakistan. The Taliban's persistent requests for India to open its Kabul embassy also indicate the urgency, from their point of view, of normalizing their relationship.[42]

While the Taliban have repeatedly tried to assuage India's security apprehensions, New Delhi remains cautious and acutely aware that Taliban attitudes could change once they feel more in control. The Taliban–Pakistan closeness is a fact that haunts India.

The question is whether India really wants to give legitimacy to the Taliban, and if so, how? With China's new initiatives to enhance its influence in the region, New Delhi clearly understands that it should not shy away from building its relationship with the Taliban. It would allow India to have a better sense of the realities on the ground, enabling it to strategize its engagement with the Taliban. For India to hold a vital stake in Afghanistan, a diplomatic presence inside the country is important. It was this realization that led to the return of a small Indian diplomatic contingent to Afghanistan in August 2022. In the words of Gautam Mukhopadhaya, a former Indian ambassador to Afghanistan,

"It's an opening gambit so to speak, in some ways you are back in the game."[43]

Turkey

Turkey shares a significant history with Afghanistan dating back to the days of the Ottoman Empire. Since the early 1900s, the two countries have attributed significant importance to their bilateral trade and established diplomatic ties for nation-building. From helping Afghanistan draft its first constitution to providing military, educational and financial aid, Turkey has certainly proved its "all-weather friendship" with Afghanistan.

Turkey, being the biggest Muslim-majority country in NATO (the only other one being Albania), had the leverage to participate in Afghanistan's politics throughout its reconstruction period in the 2000s. Its neutrality toward Afghanistan's internal affairs and diplomatic engagements had helped in facilitating dialogues between the Afghan government and the Taliban. It also commanded the International Security Assistance Force (ISAF) in 2003[44] and established an office of the Turkish Cooperation and Coordination Agency (TIKA) in Afghanistan.[45] The Turkish-speaking minority in Afghanistan also accelerated Turkey's cultural engagement in the country. All these factors shaped the building of what Turkey calls a fraternal relationship with Afghanistan. The Taliban were still skeptical about Turkish goals in Afghanistan.

Turkey's offer to provide military and security assistance at Kabul airport in June 2021 came as a surprise to the international community.[46] Although unsuccessful, the pivot shows that Turkey was prepared to recognize the Taliban as Afghanistan's main authority early on. Turkey believed that this strategic move to become the eyes and ears of the US in Afghanistan could help it in improving its bilateral relationship, given that American sanctions on Turkey for its acquisition of Russian S-400 missiles and its violation of the Countering America's Adversaries through Sanctions Act (CAATSA) had caused a significant deterioration in their relationship.[47] Turkey also aims to gain long-term geopolitical leverage through the joint operation of Kabul airport alongside Qatar, thus benefitting from the Qatar–Taliban connection. However, it is facing stiff competition from the UAE in this battle which has taken many twists and turns.

Nevertheless, just like other regional powers, Turkey's policy toward Afghanistan is at best tentative. From asking the Taliban to "end the occupation"[48] to being optimistic about cooperation with the group,[49] Turkey has been testing the waters. Prudent in its diplomatic engagements, it maintained an open dialogue to support the new ruling power in Afghanistan. The sudden shift in Ankara's policies and acceptance of the change in Afghanistan are shaped by diplomatic, economic and humanitarian interests. Turkey's engagement with the Taliban is geared towards becoming a key regional influence in Afghanistan and Central Asia.

Like others, Turkey has some security concerns in dealing with terrorism and extremism coming out of Afghanistan, but its economic interests take priority. These include private investments in the country by the Turkish Independent Industrialists and Businessmen's Association (MUSIAD)[50] and the Afghan–Turkish business association.[51] These collaborations are building strong partnerships to invest in development projects in the areas of power, energy and gas. Turkey's construction of the Kajaki hydro-electric power plant in Kabul has already demonstrated Ankara's interest in investing in Afghanistan.[52] The strategic Lapis Lazuli transit corridor, which runs from Afghanistan to Turkey via other Central Asian countries, will further enhance significant trade and transits in Central Asia.[53] This would offer opportunities for the Taliban to build strong bilateral ties with other nations and show their legitimate efforts to address their security concerns. The Taliban are hoping for investments from Turkey for economic reconstruction, which will probably attract other regional countries to do the same. Regardless, every country intends to become an economic beneficiary of Afghanistan's mineral-rich resources. Sadly, even the extension of humanitarian aid—of human compassion—must come as a trade.

Turkey has intensively used soft power diplomacy by inviting the Taliban delegation to Ankara, facilitating meetings with religious institutions and scholars, and even providing humanitarian aid following the Kabul earthquake. Along with its existing operations in Kabul, Turkey has reopened its consular services in major cities like Mazar-e-Sharif[54] to show its strong intent of collaborating and creating cross-network educational institutions. Furthermore, the Taliban's (now former) minister of education, Abdul Baqi Haqqani, met the Turkish ambassador in March 2022 to build a religious and modern sciences curriculum.[55] All these instances highlight the Taliban's significant efforts to build a relationship with Turkey—they are not ignorant of the fact that Turkey could become a key entry point for them to attain international legitimacy. Being the major Muslim NATO member, Turkey's political engagements with the Taliban hold the power to shape and change the behavior of other NATO members as well.

While this ambition is optimistic, Turkey would be wise to think realistically about its engagement with the Taliban as it does pose genuine problems for its domestic security. Turkey already hosts the largest refugee population in the world—as tragic as it is, accepting more poses a real challenge to its economy, domestic stability and, potentially, national security. Already the government faces much criticism from the domestic population for its engagement with the Taliban.[56] With the recent tragic memories of the perils of Syrian refugees, and the attitudes of their own population, perhaps Turkey might take a more cautious approach when considering hosting more asylum seekers and refugees.

As Turkey aims to leverage its relationship and establish itself strongly in Central Asia, its overreach in Afghanistan could become counterproductive. President Erdogan appeared to be cognizant of the risks involved when he said: "Turkey is ready to lend all kinds of support for Afghanistan's unity but will follow a very cautious path."[57]

Emerging Taliban Foreign Policy

The Taliban have put themselves in an unprecedented situation—becoming the very thing they tried to destroy. They have put on the shoes of politicians, taken on the task of being governors, when their entire life so far has been defined by their efforts against such people. They have dreamt of this for a long time, but when eventually a dream becomes a reality, it's time to wake up—can they deal with the reality of life in power? A movement whose historical mode of operation has been insurgency is now in complete control of a nation drowning in deep water. Afghanistan today has fractured institutions, faces some of the world's worst humanitarian crises and is undergoing severe economic turmoil among a myriad of challenges. Moreover, divisions within the Taliban have led to a lack of cohesion in its actions and domestic policies, making the group's new job even harder. While the international community asks for more inclusivity in its governance and respect for human rights, such expectations are futile. They have enough on their plate—to add more means potentially to make an overflowing mess.

To construct any projections regarding the Taliban's future in power, their governance performance must be constantly evaluated. Afghanistan needs a formal, established, legal economy—and the prospects for this, given their current economic plight, appear to be bleak.

The strategic nature of its location, coupled with the tantalizing desire to exploit its resources, seals Afghanistan's fate as a sought-after prize for competing nations. With the vested interests of China, Iran, Turkey, Qatar, UAE, Pakistan, India and Russia, besides other Central Asian states, instability due to rivalries could plague Afghanistan. With ISK in the background, and the likelihood of a resurgence of other militant groups, the Taliban cannot expect a smooth ride.

As the West weighs its options in Afghanistan, many neighbouring countries are also in wait-and-see mode. In the interim, diplomatic engagements are key to protecting their security interests. They can certainly do so while hoping for the best. As nations bide their time in giving recognition to the Taliban, a collective strategic posture has a higher likelihood of engaging the Taliban effectively.

By mid 2024, the Taliban had skillfully engaged with not only their neighboring states but with China and various international organizations, including the EU and UN. While recognition remains evasive, around 40 states nevertheless have their representatives present in Afghanistan today. This has been a hopeful sign for them, a motivator even. Drawing some strength from these regular interactions with states and international organizations, the Taliban felt confident enough to decline participation in a UN conference in Doha in February 2024 focusing on the humanitarian and human rights crisis in Afghanistan. As their demands to be accepted as the sole representatives of Afghanistan were ignored, Taliban never showed up—but interestingly, UN Secretary General Guterres remarked on their absence in a way that suggests the group will likely get what they want eventually. Guterres said that while conversations with the 'de facto authorities' didn't take place that day, "it will happen in the near future."[58]

Conclusion

The Future of the Taliban

The West's strategy of aid conditionality—asking the
Taliban to moderate their behaviour on women's rights
and other issues in return for funding—has clearly failed.
It is imperative for the West to develop mechanisms that
prevent the Afghan population from being punished for
the Taliban's takeover . . .

> —Hamid Hakimi and Gareth Price, Chatham House[1]

The reality of the Taliban is right before us, in all their gore
and grit. But now, the question remains: where do we go
from here, when the road is anything but clear? They
face their most daunting challenge yet in figuring out
how to move from a globally condemned insurgency to a
recognized political organization responsible for governing
Afghanistan. Beyond that, they have to tackle the problem
of all the varying perspectives within their network. To put
it simply, and mildly, if they want to continue in power, they
will have to make sure all their team members are on the
same page. The problem is that the Taliban's rank and file

have been motivated by a set of ideals based on an anti-Western, anti-modern attitude. To cooperate with those very elements, the Taliban will now have to make a concerted effort to reshape their worldview and internalize it first. And finally, as responsible managers of a new state, they require a different skill set and approach from the one they are so accustomed to. Such a reconstruction of their political philosophy will not be so simple, either. Whether they have that in them at all, only time will tell. If they can make these transitions in the next three to five years, their project will likely start to gain credibility. All they must do is govern just well enough to minimize any terrorist-induced chaos, disable criminal networks and manage the humanitarian crises that are knocking on their doors. If they can pull that off, or at least be seen as making genuine efforts in this direction, perhaps not just their neighbors but the whole international community will start adjusting to their reality. It is a tall order indeed but not impossible.

Throughout the book, the primary issues that the Taliban are facing and will continue to face have been examined in some detail. Even though their leaders have shown repeatedly, as was the case in the Doha negotiations, that they can compromise and engage with the West—for their men on the ground, the foot soldiers, especially those hailing from the rural areas, it will be a very hard sell. The last thing the leaders in Kabul need is to be disconnected from their network on the ground across the country. If they are out of sync, the possibility of the group splintering into different factions becomes a very real one. However, it is not fair to assume that all those from rural areas, or all the lower-ranking members, are of such a mindset. There are also many members from these areas with significantly more exposure to the world beyond Afghanistan, and educational credentials to their name, which will benefit the group in creating a balance.

Another complicating factor is how to honestly qualify and quantify the Taliban. My findings, based on conversations with Taliban on this point, is that hardly 30 percent—to a maximum of 40 percent—are ideological in orientation, the rest are merely their relatives, sympathizers and friends who either pose or are viewed as Taliban in a social sense if not a military one. Another group assuming the Taliban label, though, are thieves and criminals. Small local warlords should also be factored in—ultimately, a lot of them are using the opportunity to make money. How long they will stay loyal to the Taliban depends on the economic opportunities and crime opportunities they will gain.

Within the Taliban, even today, the most important credential one can possess is the clerical or *Mullah* status. Going by the book, religious knowledge determines your position and reputation. Even if in disagreement, the leader's religious credentials matter beyond anything else, and ultimately trump political connections. The NATO and US approach in Afghanistan had many flaws and they made many grand miscalculations, yes, but perhaps the most central one came down to their lack of knowledge as to how the Taliban hierarchy worked in practice. That is, they failed to follow the rule #1 in war: know your enemy! The US team in Doha was expecting Mullah Baradar to get the top slot once the Taliban were back in Kabul without realizing his rank did not exactly align with it. The world witnessed the victory of the Taliban, but how they managed it still escapes us all, it appears.

In a conversation I had with an important ideologue of the Taliban, he shared fascinating insights into the reality of Taliban leaders' time spent in Pakistan. When I made the assumption that because Habitullah and some other top leaders lived in Pakistan they were inevitably influenced by it, he told me a very interesting fact. He said that these leaders lived in small self-made reflections of Afghanistan, made up of small camps across the country, spanning from KPK to Punjab to Quetta. They made a mini-Afghanistan within Pakistan wherever they went—and because their trust primarily only extended to Afghans, they seldom even interacted with those outside their camps. This is particularly the case for Taliban middle- and senior-level operators who lived in Pakistan. The point here is that Taliban narratives sanctioned by the top Taliban leaders continued to be taught and enforced among the Taliban cadres unfiltered, and without being diluted due to different settings and environment. The environment in which Taliban middle- and senior-ranking officials operate, whether within or outside Afghanistan, remains controlled—as much as possible.

Ultimately, understanding and predicting the power struggle between the "old" Taliban—those we have watched over the past thirty years—and the new generation of the Taliban, lies at the core of this analysis. To avoid the mistakes of our past, we must reexamine in depth and analyze the reality of the rebranded Taliban—their demographics, psychology, inheritance and, even more, the factors that have led to their current state, ranging from external players to internal issues. In doing this, the book aims to reframe, in a sense, the current perspective to accommodate not only more nuance but some optimism too. The goal is to recognize the psyche of the present generation of Taliban and work with that. Additionally, in recognizing the new threats in the region, such as ISK, and analyzing the ensuing power struggles, we can further capture the dynamics of the region and its security future.

Let us examine some key differences between the old and "new" Taliban, for the lack of any other word to label the contemporary version of the Taliban. First, the original group from 1996 to 1999 were notoriously comfortable with keeping themselves within an introverted reality, whereas the Taliban of today have an established and forward-looking sense of international relations. They have moved past their reputation as isolationists, becoming willing interactors with a global view of engagement. On that same front, the former had very little interest in working with development agencies like the UN. Today, with new institutions and infrastructure in place (and credit will have to be given where it is due: to the US and its NATO allies), the contemporary Taliban inevitably have realized they cannot go on like their predecessors in 1990s. To live without the features of the modern era, the ease of high-speed internet and all the rest, is not realistic for them. So they took it from where they could get it. Their electricity, for instance, is provided by Uzbekistan and Tajikistan—and they are continuously engaging and negotiating with them for its supply without disruption.[2] Taliban leaders have also been demanding from both these Central Asian states the return of the helicopters and aircraft that were flown there by former members of the Afghan security forces while escaping from Afghanistan in and around August 2021. It is believed that 46 aircraft are in the possession of Uzbekistan and 18 in Tajikistan.[3] Even though Taliban defense minister Mullah Yaqoob warned both countries not to test Taliban patience and force them to take retaliatory steps,[4] so far the Taliban have only pursued diplomatic avenues.

The Tajikistan–Taliban border tensions are another tough challenge for the Taliban. Both sides are housing the other's enemies, and in any case their 800-mile border is hard to monitor and manage.[5] Both sides accuse the other of causing instability across the border.

All of this speaks to the Taliban's estimation of why they cannot remain aloof from their neighborhood as well as to their concerns and fears. Taliban 1.0 would gasp in horror at the thought, as they saw outsiders as spies or negative influences. To see the fruits of their labor move so far off course as to trust others would be quite unpalatable for them. Additionally, regarding the media, the former group was far more conservative when approaching media freedoms. In the new Afghanistan, the number of Western journalists being allowed to operate is a big change, as there are many international and especially regional news networks still carrying on with their coverage. Of course, there are major issues, with increasing control being asserted, and women not having the same opportunities as men, and a gradual increase in the filtering of narratives on state media, but, ultimately, the media world is still functional. This is a product of new times that will have a big impact on the extent to which the Taliban can control knowledge and information, and it is also happening through social media—something we are already seeing with their usage of Twitter and Facebook. Comparing Taliban media freedoms with Western standards would be grossly unfair. Some Middle Eastern and Central Asian states with whom the West happily engages day in and day out offer better examples for the purposes of comparison.

Moreover, the 1990s Taliban had a dangerous religious militant agenda targeting both regional and global locations—they were, after all, the offspring of the Afghan Mujahideen, many of whom came from different countries from across the world: from Indonesia and Malaysia at one corner to Egypt and Sudan on the other, and everywhere in between. We know enough about how the Al-Qaeda–Taliban marriage of convenience produced terrorism. While the Taliban, especially the Haqqani faction, still have some sympathy for Al-Qaeda, as exposed by their hosting of Al-Qaeda top leader Ayman Al-Zawahiri in Kabul, today the new generation of Taliban, lacking access to the old global Mujahideen-era network, are more focused on their identity as Afghans. Nationalism is a key identity marker now, more so than a universal religious mission.

Additionally, the old Taliban were more fixated on sectarianism, partly because of the Al-Qaeda influence and Arab militants—for whom sectarian divisions, especially Sunni versus Shia, were important. Hazara Shias, constituting one-fifth of the nation's population, for instance, faced massacres during the late 1990s at the hands of

Taliban. Although Hazaras are still facing discrimination and violence, today's Taliban have tried to reach out to the Hazara Shias, both in Kabul and in the northern areas of the country.[6] I was told during an interview that the Pakistani Shia leader Sajid Naqvi had received a message from Mullah Baradar during a visit he made to Pakistan, to emphasize that the Taliban had reached out to the Hazara Shias.[7] He wanted to convey this message to Pakistani Shia leaders as well—to let them know that they should not be concerned about sectarianism in Afghanistan—and to convey it to Afghan Shias through their channels as well. One cannot take such outreach at face value but nonetheless these efforts to cooperate with and support this persecuted Muslim and ethnic minority group indicate an important policy shift— or perhaps one in the making. There are many non-Hazara Shia communities in Afghanistan as well, who were generally aligned with anti-Taliban forces, so this is not an easy decision for the Taliban in political terms.

On this note of religion, the old Taliban, with their Deobandi-Hanafi roots, were the dominant religious group operating in Afghanistan but they had witnessed a potent dogmatic intervention from Al-Qaeda's Salafi narratives. The result was a highly militant version of Deobandism that was not in line with the original teachings, as discussed earlier in the book. Since running the insurgency in Afghanistan, largely on its own, though aided and abetted by drug mafia as well as Pakistan, the Taliban today are relatively more independent in their religious thinking. This return of sorts to nineteenth-century Deobandi roots, which historically was accommodative of even Sufi groups in Afghanistan, also explains the growing Taliban tensions with ISK. Now, they are faced with a group which is not only more extreme, but in fact—from a religious perspective—strongly anti-Deobandi in its outlook. ISK has even published booklets for public dissemination in Afghanistan and Pakistan directly challenging the Deobandi school of thought. To say they are opponents is not quite accurate—they are sworn enemies.

Finally, the former Taliban was a warrior movement at heart. The present-day Taliban benefit from running shadow governments across the country, with many members operating in organized hierarchies. In my conversation with an Afghan Taliban member, I was told that the Taliban are facing a challenge from these dime-a-dozen weapon-wielding individuals claiming they are the Taliban.[8] They are not authorized to do that but the Taliban lack enforcement measures. However, they are actively engaged in organizing themselves to govern better and have started assigning different factions and cadres to wear specific uniforms. A senior Taliban official told me in August 2022 that they would soon start arresting people brandishing weapons at checkpoints and major crossroads in Kabul. This is at least a gradual attempt to institutionalize—a stark contrast from the tactics of the earlier brand of Taliban. Various ministries and government offices are being populated; a structure is in place and the Taliban are trying their best to sustain what was built over the last two decades. Well, it is easy to fill roles—but to adapt to an administrative and institutional setup that they are not familiar with is new territory for them, and surely one where they are breaking new ground.

Slowly, we are beginning to see the shedding of the old Taliban's skin—and maybe it is turning into something not seen before.

A Taliban cleric who taught and trained many of the new generation of middle-ranking Taliban leaders told me that the Taliban foot soldiers who fought—and ultimately won the war for them—are a priority to be accommodated in government positions. For cabinet positions, he further added, "the central criterion was how deep one's piety and loyalty to core Taliban values and ideology was."[9] He insisted that the younger generation is open-minded when it comes to engagements and interactions, even with those they disagree with. At the same time though, they are very conservative and continue to be plagued by tribal thinking. When I asked how Taliban hailing from different ethnic and tribal backgrounds are expected to work together for a common cause of developing and stabilizing Afghanistan, he confessed that the biggest challenge new leaders face is the entrenched urban versus rural divide. While many leaders have experienced living in urban centers in Afghanistan, Pakistan and Qatar, most of their foot soldiers come from rural backgrounds—so for them, urban centers like Kabul are a new world. These are men for whom *purdah* (the veil) is a core Islamic tradition on which there can be no compromise and they are heavily influenced by patriarchal ideas of women. They cannot accept a relatively open society in an urban setting, where men and women work side by side. For Taliban leaders with international exposure, it is hard to reeducate their cadres, even if they really want to—which is why it is so important for their Western and regional interlocutors to remember this dilemma when issuing policy statements on matters sensitive to them. These pronouncements, in any case, are mostly directed at local Western audiences. Realistically, under the Taliban meaningful progress in this arena is a long way off.

My recommendation—knowing full well this is going to be controversial—is to increase engagement with the Taliban. In fact, engaging in conversations with them on what is required by the international community for them to be formally recognized is perhaps the only way forward in the muddled reality we have now. My argument is that any effective, sustained and meaningful engagement with them has the real capacity to empower the relatively pragmatic and moderate elements among them. *Not* engaging is going to support the view of hardliners that the world is against them—and consequently they will rise further within the organization. The older generation of the Taliban, the comrades of Mullah Omar, are on their way out over the next five years or so. The newer Taliban, by virtue of social media and their digital access to the globe, are the ones who will be the movers and shakers in Afghanistan. We can allow them to move around in the dark, or offer them a way out. The tens of billions of dollars invested in Afghanistan created an infrastructure now at the disposal of the Taliban, and this we cannot ignore. They will need engagement, better skills, and capacity building to use it and run a government. It will inevitably force them to engage with people of different views and ethnic groups in Afghanistan—and that may even lead to a diversified government. Earlier Western "demands" along these lines fell on deaf ears, but the Taliban will be forced to consider these when confronted with practical challenges of governance—and that is happening. This is an optimistic projection, though, I must admit.

Offering the Taliban some level of legitimacy does not have to equate to accepting their flaws—of which there are many. It is worthwhile to note that there are a large number of states with atrocious human rights records recognized by the international community. What makes Afghanistan stand out? And is it so bad to assume—to hope—that they can change, for the better? If anything, for the sake of the Afghan people, who have been treated so terribly in all of this—do we not owe them even an attempt to offer some light?

While conversing with a former senior US official who follows the Afghan crisis very closely and was involved in diplomatic engagements with South Asia, including Afghanistan, I was startled by the tone of assessment: "We have demonstrated in a spectacular way to the Afghan people that we don't give a shit about Afghanistan. The Taliban are not like us, not in terms of policies or values, but we also know they are sick of hearing our lectures about women's rights and morality. They tell us hey—we are not lecturing you on what we think you are doing wrong. Our narrative is simply annoying and unhelpful to them."[10] This person still did not recommend recognizing the Taliban as the legitimate government of Afghanistan—and believed that it is inconceivable to expect the Biden administration to take that route. Given political polarization and extremism trends across the world, it is quite hypocritical of the international community, and especially the West, to expect the Taliban to follow a reform agenda that is seen by them as alien.

Moreover, let us stop for a moment with all these rushed plans and acknowledge that we are not going *anywhere* with the current US policy toward Afghanistan. We are not accomplishing anything by giving a "to-do list" to the Taliban that they cannot agree to—not to mention that they cannot even be publicly seen to be meeting with US officials. The best way to promote and protect international interests, for the sake of stability in Afghanistan, and for it not to turn into a hub of terrorism again, is to start by scrapping the moral lectures. Then to proceed with structured engagement that involves direct communication with Taliban leaders both in Kabul and Kandahar. Mullah Baradar and Abbas Stanikzai, as skilled as they are, are not the lead policy decision-makers of Afghanistan today. Hibatullah and Siraj Haqqani are—and no Western capital is in direct communication with them, especially Hibatullah, as yet.

Despite their dysfunction and intense internal rivalries, the Taliban's grip on the steering wheel is not about to loosen any time soon. They will now and forever look at themselves only through the lens of their recent victory—they are the glorious David who overcame the monstrous Goliath, and so this sense of themselves will be forever etched in their memory. They waited a long time to get what they have now, and they will not let anyone or anything—especially not their own differences or dynamics—get in the way of that. Their outward projection of unity and following Hibatullah's commands—despite growing internal divisions—is their power, their secret weapon. Their commitment to their cause, and their ability to overlook their differences—no matter how personally distasteful—is, to them, what makes them so special. So if listening to the top leader who is following guidance from a handful of extreme clerics in Kandahar leaves a bad taste in their mouth, they will gladly accept it because that is the reason they were able to return to Kabul—and they don't want to vacate it again. The tragic truth, though, is that the resistance they now face from rivals such as ISK is also their life support. It only strengthens them, knowing that there are people who pose a theological as well as political challenge to their authority—it makes them all the more possessive, and protective, of it. This has the deadly potential to further militarize them and fuel a new wave of violent conflict in the future.

To move forward, we must accept hard truths. The Doha negotiations showed that engaging with the Taliban is possible, that they are not only capable of rational discourse but also believe in give and take. Clinging to the image of Mullah Omar from decades ago only means staying stuck in denial that a new reality lies before us. The Taliban are now reaching out to the UN, asking for money, and looking to cooperate with other states, from China and India on the one hand to the European Union and US on the other. They are clearly making an effort. Sure, those in Kandahar are out of touch with the reality of the international order, and Siraj Haqqani was caught with his pants down while secretly hosting Ayman Al-Zawahiri; most of those in Kabul are in a learning mode. They are catching up, and those among the Taliban leadership who are still stationed in Doha need to return to Kabul with their families and help with the transition. The West, for its part, needs to accept the reality and move on to the final stage of their grief: acceptance.

In conclusion, the Taliban have a long way ahead of them, due to their own rigidity and bigotry, more than anything else. The variations within their vast network pose the most significant challenge to their movement. It is only a matter of time until power politics starts to impact their cohesion; if it comes down to it, this may be their kryptonite. Additionally, the dangers posed by ISK are growing each day. The threat is indeed very serious, but not existential. They will remain an ugly sight in their peripheral vision, creating terror where they can and irritating the Taliban to the best of their ability. The tensions there, plus the added strain of the complicated relationships with Pakistan and the Pakistani Taliban, make for an interesting, but stressful, future for them in terms of regional security. Losing the goodwill of Pakistani intelligence could be deadly for them, but trying to retain their support (and their image as Pakistan's proxy) could be politically unsustainable given the tribal dynamics of Afghanistan.

Finally, the most significant factor: the new generation of Taliban—or Taliban Generation Z—already constituting a majority of Taliban cadres, is likely to have a huge influence over the Taliban's policy-making. Their awareness of global movements, tech-savvy nature and dreams influenced more by the greater world than religious dogma are undoubtedly going to change the nature of the group as we know it. As regards religion, despite the great divisions in belief, the historical legacies of Afghanistan's rich landscape of faith still stand. The Taliban will eventually have to reform, growing in their religious inclusivity and accommodations if they want to be taken seriously by the ordinary

Afghan people. The Taliban's success has certainly inspired other groups across the world and they are all watching them closely. If the Taliban want to succeed in building a stable and independent Afghanistan they will have to part ways with rigidity, exclusivity and use of oppressive tools.

Money does make the world go round—the Taliban's financial management will play the biggest role in their success or failure. If they are telling the people not to worry, they have to give them reasons not to—people need some proof that they can feel secure. If they cannot help ordinary Afghans make ends meet, public protests will become inevitable, shaking the ground even more. The best-case scenario remains that the Taliban properly build upon the relative peace that has come to Afghanistan—in comparison to previous years—and that the moderates among them rise to the top. Some among them will eventually push for reform, including in the theological arena, otherwise, their power will be short-lived, as all moderates know. The worst-case scenario, on the other hand, is if the rigidity that we have seen signs of from the likes of Hibatullah and chief justice Hakim continues. And if their internal rifts lead to violence and division, that possibility becomes dangerously real, particularly if the Taliban delay in making the best use of their time. The Taliban often used to say, "You have the watches, but we have the time." All we can do now is watch what they do with the time they have and hope, for the sake of humanity, that the best-case scenario triumphs after all.

Ultimately, perhaps if those tasked with deciding the fate of Afghanistan were more compassionate and more thoughtful, things would be different today. Sadly, that is not the case. But there are more pages to be written, a destiny still to be fulfilled. Only time will tell what the new fate-creators will do with their pens—one can only hope they will write in the language of peace and poetry, not the dogma, strife and sorrow of yesterday's hands. Perhaps the issue at heart was our naïve optimism. Have foreign interventions dangerously reminiscent of colonial endeavors proved to be effective? If there is anything to be said definitively, it is that the Afghan people deserved better, and that hope is not lost. We need to reimagine what—and *who*—the Taliban are today. It is worth remembering that shifting the lens from one of guns and graveyards to one of *potential* and *peace* is a burning desire—and long-awaited right—of the people of Afghanistan. In the land of poets, mystics and melodies, peace is not—and cannot—be impossible.

Epilogue

Between Despair and Hope

An Overview: Are the Taliban Succeeding?

It has been both a long and short last three years for Afghanistan. For the Taliban, the new rulers, they have had time to establish themselves and find their footing. Or have they? The Taliban argue that they have brought security and stability to the country and this claim is not without its merits. For the 40 million ordinary Afghans, however, it has proved to be a challenging time to make ends meet; the population has experienced humanitarian crises and increasing restrictions, while being politically isolated from the world. Girls are still barred from school, tragically, but perhaps unsurprisingly. Generally, though, the ruling Taliban has done better than was expected in certain areas. They were neither prepared nor believed to have the capacity or skill set to govern. Yet here they are, ruling Afghanistan without any significant political opposition, and seemingly, without an end in sight for their reign.

Their regional and global engagement is expanding: notably, the Chinese have upgraded their relations with them by accepting the credentials of the Taliban's newly appointed Afghan ambassador to China. This does not amount to formal recognition of the Taliban, but it is a significant step in that direction. Taliban leaders are constantly engaged regionally, and are slowly but surely being accepted as a de facto government. They sent diplomatic missions to fourteen countries and are interacting with many more states through diplomatic outreach—a very different scenario than they faced during their first stint in government.[1]

Potentially, this increase in engagement has the power to be the only peaceful way to impact Taliban policies moving forward. Additionally, their revenue collection has been far better than expected "as evidenced by the stable exchange rate, low inflation, effective revenue collection and rising exports," according to an assessment in 2023 from the United States Institute of Peace (USIP).[2] Development projects are underway, including the construction of railways, thanks to significant investment from Iran. The Taliban's ban on drugs, a counter-narcotics victory, resulted in a 95 percent drop in the cultivation of opium and poppies.[3] This will help deal with a widespread addiction problem within the country and serves as a good omen for the immediate neighborhood where opium consumption has been on the rise. However, serious concerns persist as production of methamphetamine—another dangerous drug—has intensified according to United Nations Office of Drugs and Crime.[4] Overall, there is less corruption and less violence between militants—even though the Islamic State of Khurasan (ISK) continues to ambush the Taliban whenever they can. Perhaps what is most prominent, though, and retrogressive, is the ever-presence of the group's dogmatic views regarding women. These views are still deeply entrenched. Despite so many promises made, girls are still out of school and women have no place in the government. The views of the old-school Taliban leaders, now well established in Kandahar power corridors, continue to take precedence.

Changes in Everyday Life in Afghanistan

Things are changing in many sectors but not necessarily for the better. Of course, the immense suffering of people has not changed for the better: young children sell pens and collect recycled items to make barely a dollar a day. People live without basic necessities and struggle for food. The desperation and devastation wrought by the humanitarian crises define daily life more than anything.

A group of Pakistani independent journalists and writers visited Afghanistan and wrote a series of blogs (named *Tahqiqaat*, meaning investigations) on their experience.[5] I had a chance to converse with them and some of the topics covered in their posts are quite insightful. For instance, they say they found Kabul to be cleaner than expected, the number of check posts has decreased since 2021, and there were fewer drug addicts visible on the roads. Overall, there's relative calm and a general perception that corruption has declined. Local administrative Taliban have also adopted a platform for public hearings for complaints. In a rather interesting and surprising move, if a complainant finds no response to three requests, they can take it up directly with top leadership in Kandahar. However, it is hard to know if this last one is being implemented.

Another important administrative change is that the consultative Shura that used to make major decisions is no longer active. The cabinet has now taken its place. To nobody's surprise, women are no longer employed in any government jobs, but those previously employed by the government continued to receive salaries until late December 2023 (they have since stopped). Not only are women's employment options severely diminished, but they are also further subjugated under a ruling barring them from traveling for work alone beyond 78 kilometers without a male escort. Any woman in violation of said ruling is warned thrice before strict action is taken. Essentially, women have little space to breathe.

Taliban cabinet members and influential people who are known to have excellent relationships with Pakistan are now avoiding seeing Pakistani officials and even visiting friends from Pakistan! Because of this suspicion about them, things have changed quite a bit in that sense.

Additionally, observations from visitors about the perspectives of Afghans who live in Kabul and those who are from the broader Kandahar area (i.e. those belonging to Nangarhar Khost, Paktika, etc.) are also different. The tone and tenor of those from Kandahar are a bit hard and generally lack an understanding of international affairs, clearly not unlike their fellow Kandahari supreme leader Haibatullah.

One issue as regards this book's earlier discussion on Deobandism is that Afghan Deobandis believe that the

Pakistani Deobandis have given up on their religious traditional inclinations and are somehow "lesser" Deobandis than them.

Lastly and most crucially is how the Taliban view their own image—and this is obvious from how much they value social media. They regularly follow international media alerts about them and their social accounts. Effectively, Taliban leaders—such as Zabihullah Mujahid—continue to engage with international statements about the Taliban quite regularly and efficiently. One can assume that this perhaps impacts the moves they make.

The marketplace, even though not vibrant, is still getting more active with trade taking place. However, as Pakistani influence seems to be diminishing, Iranian traders seem to have taken their place with more activity in the marketplace. Slowly but surely, in all aspects, the nature of the ruling dynamics is shifting.

Interpreting the Latest Developments in Afghanistan

Contrary to what many had assumed, the Taliban are making concerted efforts to adjust to their new roles as rulers. Each passing day since August 2021 has made the new suits they wear fit just a little better and helped their new shoes break in. Blistered they may be, sure, but they are still standing. Expansion in all aspects of their rule has taken place, for better or worse. If anything, they have gained a clear understanding of what faces them and what they must prioritize. Years of sitting on the sidelines, waiting for battle, are gone. This moment is what they have been waiting to see.

Decision-making, however, is still sporadic, and self-imposed ideological constraints serve as a massive hindrance to progress and harmony. Policy-making for effective governance is different from battlefield planning and conducting disruptive operations. The Taliban will have to reinvent some of its cadres, and signs indicate that they are recognizing this need. Ordinary Afghans are more scared than impressed by the developing Taliban governance model. Traumatic memories of an ugly past are all too real, haunting them each and every day.

Who is really in charge?

Mullah Hibatullah—or *Ameer* (leader) as he is now widely referred to inside Afghanistan—is *the* man in charge of all policy and administrative affairs. He oversees financial issues and keeps an eye on ministries in Kabul. According to an insider source, he has an eye on each ministry via secret representatives strategically placed all over. Often the minister in charge has no clue who that is. So, after Hibatullah gets his regular updates, he confronts ministers when needed and at times even strips them of their powers, depending on what he has heard. Minister for mining and petroleum Shabuddin Delawer is one example—known once upon a time to be very influential and important, but once the telephones rang with some complaints about his nepotism, Delawer's wings were swiftly clipped. He had managed to get his son appointed as the Taliban's ambassador to Uzbekistan, while another son and son-in-law are also holding important government positions in Kabul.[6]

Mullah Hibatullah's office is a vibrantly occupied space where government officials from across the country are often called in. Many ordinary Afghans are also seen queuing, hoping the supreme leader will provide aid in the form of financial giveaways. According to some insiders I interviewed, Hibatullah spends most of his time with a few of his close associates—strategists who constantly advise him about directives he needs to issue regularly to various ministries and offices in Kabul. The second group that takes a significant chunk of his time are local orthodox, conservative-minded mullahs and religious leaders who look at Hibatullah as one of their own. They continue to ask him for religious edicts on issues relating to day-to-day affairs and, even though Hibatullah finds himself more comfortable with the second group given his clerical training, he has started enjoying the thought of himself as a ruler who has veto power over everything.

Even though he often calls the prime minister and deputy prime ministers for briefing, Hibatullah's understanding of governmental affairs and administrative issues is quite rudimentary. In order to prove to everyone that he is indeed the man in charge, he has taken a few steps clearly reflecting his dogmatic worldview. First, as a show of power, he is building up a new security force in Kandahar that will be only answerable and loyal to him. Interestingly, most of the people employed in this new force belong to his own Nurzai tribe, indicating that he is fully conscious of the relevance of tribal identity. This tribe has strong roots in the south of Afghanistan and is seen as highly influential which further adds to the strength of his support network. Even though the Taliban claim legitimacy based on their ideological roots and take pride in their Pashtun identity, the inter-tribal rivalries remain highly relevant. Beyond that, he is aware of the need for a force at his disposal that can not only defend him but can act as an extension of his power in case Kabul or other actors challenge his power. This approach is clearly a Machiavellian tactic.

Among those who do have significant influence over Hibatullah is Mullah Shirin Akhund, the governor of Kandahar, who acts as the supreme leader's eyes and ears and is responsible for conveying critical messages on his behalf, both domestically and internationally.[7] For instance, when it comes to the Taliban's engagement with Pakistan, he is the middleman, as Hibatullah routinely declines meetings with intelligence and political leaders from Pakistan. Zabihullah Mujahid, the official spokesperson of the Taliban, who was ordered to move to Kandahar from Kabul some time ago, is the other person with regular direct access to Hibatullah and who communicates his important messages.

Finally, Hibatullah, while reinforcing his position, is cognizant of the challenges to his authoritarian style. In his April 2024 Eid message, for instance, he emphasized the need for the Taliban to set aside their differences and focus on better governance. Criticism about his dogmatic policy choices, especially about women, is meanwhile increasing within the power corridors of Kabul.[8]

New Security Protocols and ISK

When it comes to handling their personal security, the Taliban have done their part in establishing solid protocols.

The red zone in Kabul is a prime example, as the area with the highest level of security. Among cabinet members, interior minister Siraj Haqqani is known to have the most extensive security paraphernalia surrounding his space. Special documentation is needed just to enter the general area around Haqqani's office—merely showing a special ID card is not enough. Anyone entering the area must first inform the gate, and only then do senior officials, including personal secretaries, go forth. I have been told Haqqani has several personal assistants to deal with different affairs for all practical purposes. Ultimately, he stands as the most influential political leader in Kabul, while Hibatullah remains the most powerful overall.

As regards the ISK, it does not pose an existential threat to the Taliban, yet it is still a very serious threat that the Taliban cannot ignore at all. The horrific terrorist attack outside Moscow on March 22, 2024 killing around 140 people, which was claimed by ISK, shows this group's growing ambitions and reach. The number of ISK attacks targeting Taliban leaders and Taliban-controlled institutions is another case in point—ISK has conducted nearly 350 attacks inside Afghanistan since mid-August 2021.[9] ISK, it is worth remembering, comprises a number of disgruntled former Taliban leaders, as well as members of the regional defunct terrorist organizations who have a fair idea about how the Taliban operate. This is one important reason the Taliban are struggling to successfully resist the growing challenge from this group: it is really difficult to confront an enemy who was once a part of you. Since the takeover in August 2021, the Taliban went after all the ISK supporters and sympathizers, ranging from Salafi (and Ahl-e-hadith) scholars, activists and associated seminaries in Kabul and its surroundings to those operating in the hubs of ISK in Nangarhar and Kunar, quite strongly. In many cases, they were ruthless and downright brutal—and that is what their security policy is defined by.[10]

Consequently, the Taliban are gradually building a security state, where dissent is criminalized, and political expression is suppressed. And obviously religion is being used to sanctify all of this. While political opposition to the Taliban inside Afghanistan remains weak and disjointed, ISK's ideological challenge to the Taliban worldview is hard-hitting. ISK are adapting to changing dynamics and evolving to survive hurdles. While resiliently facing Taliban military onslaught, ISK is shifting its focus to vilify the credentials of Taliban leaders in ideological terms, and also alleging that the Taliban are secretly allied with the West. For this, ISK is leveraging various forms of media to stay politically relevant. One example is ISK framing the Taliban's increased interaction with Western diplomats as "abandonment of true Jihad."

Terrorist Sanctuaries in Afghanistan—Insights from Minister Siraj Haqqani

The Taliban's policy towards the Pakistani Taliban (Tehrik-i-Taliban Pakistan—TTP) remains in flux. Because the TTP's criminal activities and terrorist operations inside Pakistan have not only significantly increased but in many cases quadrupled in comparison to a year ago, this is a matter of urgency and monumental significance for Pakistan. Many local militant groups in Pakistan are now reconnected to the TTP, posing a severe security threat to the Pakistani state. Many parts of Waziristan are now TTP hubs, and even in and around urban areas of Khyber Pakhtunkhwa province TTP militants are active collecting tolls at gun point and conducting kidnappings for ransom. For Pakistan, the Afghan Taliban's leniency in the matter is unforgivable, but should it be surprising? Their naivety has apparently not caught their own attention yet.

Despite serious threats from Pakistan and demands for the handing over or elimination of TTP cadres, the Afghan Taliban insists that Pakistan needs to negotiate with the group. When Siraj Haqqani was approached by a friend in a face-to-face meeting in early 2024, he made a strong case that Pakistan must figure out a way to directly settle with the TTP rather than employing force. Haqqani's argument was quite interesting: if the Afghan Taliban could negotiate with the Americans in Doha, why can't Pakistan negotiate with the TTP? Touché, one could say. In the same conversation, he went on to mention that according to the Afghan Taliban, there are an estimated ten to twelve thousand warriors residing in Afghanistan, and if you include their families, you are looking at thirty thousand people. The Afghan Taliban cannot arrest them, nor would they like to militarily confront them. He also mentioned that, unlike the Afghan Taliban who have common ideological leanings and shared tribal networks, the TTP is much more diverse with many internal factions—and any pressure from the Taliban on them may push them towards ISK, something they are desperate to avoid. Thus, the dilemma leaves them at a cross-roads. Haqqani even mentioned that he had arranged a meeting between TTP leader Noor Wali Mehsud and leading Pakistani cleric Taqi Usmani (representing Pakistan), in which Usmani almost convinced him that the TTP would be better off not challenging the constitution and raison d'etre of Pakistan, as that would be the point of no return. Mehsud agreed and asked for time to have conversations with his companions, but the dialogue somehow broke at that point.

One pending issue that remained was the status of the Pakistani tribal areas. Notably, the TTP is deeply opposed to any merger of the tribal areas into Pakistan's Khyber Pukhtunkhwa (KPK) province, because that has allowed Islamabad and the provincial government in Peshawar to gain control. Understandably, the TTP wants the freedom of movement and semi-autonomous status that they had enjoyed in the past. So, yet another issue remains unresolved. In the midst of all this, the Afghan Taliban are far from interested in tackling the TTP, while Pakistan is rigid in its demands that they nevertheless comply. The Afghan Taliban though, as we know, is not known to be subservient to Islamabad. This increasingly tense dynamic continues to unfold, quite chaotically.

Some lip service was offered by Mullah Yaqoob, the Afghan defense minister, categorically calling on his fighters to obey a recent decree by their supreme leader that forbids them from engaging in "Jihad" outside Afghanistan. He declared: "If someone still leaves Afghanistan intending to wage Jihad abroad, it cannot be considered Jihad anymore. If Mujahideen [Taliban forces] continue to fight despite orders from the Emir to stop, it is not Jihad but rather hostility."[11]

Dealing with Administrative Challenges

For Siraj Haqqani and the Kabul government though, the bigger challenge at the moment is figuring out how to pay salaries or stipends to about 70–80,000 Afghan foot soldiers, who are either jobless or waiting to be accommodated. Fascinatingly, in an act of real governance, they made a case to the UN—reportedly still under consideration—for some development funds to employ this force, because they are concerned that someone else—like ISK—might swoop in and offer what they cannot. If only they could afford the same energy and concern to the 40 million other souls under their rule who need their help. Poor human resource management is a serious challenge. According to a senior official in Kabul, nepotism is also a serious challenge in this sphere. For instance, lately many officials who were trained for police jobs used their contacts, sans permission, to join the military. The absence of a verification system allows this lateral movement of Taliban officials in a way that only causes unnecessary gaps and confusion. Afghanistan still lacks a system that properly employs, manages and monitors these Taliban foot soldiers, and it is only a matter of time before this chaos manifests into something they cannot handle.

In the financial arena, the Taliban have improved their financial management to the extent possible with limited resources. Salaries to government officials are no longer handed over through cash, as was the case during the first two years, and they now receive salaries via their bank accounts. Only funds for food provision are offered through cash disbursements. The salaries of various ministers and upper-level bureaucrats vary depending on their networks, influence and outreach capabilities. For instance, those like Siraj and Yaqub, who regularly host guests, receive higher salaries to be able to cater to their unique hospitality requirements. Additionally, they now have a functional auditing system.

No Progress on Girls' Education

On the tragically sensitive issue of girls' education, Hibatullah continues to drag his feet. It is reported that some institutions catering to women's needs like nursing and medical schools have recently been opened for women, but Kandahar insisted that no announcement of it should be made, because Hibatullah is concerned his hardliner constituents, who do not want girls to be educated, will cause a ruckus. Based on my conversations and insights gleaned from many visitors to Kabul, several cabinet members and senior officials are very defensive when it comes to girls' education, and behind closed doors whisper complaints and critiques of Hibatullah and his stubbornness on the issue.

In one instance, several cabinet ministers decided to visit Hibatullah all together and insisted that for international recognition, they needed some flexibility on the subject. They had even hoped that, as was the case generally whenever confronted, Hibatullah would say "Why don't you pick someone else as top leader? I'm ready to step aside." They were hoping, naively, that they would hear those words and immediately decide on another top leader for his place. Somehow, though, Hibatullah got intelligence ahead of time. When this group approached him in Kandahar, plan ready, he simply told them to wait and that he would meet each one-on-one. The plan fizzled out. It is doubtful if Hibatullah would ever consider stepping aside—and his reported statement "Why don't you pick someone else as top leader?" likely was a rhetorical way to make a point. In case he is eliminated through an internal coup, orchestrated by one of the powerful ministers in Kabul (which is now less likely), or by the ISK, or someone else succeeds in assassinating him, there will be no power-vacuum as the Taliban are quite well organized to deal with such a scenario.

The divisions thus previously spoken of still exist but are apparently not as potent anymore. Many Taliban cabinet members were carefully conveying to Hibatullah meanwhile that they needed to do something in the face of mounting global and regional demands about women's rights in the country. Realizing the pressure, Hibatullah used an incident to push back strongly. When some conservatives approached him readily equipped with an innocent video of young men and women at a university event, showing him what they deemed to be profane, they asked, "Just like the West—is this what our revolution was for?" Consequently, Hibatullah used that one video to announce a further clampdown on girls' education. Minister for higher education Baqi Haqqani challenged this decision according to someone directly privy to this development, but in response he was removed from the education ministry. Interestingly, Baqi has been put on a travel ban list by the US. Despite being among the few who wanted to change policy, echoing the demands of the Western world, he is now on the hit list of not only Hibatullah but those very Western powers. While this perhaps could be attributed to the ignorance on the part of those who put him on the list, the ridiculous conspiracy within some Afghan circles is that Americans do not *want* girls to go to school.

The tragedy of the Taliban looking down on women continues to unravel in horrific ways, costing women and girls across the country their chance to live with dignity and equality. There is a strong fear that the Taliban 1.0—which was a more dogmatic version—is being reintroduced as they gain strength. Whether those in Kabul who object to this policy will take a stand against this, time will tell.

In comparison, seminary education for boys is a priority. Establishment of a new Madrassa chain across Afghanistan's provinces, named Madrassa Jihadiya, is receiving priority funding. Hibatullah himself is directly appointing the top positions in each district, and managing their oversight. The purpose is to create a new generation of religious clerics who can lead the future Taliban movement.

Relations with Pakistan in Flux

Pakistan's relationship with Afghanistan has notably deteriorated, rather significantly and quickly. Pakistan's response to non-cooperation from Kabul, as discussed above, has resulted at times in targeted air strikes against TTP hideouts and in a more consequential way, forced the return of Afghan refugees from Pakistan. Thousands of these Afghan refugees had been living in Pakistan for over three decades or so, and in many cases they had been part and parcel of local communities. Pakistan started by forcefully returning those Afghans who lacked any legal documents. Sadly, many others fled the only home they ever knew, scared of being arrested. Thousands of them returned to Kabul without any resources in their hands. This move was meant to act as a strong message to the Afghan Taliban, who were initially taken by surprise—but to say it's backfiring wouldn't be too off course.

Some Pakistani officials I interviewed, particularly those belonging to the Pashtun community, shared their serious concerns about this policy, which they deemed counterproductive. One official who had served in a leading security role quipped that this thoughtless strategy from Islamabad could lead to a terrible blowback, as Afghan refugees have strong networks in Pakistan. Moreover, the Pakistani Taliban are also operating with impunity. He shared a projection that was being talked about among those who follow these things closely, believing that the coming Taliban wave will be so ferocious that it will take control of Pakistani Pashtun areas—including KPK—and Pakistani security forces may have to stop them at the Attock River (which divides Punjab from the Pashtun dominated areas of Pakistan). When I shared this assessment with a former senior Afghan official, he said he was reminded of something President Karzai used to say to his close associates: "Whether in ties or turbans, Afghans will reach the Attock

River someday." This underlines an old fear Pakistan has always kept in its back pocket: what if the Pashtuns of both sides joined hands? What if the radicals and revolutionaries were to merge at last—and what would that mean for the integrity and sovereignty of Pakistan? It still seems unlikely in the near future, but it is hard to predict how things will proceed if divisive politics and conflict continue in this area.

The impression in Afghanistan is that Pakistan is being very harsh with Afghan refugees (which is quite true), creating further discord between the two. To contribute so deeply to a war that's displaced millions of people and then kick these people out of their only refuge is nothing short of cruelty—but as is often the case with Pakistan, rather unsurprising.

Progress on the Diplomatic Front

It is regional diplomacy where the Taliban continue to do very well in relative terms. The Taliban's foreign minister, Mullah Muttaqi, is turning out to be an effective communicator of the Taliban's needs, expectations and hopes. At 52 years of age, he is emerging as the most important of the younger generation of Taliban leaders and he has the trust of both Kandahar and Kabul—two crucial pillars of the Taliban hierarchy. He is liked by both Indians and Pakistani interlocutors—a hard status to achieve. This role has prepared him well to be a strong contender for a future leadership position when his generation's time comes to hold political power in Kabul. Those who interact with him see him as a relatively open-minded and flexible person.

Still there are many challenges in the diplomatic realm. For instance, the Taliban want to work more closely with Saudi Arabia, but Riyadh is now more cautious in its dealings with the Taliban. The Saudi preference is to deal with the Taliban through the Organization of Islamic Cooperation (OIC) framework. For instance, the OIC sent a delegation to Kabul in the summer of 2022 to discuss, or rather promote, Islamic teachings of tolerance and the importance of women's education with apparently little success.[12] Meanwhile, Saudi pilgrimage diplomacy (inviting and taking care of Taliban pilgrims during the hajj season) is another track to build trust with them gradually—and some progress was made during hajj season in July 2023, but Saudis are not impressed at all by Hibatullah. How the times have changed.

It is still Qatar that continues to play the most important role in Afghanistan from among the Gulf countries. The Qatari prime minister remains the only person whose request for a meeting with the Taliban top leader Hibatullah was accepted, revealing just how strong that connection is. Little insight is available as to what was discussed in the meeting in May 2023, but it is believed that the Qataris conveyed to Hibatullah the serious Western concerns about extremism trends in Afghanistan and the need to avoid taking more dogmatic steps. Apparently, the message had little impact.

Internal divisions also exist as regards foreign policy orientation. For instance, defense minister Yaqoob, interior minister Siraj Haqqani and intelligence chief Wasiq are seen as more inclined toward engaging and even cooperating with the US and other Western nations, whereas top leader Mullah Hibatullah, while being an isolationist, looks more favorably and a bit surprisingly toward Iran. Increased engagements with China are the least controversial in Taliban circles, as they are neither criticizing Taliban policies nor seen as acting intrusively in any other way. Chinese investments are also having an impact. For instance, a 25-year-long, multimillion-dollar oil extraction contract with an estimated investment value of around $700 million in the first 4 years alone has won China many friends in Kabul.[13]

Environmental Challenges

An additional complicating challenge for the Taliban has emerged in the shape of a serious impending environmental crisis. Afghanistan is one of the nations most vulnerable to climate change impact globally. Unrelenting deforestation, land degradation and water scarcity coupled with flash floods, droughts (impacting twenty-four out of thirty-four provinces) and landslides are damaging crops, destroying livelihoods and exacerbating the humanitarian crisis. With limited expertise available to deal with this worsening environmental challenge, the Taliban regime has opted for the construction of a major irrigation canal (the Qosh Tepa Canal) on the Amu Darya River in the north. This is a major undertaking, as it is expected to be 115 miles long and 100 meters deep. Its construction is raising concerns in Uzbekistan and Turkmenistan as both countries will lose a significant volume of irrigation water available to draw from the river. The water of the Amu Darya accounts for around 80 percent of all water resources in the region. Successful completion of the project (expected in two to three years' time) will likely reinvigorate the agricultural sector in Afghanistan but not without negatively impacting Kabul's diplomatic relations with its two important neighbors. Another tough dilemma for the Taliban indeed.

Concluding Thoughts: The Future of the Taliban

Kabul today, representing the relatively pragmatic elements, hopes to instill some sense into the proceedings. They abhor Kandahar's isolationist tendencies and continue to push for engagement with the West for two reasons: a) they hope to rule out the possibility that Afghan opposition forces (mostly in exile now) can garner any international support against the Taliban, and b) to gain time to stabilize their hold on power and develop Afghanistan. They wish to stay loyal to their ideological moorings but are open to compromises in the political sphere.

It is true that there is less corruption hampering effective governance, but there is also less competence. It is beyond the capacity of the Taliban to deal with the demographic changes in Afghanistan as internal migration for economic reasons is assuming serious proportions.

The Taliban appear to be in no hurry to resolve tough security challenges, not realizing the delay in effectively dealing with groups such as ISK, Al-Qaeda remnants and the TTP will complicate the matter further. One challenge is the Taliban's lack of capacity to manage Afghanistan's borderlands, even though they would never acknowledge it. ISK rocket attacks on Uzbekistan and Tajikistan in 2022 and the TTP's regular movement across the Afghanistan–Pakistan frontier is ample evidence of that.

For the international community, in the words of *The Economist*, it is clear now that "isolating the mullahs is not working," and that "the West needs a more constructive approach."[14] The question is what that approach may look like. Primarily, it needs to be realized that the Taliban are having difficulty in understanding the language that the West speaks, which frames issues in ways that primarily target their own constituencies. Afghans, given their history, are highly skeptical of ideas that are introduced from outside. That is why trust-building is important, while recognizing that it is a process that takes time. Parallel to that, a multilateral approach is likely to be more effective. Regional countries need to come up with a collective agenda rather than pursuing their own respective interests. The Taliban are unlikely to defy a regional consensus, especially if it involves Pakistan, Qatar, Iran, Turkey, Uzbekistan and China.

Ultimately, the Taliban are not going anywhere. They are a reality, and my thesis in this book is proving to be relevant to what is transpiring in Afghanistan today. Engagement with them is a sacrifice we must be willing to make for the sake of the millions of people it has the power to benefit. The situation for the ordinary people of Afghanistan is truly one of a crossroads between hope and despair. We must ask ourselves at this point: what choice do we have other than to go the route of hope through engagement?

Engagement in the shape of dialogues and talks must continue but with less ambitious goals and expectations. More importantly, and as an April 2024 Crisis Group assessment by Graeme Smith rightly argues, there is a need for separate tracks of engagement on issues of urgency besides the rights challenges, such as economy, security, besides drugs and human smuggling—and each track should be judged on its own merits with an aim to build confidence and increase leverage.[15]

One hopes that the Taliban 3.0, still in its toddler years, adapts to the necessity of growth and learning sooner rather than later. There is no threat of a major intervention facing them, realistically, so every day that goes by, they remain in an unprecedented situation. They are on their own, tripping over their own feet (at the expense of their people), and they ought to realize they cannot keep things up the way they are going. The cruelty against women that they continue to exhibit is not only tragic, but when it comes down to it, embarrassing too. Soon enough, the acts of their own stupidity and refusal to evolve will come back to bite them, and if they have any sense, they will change course soon. Such extreme defensiveness and close-mindedness can never last long: it is a poison that kills the one holding it. They are sick of our morality lectures, of course. That's why, it has to be a conversation.

Three years have passed by quickly for those of us mere witnesses, watching through a screen. For 40 million people, it has been a painful passage of time defined by trauma and tears. It is our collective moral duty to each other and to humanity to protect each other from oppression and injustice. The world more than anything else owes this to the people of Afghanistan. To the women deprived of basic dignity and respect, the little girls robbed of an education, and every child from whom a hopeful future has been stolen.

List of Key Deputy Ministers, Heads of Departments, Governors and Military Commanders

Sher Mohammad Abbas Stanikzai, deputy foreign minister

Zabihullah Mujahid, deputy minister of information and broadcasting

Mullah Muhammad Fazil Mazloom Akhund, deputy defense minister

Mawlawi Mohammad Qasim Farid, deputy minister of defense (policy and planning)

Ibrahim Sadr, deputy interior minister

Maulvi Noor Jalal, deputy interior minister (education and personnel)

Sadar Azam Haqqani, deputy minister of agriculture

Abdullah Khan, deputy interior minister (counter-narcotics)

Maulvi Shamsuddin Mansoor, deputy interior minister (policy and strategy)

Muhammad Bashir, deputy commerce minister

Azim Sultan, deputy commerce minister

Sheikh Maulvi Abdul Hakim, deputy minister of martyrs and disabled affairs

Maulvi Saeed Ahmad Shahidkhel, deputy minister of education

Maulvi Abdul Rahman Halim, deputy minister of rural rehabilitation and development

Maulvi Atiqullah Azizi, deputy minister of information and culture (finance and administration)

Mullah Faizullah Akhund, deputy minister of information and culture (youth affairs)

Mullah Saaduddin Akhund, deputy minister of information and culture (tourism)

Mullah Nasser Akhund, deputy minister of finance

Maulvi Arefullah Aref, deputy minister of energy and water

Mujeeb-ur-Rehman, deputy minister of energy and water

Maulvi Saifuddin Tayeb, deputy minister of communications

Haji Mullah Mohammad Essa Akhund, deputy minister of minerals and petroleum

Maulvi Sharafuddin, deputy minister of disaster management

Enayatullah Shuja Haqqani, second deputy minister of disaster management

Maulvi Hamdullah Zahed, procurement director

Sheikh Abdul Rahim, deputy director of procurement

Mullah Rahmatullah Najib, deputy director national directorate of security

Tajmir Jawad, deputy director of intelligence

Maulvi Mohammad Yousef Mastari, director of prisons

Mullah Habibullah Fazli, deputy director of prisons

Maulvi Keramatullah Akhundzadah, head of the Administrative Reform and Civil Service Commission

Maulvi Ahmad Taha, deputy minister of border and tribal affairs

Engineer Najibullah, head of the Nuclear Energy Agency

Maulvi Fathullah Mansour, head of Kandahar airport

Mohammad Ismail, executive commander of the Military Court

Maulvi Esmatullah Asim, deputy head of the Red Cross

Maulvi Rahimullah Mahmoud, deputy commander of the Al-Badar Corps in Kandahar

Maulvi Abdul Samad, deputy commander of the Azam Corps in Helmand

Noorullah Munir, head of office for issuance of religious edicts

Abdul Qayyum Zakir, military commander in Panjshir to confront opposition forces aligned with previous government (earlier, briefly served as deputy defense minister as announced in September 2021)

Mufti Saeed Ahmad Mustaqim, deputy minister of rural rehabilitation and development

Maulvi Haseebullah Hamid, deputy minister of higher education (finance and administration)

Dr. Hassan Ghyasi, deputy minister of public health

Abdul Latif Nazari, deputy minister of economy

Abdul Bari Omar, director, food and drug administration

Ataullah Omari, former deputy minister of defense for technology and logistics, now serving as minister for agriculture since August 2022

Alam Gul Haqqani, head of the passport department

Mawlawi Makhdoom Abdul Salam Saadat, deputy minister of labor and social affairs

Sheikh Syed Rasool, chairman of the Supreme Audit Office

Amir Khan Haqqani, commander of Al-Fatah 209th Corps

Mullah Bari Gul Akhund, chief of staff of Al-Badr 205th
   Corps

Mullah Abdul Razzaq Akhund, chief of staff of Al-Farooq
   207th Corps

Mawlawi Hizbullah, chief of staff of the 203rd Corps

Haji Mali Khan (uncle of Sirajuddin Haqqani), governor of
   Logar province

Abdul Ghani Faiq, governor of Badakhshan province

Qudratullah Abu Hamza, governor of Balkh province

Ishaq Akhundzada, governor of Ghazni province

Maulvi Abdul Ahad Talib, governor of Helmand province

Noor Islamjar, governor of Herat province

Nisar Ahmad Nusrat, governor of Kunduz province

Daud Muzamil, governor of Nangarhar province

Maulvi Qasim Khalid, governor of Kunar province

Mohammad Ismail Turkman, governor of Takhar province

Hafizullah Pahlawan, governor of Faryab province

Bakhtiar Muaz, governor of Baghlan province

Qari Ehsanullah Baryal, governor of Kabul province

Mohammad Yousaf Wafaa, governor of Kandahar province

*Sources: Taliban government websites and official
   announcements*

Graduates of Darul Uloom Haqqania Holding Senior Official Positions in Afghanistan

Amir Khan Muttaqi, foreign minister

Abdul Hakim Akhunzada, chief justice

Abdul Qadeer Haqqani, deputy governor of the Afghan Central Bank

Mohammad Nabi Omari, governor of Khost province

Abdullah Mukhtar, governor of Paktika province

Maulvi Abdul Kabir, deputy prime minister for political affairs

Shahabuddin Delavar, minister of mines and petroleum and head of the commission to contact Afghans abroad

Abdul Baqi Haqqani, (former higher) minister of higher education

Noor Mohammad Saqib Haqqani, minister of Hajj and religious affairs

Najibullah Haqqani, minister of communications

Abdul Latif Mansoor Haqqani, water and energy minister

Abdul Salam Hanafi Sahib, deputy prime minister

Noor Jalal Haqqani, deputy interior minister

Sadar Azam Haqqani, deputy minister of agriculture

Ahmad Taha Haqqani, deputy minister of border and tribal
  affairs
Enayatullah Shuja Haqqani, deputy minister of Afghanistan
  National Disaster Management Authority
Alam Gul Haqqani, head of the passport department
Abdul Hakim Sharei, minister of justice

Source: Darul Uloom Haqqania official

Text of the "Decree of the Amir al-Mu'minin on Women's Rights," December 3, 2021

In the name of Allah, the most merciful, and the most compassionate

The Islamic Emirate's leadership instructs all relevant organizations, Ulema-e-Karam [respected scholars of Islam] and Tribal Elders to take serious action to enforce Women's Rights.

1. Adult women's consent is necessary during Nekah/marriage (though both should be equal with no risk of sedition).
   No one can force women to marry by coercion or pressure.
2. A woman is not a property, but a noble and free human being, no one can give her to anyone in exchange for peace deal and or to end animosity.
3. After the death of the husband, "Sharaie Adat" (four months and ten nights or pregnancy) passes, no one can marry a widow by force including her relatives. A widow

has the right whether to marry and or to determine/ choose her future. (Though the principle of equality and preventing sedition should be kept into consideration.)

4. It is the Sharia right of a widow to obtain, "Mahar" from her new husband.

5. A widow has heritage right and fixed share in the property of her husband, children, father and other relatives. No one can deprive a widow of her right.

6. Those with multi marriages (more than one wife) are obliged to give rights to all women in accordance with the Sharia law and maintain justice between them.

For proper implementation of this decree, relevant organizations are instructed to do the following acts:

1. The Ministry of Hajj and Religious Affairs is instructed to encourage scholars to give awareness to the people related to women's rights through their letters and preaching that oppressing women and not giving them their rights will cause Allah's dissatisfaction and his torment and anger.

2. The Ministry of Information and Culture is directed to publish articles related to women's rights through its means in writing and audio, as well as encourage writers and activists to publish useful article on women's right in order to attract attention of Ulema and people about women's Sharia rights, to prevent the ongoing oppression.

3. The Supreme Court must issue instruction to all courts to consider applications for women's rights, especially

widows' rights and their oppression in a proper and principled manner, in order not to disappoint women of getting rid of oppression and obtaining their Sharia rights.

4. Governors and district governors must cooperate comprehensively with the named ministries and the Supreme Court in the implementation of this decree.

Leadership office of Islamic Emirate
28/04/1443 Hijri Lunar
12/08/1400 Hijri Solar
03/12/2021 Gregorian

*Source: https://www.alemarahenglish.af/special-decree
-issued-by-amir-ul-momenin-on-womens-rights/*

Notes

Introduction: History Repeats Itself

1. Interview with a former interior minister of Afghanistan, who remained a close associate of both President Karzai and President Ghani, September 2022. On December 30, 2021, Ghani interestingly claimed in a BBC interview that on the day of his departure from Kabul, "Two different factions of the Taliban were closing in from two different directions," and "the possibility of a massive conflict between them that would destroy the city of five million and bring havoc to the people was enormous." For details, see: https://www.bbc.com/news/world-asia-59807737
2. Haseeba Atakpal, "Ghani's team had contact with Haqqani network in 2014 poll: Nabil," *TOLO News*, September 5, 2019, at: https://tolonews.com/afghanistan/ghani's-team-had-contact-haqqani-network-2014-poll-nabil
3. Interview with a former senior ISI military officer who was directly involved in the process, September 2022. He argued that it was a Pakistani effort to mend relations with Kabul and support a US-favored candidate (in their view) for better Pakistani–Afghan relations in the future.
4. Interview conducted by a researcher with an Afghan official present in the presidential palace in August 2021, July 2022.
5. Mohamed Madi, Ahmad Khalid and Sayed Abdullah Nizami, "Chaos and confusion: The frenzied final hours of the Afghan government," *BBC News*, September 8, 2021, at: https://www.bbc.com/news/world-asia-58477131
6. Quoted in Jennifer Hansler and Kylie Atwood, "Senior Afghan official accuses US envoy of 'delegitimizing' Afghan government," *CNN*, March 14, 2019, at: https://www.cnn.com/2019/03/14/politics/mohib-khalilzad-afghanistan-row/index.html
7. Madi et al., "Chaos and confusion: The frenzied final hours of the Afghan government."
8. Ibid.
9. Kathy Gannon, "Afghan president was isolated before slipping into exile," *AP News*, August 15, 2021, at: https://apnews.com/article/race-and-ethnicity-2901e54d6268341d3caf936fef6313db

10. Interview, Washington DC, August 15, 2021.

11. President Biden speech text, August 16, 2021, at: https://www.whitehouse. gov/briefing-room/speeches-remarks/2021/08/16/remarks-by-president-biden-on-afghanistan/

12. See Hassan Abbas, *The Taliban Revival: Violence and Extremism on the Pakistan–Afghanistan Frontier*, Yale University Press, 2015.

13. "Afghan troops suffer 'shockingly high' casualties as violence mounts," *Reuters*, June 7, 2021, at: https://www.reuters.com/world/asia-pacific/afghan-troops-suffer-shockingly-high-casualties-violence-mounts-2021-06-07/

14. Sussanah George, "U.S. watchdog details collapse of Afghan security forces," *The Washington Post*, May 18, 2022, at: https://www.washingtonpost.com/world/2022/05/18/us-watchdog-details-collapse-afghan-security-forces/

15. Quoted in Natasha Turk, Abigail Ng and Amanda Macias, "'Intelligence failure of the highest order'—How Afghanistan fell to the Taliban so quickly," *CNBC*, August 16, 2021, at: https://www.cnbc.com/2021/08/16/how-afghanistan-fell-to-the-taliban-so-quickly.html

16. See Suhail Shaheen Twitter account: https://twitter.com/suhailshaheen1

17. See Zabihullah Mujahid Twitter account: https://twitter.com/zabehulah_m33

18. Craig Timberg and Cristiano Lima, "Today's Taliban uses sophisticated social media practices that rarely violate the rules," *The Washington Post*, August 18, 2021, at: https://www.washingtonpost.com/technology/2021/08/18/taliban-social-media-success/

19. Catherine Thorbecke, "How the Taliban uses social media to seek legitimacy in the West, sow chaos at home," *ABC News*, August 19, 2021, at: https://abcnews.go.com/Technology/taliban-social-media-seek-legitimacy-west-sow-chaos/story?id=79500632

20. Clayton Thomas, "Afghanistan: Background and U.S. policy: In brief," Congressional Research Service, updated August 26, 2022, pp. 2–3, at: https://crsreports.congress.gov/product/pdf/R/R45122

21. Susannah George, "Afghanistan's military collapse: Illicit deals and mass desertions," *The Washington Post*, August 15, 2021, at: https://www.washingtonpost.com/world/2021/08/15/afghanistan-military-collapse-taliban/

22. See David Zucchino, "Collapse and conquest: The Taliban strategy that seized Afghanistan," *The New York Times*, August 18, 2021, at: https://www.nytimes.com/2021/08/18/world/asia/taliban-victory-strategy-afghanistan.html

23. Yaroslav Trofimov and Margherita Stancati, "Taliban covert operatives seized Kabul, other Afghan cities from within," *The Wall Street Journal*, November 28, 2021, at: https://www.wsj.com/articles/taliban-covert-operatives-seized-kabul-other-afghan-cities-from-within-11638095401

24. Phone interview with Kamran Bokhari, July 2022.

25. For details, see Hassan Abbas, *Pakistan's Nuclear Bomb: A Story of Defiance, Deterrence and Deviance*, Oxford University Press, 2018, pp. 172–174.

26. Hassan Abbas, "Extremism and terrorism trends in Pakistan," *CTC Sentinel*, vol. 14, no. 2 (February 2021): 44–53, at: https://ctc.usma.edu/extremism-and-terrorism-trends-in-pakistan-changing-dynamics-and-new-challenges/

27. Roger Fisher and William L. Ury, *Getting to Yes: Negotiating Agreement Without Giving In*, Penguin, second edition, 1991.

28. Abdul Hakim Haqqani, *Al-Imarah Al-Islamiah wa Nizamaha* [*The Islamic Emirate and its System*], Maktaba Dar al-aloom al-Sharia, 2022.

1 The Road to Kabul: The Secret Deal, the New Taliban and a House of Cards

1. Quoted in Ayaz Gul, "US, Taliban sign historic Afghan peace deal," *VOA*, February 29, 2020, at: https://www.voanews.com/a/south-central-asia_us-taliban-sign-historic-afghan-peace-deal/6185026.html

2. Quoted in Steve Coll and Adam Entous, "The secret history of the U.S. diplomatic failure in Afghanistan," *The New Yorker*, December 20, 2021, at: https://www.newyorker.com/magazine/2021/12/20/the-secret-history-of-the-us-diplomatic-failure-in-afghanistan

3. For details about initial challenges, see International Crisis Group, *Taking Stock of the Taliban's Perspectives on Peace*, Report No. 11, August 11, 2020, at: https://www.crisisgroup.org/asia/south-asia/afghanistan/311-taking-stock-talibans-perspectives-peace

4. Mathieu Aikins, "Inside the fall of Kabul," *The New York Times*, December 10, 2021, at: https://www.nytimes.com/2021/12/10/magazine/fall-of-kabul-afghanistan.html

5. Tahir Khan, "Taliban leader Mullah Omar died in a Karachi hospital in 2013, says Afghanistan," *Express Tribune* (Pakistan), July 19, 2015, at: https://tribune.com.pk/story/928571/afghan-taliban-leader-mullah-omar-is-dead

6. For details, see Kate Clark, "The release of Mullah Baradar: What's next for .negotiations?" *Afghanistan Analysts Network*, September 21, 2013, at: https://www.afghanistan-analysts.org/en/reports/war-and-peace/the-release-of-mullah-baradar-whats-next-for-negotiations/

7. Mark Mazzetti and Jane Perlez, "C.I.A. and Pakistan work together, but do so warily," *The New York Times*, February 25, 2010, at: https://www.nytimes.com/2010/02/25/world/asia/25intel.html?ref=todayspaper

8. "ISI hid news of Mullah Omar's death: Ex-Pentagon official," *Economic Times* (India), August 16, 2015, at: https://economictimes.indiatimes.com/news/international/world-news/isi-hid-news-of-mullah-omars-death-ex-pentagon-official/articleshow/48500725.cms?from=mdr

9. Sami Yusufzai, "New leader 'a moderate face among the Taliban'?" *CBS News*, September 10, 2015, at: https://www.cbsnews.com/news/taliban-leader-mullah-akhtar-mansoor-europe-afghanistan-peace-talks/

10. See "Security Council 1988 Sanctions Committee amends one name in its sanctions list," United Nations press release, December 23, 2016, at: https://www.un.org/press/en/2016/sc12656.doc.htm

11. Ovais Jafar, "Afghan Taliban leader frequently travelled to Dubai," *The News*, May 23, 2016, at: https://www.thenews.com.pk/latest/122118-Afghan-Taliban-leader-Mullah-Mansour-frequently-travelled-Dubai

12. Interview in Washington DC, August 2022.

13. Abdul Basit, "Future of the Afghan Taliban under Mullah Akhtar Mansoor," *Counter Terrorist Trends and Analyses*, vol. 7, no. 10 (November 2015): 9–13.

14. The fact is mentioned in Rahimullah Yusufzai, "Disunity rather than defeat," *The News*, August 9, 2015, at: https://www.thenews.com.pk/tns/detail/559174-taliban-disunity-rather-defeat

15. For details, see Rahimullah Yusufzai, "Mediation efforts on to resolve Taliban rift," *The News*, August 6, 2015, at: https://www.thenews.com.pk/print/55083-mediation-efforts-on-to-resolve-taliban-rift

16. Basit, "Future of the Afghan Taliban under Mullah Akhtar Mansoor," p. 10.

17. Joseph Goldstein, "Taliban's new leader strengthens his hold with intrigue and battlefield victory," *The New York Times*, October 4, 2015.

18. For a profile of Mullah Mansour and his choice of deputies, see M. Ilyas Khan, "Profile: Taliban leader Mullah Akhtar Mansour," *BBC News*, May 22, 2016, at: https://www.bbc.com/news/world-asia-34405035. For Admiral Mullen's quote, see "US Admiral: 'Haqqani is veritable arm of Pakistan's ISI,'" *BBC News*, September 22, 2011, at: https://www.bbc.com/news/av/world-us-canada-15026909

19. Abdul Hai Mutma'in, *Mullah Mohammad Omar, Taliban and Afghanistan*, Afghan Publishing Community (Kabul), 2017, p. 338.

20. For details, see Nic Robertson and Jamie Crawford, "Obama: Taliban leader's death marks 'milestone'," *CNN*, May 23, 2016, at: https://www.cnn.com/2016/05/21/politics/u-s-conducted-airstrike-against-taliban-leader-mullah-mansour/index.html

21. Quoted in Jon Boone and Sune Engel Rasmussen, "US drone strike in Pakistan kills Taliban leader Mullah Mansour," *The Guardian*, May 22, 2016, at: https://www.theguardian.com/world/2016/may/21/us-airstrike-taliban-leader-mullah-akhtar-mansoor

22. "Afghan Taliban splinter group names Mullah Rasool as leader," *BBC News*, November 4, 2015, at: https://www.bbc.com/news/world-asia-34719314

23. Robertson and Crawford, "Obama: Taliban leader's death marks 'milestone.'"

24. "Profile: New Taliban chief Mawlawi Hibatullah Akhundzada," *BBC News*, May 26, 2016, at: https://www.bbc.com/news/world-asia-36377008

25. "Haibatullah Akhunzada: Shadowy Taliban supreme leader whose son was suicide bomber," *Reuters*, September 7, 2021, at: https://www.reuters.com/world/haibatullah-akhundzada-shadowy-taliban-supreme-leader-whose-son-was-suicide-2021-09-07/

26. For details, see Shereena Qazi, "Who is new Taliban leader Mullah Haibatullah Akhunzada?" *Al Jazeera*, May 26, 2016, at: https://www.aljazeera.com/news/2016/5/26/who-is-new-taliban-leader-mullah-haibatullah-akhunzada

27. "Profile: New Taliban chief Mawlawi Hibatullah Akhundzada," *BBC News*.

28. Conversations with law enforcement officials who served in Quetta, Pakistan and followed his activities.

29. Carter Malkasian, *The American War in Afghanistan: A History*, Oxford University Press, 2021, p. 405.

30. Ibid., p. 408.

31. Ibid.

32. For a detailed assessment, see Atal Ahmadzai, "Dying to live: The 'love to death' narrative driving the Taliban's suicide bombings," *Perspectives on Terrorism*, vol. 15, no. 1 (February 2021): 17–38.

33. Malkasian, *The American War in Afghanistan*, p. 417.

34. Zia Ur Rehman, *Exposing the Karachi–Afghanistan Link*, Norwegian Peacebuilding Resource Centre report, December 2013, at: https://www.files.ethz.ch/isn/175236/62255901a49df8d77e0e33b4611a4270.pdf; also see Jeff Stein, "Report: Pakistani spy agency rushed Mullah Omar to hospital," *The Washington Post*, January 18, 2011, at: http://voices.washingtonpost.com/spy-talk/2011/01/mullah_omar_treated_for_heart.html

35. Lynne O'Donnell and Mirwais Khan, "Taliban leadership in disarray on verge of peace talks," *Foreign Policy*, May 29, 2020, at: https://foreignpolicy.com/2020/05/29/taliban-leadership-disarray-coronavirus-covid-peace-talks/

36. Dawood Azami, "How Qatar came to host the Taliban," *BBC News*, June 22, 2013, at: https://www.bbc.com/news/world-asia-23007401

37. Nazr Mohammed Mutmain, *Six Days with Taliban Leaders*, Danish Publishing Community (Kabul), 2019, p. 173, as described in detail in Malkasian, *The American War in Afghanistan*, pp. 307–309.

38. Abdul Hai Mutma'in, *Taliban: A Critical History from Within*, edited by Alex Strick van Linschoten, Saba Imtiaz and Felix Kuehn, First Draft Publishing, 2019, pp. 261–263.

39. See Memphis Barker and Julian Borger, "Taliban publish letter calling on US to start Afghan peace talks," *The Guardian*, February 14, 2018, at: https://www.theguardian.com/world/2018/feb/14/taliban-publish-letter-calling-us-start-afghan-peace-talks

40. Ibid. The Trump strategy at the time offered greater authority to US military commanders to use military force targeting Taliban strongholds.

41. Ibid.

42. See Daniel Byman and Steven Simon, "Trump's surge in Afghanistan," *Foreign Affairs*, September 2017, at: https://www.foreignaffairs.com/articles/afghanistan/2017-09-18/trumps-surge-afghanistan

43. See Kevin Ponniah, "Counting the cost of Trump's air war in Afghanistan," *BBC News*, June 7, 2018, at: https://www.bbc.com/news/world-asia-44282098

44. Malkasian, *The American War in Afghanistan*, pp. 408–410.

45. Shereena Qazi, "Afghanistan: Taliban resume fighting as Eid ceasefire ends," *Al Jazeera*, June 18, 2018, at: https://www.aljazeera.com/news/2018/6/18/afghanistan-taliban-resume-fighting-as-eid-ceasefire-ends

46. Malkasian, *The American War in Afghanistan*, pp. 424–425.

47. Ibid.

48. Mujib Mashal and Taimoor Shah, "Taliban offer to reduce violence in Afghanistan ahead of deal with U.S.," *The New York Times*, January 16, 2020, at: https://www.nytimes.com/2020/01/16/world/asia/afghanistan-taliban-agreement.html

49. For instance, see Andrew Watkins, "Taliban fragmentation: A figment of your imagination?" *War on the Rocks*, September 4, 2019, at: https://warontherocks.com/2019/09/taliban-fragmentation-a-figment-of-your-imagination/

50. Malkasian, *The American War in Afghanistan*, p. 427.

51. Susannah George, "Shadow politicians, clerics and Soviet-era fighters: The Taliban's team negotiating peace," *The Washington Post*, September 20, 2020, at: https://www.washingtonpost.com/world/asia_pacific/afghan-taliban-peace-talks/2020/09/30/a5333540-f859-11ea-85f7-5941188a98cd_story.html

52. Profile of Sher Mohammad Abbas Stanikzai, see: http://www.afghan-bios.info/index.php?option=com_afghanbios&id=2486&task=view&total=39&start=34&Itemid=2

53. Simrin Sirur, "Who is Sher Mohammad Abbas Stanikzai, the Taliban leader who trained at IMA in Dehradun," *The Print*, August 29, 2021, at: https://theprint.in/world/who-is-sher-mohammad-abbas-stanikzai-the-taliban-leader-who-trained-at-ima-in-dehradun/724264/

54. Interview with a US official familiar with the negotiations, Washington DC, June 13, 2022.

55. Malkasian, *The American War in Afghanistan*, p. 426.

56. Mashal and Shah, "Taliban offer to reduce violence in Afghanistan ahead of deal with U.S."

57. Interview in Islamabad, September 2022.

58. Malkasian, *The American War in Afghanistan*, p. 431.

59. Ibid.

60. Craig Whitlock, *The Afghanistan Papers: A Secret History of the War*, Simon & Schuster, 2021, p. 272.

61. Mujib Mashal, "Once jailed in Guantánamo, 5 Taliban now face U.S. at peace talks," *The New York Times*, March 26, 2019, at: https://www.nytimes.com/2019/03/26/world/asia/taliban-guantanamo-afghanistan-peace-talks.html

62. Ibid.

63. Malkasian, *The American War in Afghanistan*, p. 435.

64. Interview, London, October 2020.

65. Malkasian, *The American War in Afghanistan*, p. 409.

66. For details, see Jonathan Schroden, "Lessons from the collapse of Afghanistan's security forces," *CTC Sentinel*, vol. 14, no. 8 (October 2021): 45–61, at: https://ctc.westpoint.edu/lessons-from-the-collapse-of-afghanistans-security-forces/

67. Ayaz Gul, "Taliban rejects Ghani's call for political reconciliation," *VOA*, April 16, 2018, at: https://www.voanews.com/a/taliban-rejects-ghani-call-for-political-reconciliation/4349927.html

68. Mujib Mashal, "The president, the envoy and the Talib: 3 lives shaped by war and study abroad," *The New York Times*, February 16, 2019, at: https://www.nytimes.com/2019/02/16/world/asia/afghanistan-ghani-khalilzad-stanekzai.html

69. Ibid.

70. Details of the meeting mentioned in Luke Mogelson, "The shattered Afghan dream of peace," *The New Yorker*, October 21, 2019, at: https://www.newyorker.com/magazine/2019/10/28/the-shattered-afghan-dream-of-peace

71. Whitlock, *The Afghanistan Papers*, p. 272.

72. Lindsey Graham and Jack Keane, "We can't outsource our security to anyone—especially the Taliban," *The Washington Post*, August 28, 2019, at: https://www.washingtonpost.com/opinions/2019/08/28/afghan-war-must-end-our-terms-not-talibans/?noredirect=on

73. Mogelson, "The shattered Afghan dream of peace."

74. Malkasian, *The American War in Afghanistan*, p. 437.
75. Ibid., p. 440.
76. Ibid., p. 446.
77. Interview with a DC-based South Asia expert who interviewed Khalilzad multiple times regarding the negotiations, July 2022.
78. Malkasian, *The American War in Afghanistan*, p. 458.
79. For the complete text of the agreement on the US Department of State website, see: https://www.state.gov/wp-content/uploads/2020/02/Agreement-For-Bringing-Peace-to-Afghanistan-02.29.20.pdf
80. Steve Coll and Adam Entous, "The secret history of the US diplomatic failure in Pakistan," *The New Yorker*, December 10, 2021, at: https://www.newyorker.com/magazine/2021/12/20/the-secret-history-of-the-us-diplomatic-failure-in-afghanistan
81. Frud Bezhan, "Why did the Taliban appoint a hard-line chief negotiator for intra-Afghan talks?" *Radio Free Europe*, September 10, 2020, at: https://www.rferl.org/a/why-did-the-taliban-appoint-a-hard-line-chief-negotiator-for-intra-afghan-talks-/30832252.html
82. Shahzada Zulfiqar, "Taliban vs Islamic State," *The News*, January 19, 2020, at: https://www.thenews.com.pk/tns/detail/599989-taliban-vs-islamic-state
83. Quoted in Aikins, "Inside the fall of Kabul."
84. "Remarks by President Biden on the drawdown of U.S. forces in Afghanistan," White House, July 8, 2021, at: https://www.whitehouse.gov/briefing-room/speeches-remarks/2021/07/08/remarks-by-president-biden-on-the-drawdown-of-u-s-forces-in-afghanistan/
85. Whitlock, *The Afghanistan Papers*, p. 274.
86. "Remarks by President Biden in Press Conference," White House, January 19, 2022, at: https://www.whitehouse.gov/briefing-room/speeches-remarks/2022/01/19/remarks-by-president-biden-in-press-conference-6/
87. Peter Bergen, "Opinion: Biden's Afghanistan exit decision looks even worse a year later," *CNN*, August 12, 2022, at: https://www.cnn.com/2022/08/09/opinions/afghanistan-exit-a-year-later-bergen; on Ghani government performance: see: "Afghanistan Country Report 2022," BTI, at: https://bti-project.org/en/reports/country-report/AFG

2 From Insurgency to Governance: Who's Who in Afghanistan Today

1. Quoted in Ayesha Tanzeem and Ayaz Gul, "Reports: Taliban enter Kabul," *VOA*, August 15, 2021, at: https://www.voanews.com/a/us-afghanistan-troop-withdrawal_reports-taliban-enter-kabul/6209594.html
2. Jim Sciutto, Zachary Cohen and Kylie Atwood, "US intel assessments on Afghanistan warn of 'accelerating pace' of Taliban hold on country," *CNN*, July 16, 2021, at: https://www.cnn.com/2021/07/16/politics/us-intel-kabul-taliban/index.html
3. Quoted in "Biden says Afghan leaders must 'fight for their nation' as Taliban gains," *Reuters*, August 10, 2021, at: https://www.reuters.com/world/asia-pacific/taliban-tighten-control-afghan-north-residents-weigh-options-2021-08-10/
4. For details, see David Zucchino and Fahim Abed, "On Afghan highways, even the police fear the Taliban's toll collectors," *The New York Times*, November 1,

2020, at: https://www.nytimes.com/2020/11/01/world/asia/afghanistan-taliban-bribery.html

5. For images of the Taliban takeover and resultant chaos, see "Kabul the day after the Taliban takeover," *Al Jazeera*, August 16, 2021, at: https://www.aljazeera.com/gallery/2021/8/16/in-pictures-kabul-the-day-after-the-taliban-takeover

6. "Frantic scenes at Kabul airport as Afghans try to flee Taliban," *Reuters*, August 16, 2021, at: https://www.reuters.com/world/asia-pacific/frantic-scenes-kabul-airport-afghans-try-flee-taliban-2021-08-16/

7. Quoted in Hassan Abbas, "Political trends in Pakistan and what to expect from the Kabul–Taliban negotiations: A conversation with South Asia scholar Dr. Marvin Weinbaum," *Near East South Asia Center for Strategic Studies Interview Series*, October 2020, at: https://nesa-center.org/political-trends-in-pakistan-and-what-to-expect-from-the-kabul-taliban-negotiations-a-conversation-with-south-asia-scholar-dr-marvin-weinbaum/

8. Hamza Mohamed and Ramy Allahoum, "Taliban enters Afghan presidential palace after Ghani flees," *Al Jazeera*, August 15, 2021, at: https://www.aljazeera.com/news/2021/8/15/taliban-continues-advances-captures-key-city-of-jalalabad

9. Ibid.

10. Aikins, "Inside the fall of Kabul."

11. Ibid.

12. Naveed Siddiqui, "'Don't worry, everything will be okay': ISI chief during Kabul visit," *Dawn*, September 4, 2021, at: https://www.dawn.com/news/1644463

13. Habib Akram, *Hum, Taliban Aur Afghanistan*, AKS Publications, 2022, pp. 229–230.

14. Ibid., p. 234.

15. Ibid., p. 233.

16. Ibid.

17. Quoted in Jon Lee Anderson, "The Taliban confront the realities of power," *The New Yorker*, February 28, 2022, at: https://www.newyorker.com/magazine/2022/02/28/the-taliban-confront-the-realities-of-power-afghanistan

18. John Hudson, "CIA Director William Burns held secret meeting in Kabul with Taliban leader Abdul Ghani Baradar," *The Washington Post*, August 24, 2021, at: https://www.washingtonpost.com/national-security/burns-afghanistan-baradar-biden/2021/08/24/c96bee5c-04ba-11ec-ba15-9c4f59a60478_story.html

19. "Taliban announces 'amnesty,' reaches out to women," *Al Jazeera*, August 17, 2021, at: https://www.aljazeera.com/news/2021/8/17/taliban-announces-amnesty-urges-women-to-join-government

20. Quoted in George Wright, "Afghanistan: Mysterious Taliban spokesman finally shows his face," *BBC News*, August 17, 2021, at: https://www.bbc.com/news/world-asia-58250607

21. "Transcript of Taliban's first news conference in Kabul," *Al Jazeera*, August 17, 2021, at: https://www.aljazeera.com/news/2021/8/17/transcript-of-talibans-first-press-conference-in-kabul

22. Ibid.

23. Ahmad Elhamy, Patricia Zengerle and Michael Martina, "Kabul attacks put bitter adversary Islamic State back into U.S. sights," *Al Jazeera*, August 26, 2021, at: https://www.reuters.com/world/islamic-state-claims-responsibility-kabul-airport-attack-2021-08-26/

24. Anderson, "The Taliban confront the realities of power."

25. See Lyse Doucet, "Hardliners get key posts in new Taliban government," *BBC News*, September 7, 2021, at: https://www.bbc.com/news/world-asia-58479750

26. "Profile: Mohammad Hasan Akhund, the head of Taliban government," *Al Jazeera*, September 7, 2021, at: https://www.aljazeera.com/news/2021/9/7/profile-mohammad-hassan-akhund-the-head-of-taliban-government

27. Interviews with Mohammad Israr Madani, December 2021. Also see "Factbox: Mohammad Hasan Akhund: Veteran Taliban leader becomes acting Afghan PM," *Reuters*, September 7, 2021, at: https://www.reuters.com/world/mohammad-hasan-akhund-veteran-taliban-leader-becomes-acting-afghan-pm-2021-09-07/

28. See Pallabi Munsi, "The Taliban's hidden moderate," *OZY, Daily Dose*, September 11, 2019, at: https://www.ozy.com/news-and-politics/is-the-man-who-blocked-girls-education-the-talibans-moderate/96449/

29. Quoted in Frud Bezhan, "The Rise of Mullah Yaqoob, the Taliban's new military chief," *Radio Free Europe*, August 27, 2020, at: https://www.rferl.org/a/the-rise-of-mullah-yaqoob-the-taliban-new-military-chief/30805362.html

30. Ibid.

31. Abdul Sayed, "How are Taliban organized," *VOA*, September 5, 2021, at: https://www.voanews.com/a/us-afghanistan-troop-withdrawal_analysis-how-are-taliban-organized/6219266.html

32. Andrew Watkins, "Five questions on the Taliban's caretaker government," *USIP*, September 9, 2021, at: https://www.usip.org/publications/2021/09/five-questions-talibans-caretaker-government

33. See https://twitter.com/ImranKhanPTI/status/1439158625243648002

34. For the first cabinet expansion, see "Taliban names deputy ministers, double down on all-male cabinet, *Al Jazeera*, September 21, 2021, at: https://www.aljazeera.com/news/2021/9/21/taliban-name-deputy-ministers-double-down-on-all-male-cabinet; for details of second expansion of November 23, 2021, see: "Taliban expand interim cabinet, 27 new members named," *WION*, November 23, 2021, at: https://www.wionews.com/south-asia/taliban-expand-interim-cabinet-27-new-members-named-431429

35. "Afghanistan's acting Taliban cabinet holds first meeting," *Radio Free Europe–Radio Liberty*, October 4, 2021, at: https://gandhara.rferl.org/a/afghanistan-taliiban-first-cabinet-meeting/31492503.html

36. Biography of Dr. Abdul Latif Nazari, at: http://www.afghan-bios.info/index.php?option=com_afghanbios&id=5145&task=view&total=809&start=536&Itemid=2

37. Zia ur-Rehman, "Where Afghanistan's new Taliban leaders went to school," *The New York Times,* November 25, 2021, at: https://www.nytimes.com/2021/11/25/world/asia/pakistan-taliban-afghanistan-madrasa.html

38. "Fact-check: PM Imran is wrong. 'Haqqani' is not a tribe in Afghanistan," *Friday Times*, September 15, 2021, at: https://www.thefridaytimes.com/

2021/09/15/fact-check-pm-imran-is-wrong-haqqani-is-not-a-tribe-in-afghanistan/

39. See profile of Abdul Hakim Sharei at: https://moj.gov.af/en/brief-biography-his-excellency-shaikh-al-hadith-mawlawi-abdul-hakim-sharei-acting-justice-minister

40. For details, see Shafiq Ahmed, "Who's who in Taliban's interim government," *AA*, September 9, 2021, at: https://www.aa.com.tr/en/asia-pacific/whos-who-in-taliban-interim-government/2360424; for short profiles, see: https://www.aa.com.tr/en/asia-pacific/key-leaders-of-taliban-the-students-of-warfare/2338048

41. "Afghan cricket board chief sacked," *Dawn*, September 22, 2021, at: https://www.dawn.com/news/1647685

42. For the detailed comments of Antonio Giustozzi, see "Conflict in Afghanistan: A new regional security map and state building implications since the Taliban takeover," IISS event video, May 11, 2022, at: https://www.iiss.org/events/2022/05/conflict-in-afghanistan

43. For a history of Afghan flags, see Alia Chughtai and Hashmat Moslih, "Infographic: Afghanistan's flags over the years," *Al Jazeera*, August 19, 2021, at: https://www.aljazeera.com/news/2021/8/19/infographic-what-afghanistans-new-flag-looks-like-interactive

44. For a general review of the book, see Jawad Borhani, "The Islamic Emirate and systems: An overview of the Taliban's manifesto of statehood," June 2022, at: https://reporterly.net/latest-stories/the-islamic-emirate-and-systems-an-overview-of-the-talibans-manifesto-of-statehood1/

45. "A look at Abdul Hakim Haqqani's book," *Institute for East Strategic Studies*, Iran, October 16, 2022, at: https://www.iess.ir/en/analysis/3149/

46. Ahmed Mukhtar, "Taliban blocks women from college entrance exams in subjects deemed 'too difficult,'" *CBS News*, October 14, 2022, at: https://www.cbsnews.com/news/taliban-blocks-women-college-entrance-exams-subjects-too-difficult/

3 Taliban.gov: Policies, Politics and Internal Rivalries

1. For details, see "'Necessary for security': Veteran Taliban enforcer says amputations will resume," *The Guardian*, September 24, 2021, at: https://www.theguardian.com/world/2021/sep/24/afghanistan-taliban-enforcer-says-amputations-will-resume

2. Ibid.

3. "Tashkent summit: Muttaqi urges the world to recognize IEA as new govt," *Ariana News*, July 26, 2022, at: https://www.ariananews.af/tashkent-summit-muttaqi-urges-the-world-to-recognize-iea-as-new-govt/

4. Saphora Smith, "In Afghanistan's 'moment of reckoning,' the Taliban lead a harsher-than-promised crackdown," *NBC News*, September 23, 2021, at: https://www.nbcnews.com/news/world/afghanistan-s-moment-reckoning-taliban-lead-harsher-promised-crackdown-n1279862

5. See Diaa Hadid, "The Taliban orders women to wear head-to-toe clothing in public," *NPR, All Things Considered*, May 7, 2022, at: https://www.npr.org/2022/05/07/1097382550/taliban-women-burqa-decree

6. "Taliban says all Afghan girls will be back in school by March," *Al Jazeera*, January 17, 2022, at: https://www.aljazeera.com/news/2022/1/17/taliban-says-will-open-all-schools-for-girls-across-country

7. See "No long-distance travel for women without male relative: Taliban," *Al Jazeera*, 26 December, 2021, at: https://www.aljazeera.com/news/2021/12/26/afghanistan-long-distance-travel-women-without-male-escort-taliban

8. Ashley Jackson, "The Ban of Older Girl's Education: The Taleban conservatives ascendant and a leadership in disarray," Afghanistan Analysts Network, March 29, 2022.

9. For details, see: https://www.nytimes.com/2022/03/23/world/asia/afghanistan-girls-schools-taliban.html

10. Interview with B, February 2022.

11. "Girls' education ban reveals deep rifts within Taliban," *VOA*, April 15, 2022, at: https://www.voanews.com/a/girls-education-ban-reveals-deep-rifts-within-taliban/6532038.html

12. Quoted in "Girls' education ban reveals deep rifts within Taliban," *France 24*, April 15, 2022, at: https://www.france24.com/en/live-news/20220415-girls-education-ban-reveals-deep-rifts-within-taliban

13. For details, see Fazel Minallah Qaziziai and Diaa Hadid, "Afghans who want teen girls back in school have new allies: Taliban-affiliated clerics," *NPR*, May 5, 2022, at: https://www.npr.org/sections/goatsandsoda/2022/05/05/1096634192/afghans-who-want-teen-girls-back-in-school-have-new-allies-taliban-affiliated-cl

14. "Taliban decree an end to forced marriages in Afghanistan," *The New York Times*, December 3, 2021, at: https://www.nytimes.com/2021/12/03/world/asia/taliban-women-marriage.html

15. For details, see Mohammad Hussain Hasrat, "Over a century of persecution: Massive human rights violations against Hazaras in Afghanistan," February 2019, at: https://www.ohchr.org/Documents/Issues/Racism/SR/Call/mhhasrat.pdf

16. Farkhondeh Akbari, "The risks facing Hazaras in Taliban-ruled Afghanistan," *George Washington University Program on Extremism*, March 7, 2022, at: https://extremism.gwu.edu/risks-facing-hazaras-taliban-ruled-afghanistan

17. "Despite mistrust, Afghan Shiites seek Taliban protection," *VOA*, November 16, 2021, at: https://www.voanews.com/a/despite-mistrust-afghan-shiites-seek-taliban-protection-/6315097.html

18. "Afghanistan: Taliban forcibly evict minority Shia," *Human Rights Watch*, October 22, 2021, at: https://www.hrw.org/news/2021/10/22/afghanistan-taliban-forcibly-evict-minority-shia

19. Sitarah Mohammadi and Sajjad Askary, "Why the Hazara people fear genocide in Afghanistan," *Al Jazeera*, October 27, 2021, at: https://www.aljazeera.com/opinions/2021/10/27/why-the-hazara-people-fear-genocide-in-afghanistan

20. See Zareen Taj, "The U.S. has a moral obligation toward Afghan women," *Ms. Magazine*, December 13, 2021, at: https://msmagazine.com/2021/12/13/taliban-united-states-women-afghanistan-hazara/

21. Interview with S, August 2022.

22. Quoted in Anderson, "The Taliban confront the realities of power."
23. Charlotte Greenfield, "Afghanistan lifts coal prices as exports to neighbouring Pakistan boom," *Reuters*, July 6, 2022, at: https://www.reuters.com/article/afghanistan-conflict-coal/afghanistan-lifts-coal-prices-as-exports-to-neighbouring-pakistan-boom-idUSL4N2YN2MF
24. For details, see David Mansfield, "Changing the rules of the game: How the Taliban regulated cross-border trade and upended Afghanistan's political economy," *XCEPT*, July 25, 2022, at: https://xcept-research.org/publication/changing-the-rules-of-the-game-how-the-taliban-regulated-cross-border-trade-and-upended-afghanistans-political-economy/
25. Ibid.
26. William Byrd, "One year later, Taliban unable to reverse Afghanistan's economic decline," *USIP*, August 8, 2022, at: https://www.usip.org/publications/2022/08/one-year-later-taliban-unable-reverse-afghanistans-economic-decline
27. "Afghanistan: Nearly 20 million going hungry," *UN News*, May 9, 2022, at: https://news.un.org/en/story/2022/05/1117812
28. "The Taliban government has proved surprisingly good at raising money," *The Economist*, June 8, 2022, at: https://www.economist.com/asia/2022/06/08/the-taliban-government-has-proved-surprisingly-good-at-raising-money
29. Ben Farmer and Simon Townsley, "Middle-class Afghans facing starvation as aid runs out," *The Telegraph*, June 4, 2022, at: https://www.telegraph.co.uk/global-health/climate-and-people/middle-class-afghans-facing-starvation-aid-runs/
30. N. Vinoth Kumar, "'The war will end ... but I saw who paid the price': Darwish's poem goes viral," *The Federal*, March 3, 2022, at: https://thefederal.com/news/the-war-will-end-but-i-saw-who-paid-the-price-darwishs-poem-goes-viral/
31. Steve Coll, "A year after the fall of Kabul," *The New Yorker*, August 27, 2022, at: https://www.newyorker.com/news/daily-comment/a-year-after-the-fall-of-kabul
32. "One certainty for Afghans: The Taliban and taxes," *Radio Free Europe–Radio Azadi*, June 16, 2022, at: https://gandhara.rferl.org/a/afghanistan-taliban-taxes-revenue-services/31901313.html
33. "The Taliban government has proved surprisingly good at raising money," *The Economist*, June 8, 2022.
34. Ibid.
35. "Overview: Afghanistan," *World Bank*, October 7, 2022, at: https://www.worldbank.org/en/country/afghanistan/overview
36. The letter is available at: https://static1.squarespace.com/static/5f32f67de5c10461a46e0ce0/t/62f3e3153ff7460c4ec1e97e/1660150549225/2022-08-10%2C+Economists%27+Letter+Afghanistan+.pdf
37. See William Byrd, "Demands for prompt return of Afghan Central Bank reserves miss the full picture," *USIP*, August 15, 2022, at: https://www.usip.org/publications/2022/08/demands-prompt-return-afghan-central-bank-reserves-miss-full-picture
38. Interview with a US official, Washington DC, August 2022.
39. Ibid.

40. Interview in Islamabad, September 15, 2022.

41. Khudai Noor Nasar, "Afghanistan: Taliban leaders in bust-up at presidential palace, sources say," *BBC*, September 15, 2021, at: https://www.bbc.com/news/world-asia-58560923

42. Steve Inskeep and Fazelminallah Qazizai, "We visited a Taliban leader's compound to examine his vision for Afghanistan," *NPR*, August 5, 2022, at: https://www.npr.org/2022/08/05/1115388675/taliban-afghanistan-leader-us-relationship

43. For details, see "Exclusive: Amanpour speaks with Taliban deputy leader," *CNN*, May 16, 2021, at: https://www.cnn.com/videos/world/2022/05/16/amanpour-sirajuddin-haqqani-interview-part-1-intl-vpx.cnn

44. Andrew Watkins, "Taliban fragmentation: Fact, fiction and future," *USIP*, *Peaceworks*, no. 160 (March 2020), at: https://www.usip.org/sites/default/files/2020-03/pw_160-taliban_fragmentation_fact_fiction_and_future-pw.pdf

45. Interview with Taliban leader C, December 2022.

46. Leo Sands, "Rahimullah Haqqani: Afghan cleric killed by bomb hidden in artificial leg—reports," *BBC*, August 11, 2022, at: https://www.bbc.com/news/world-asia-62508070

47. Abubakar Siddique, " 'Unprecedented differences': Rifts within the Taliban come out in the open," *Radio Free Europe–Radio Liberty*, June 2, 2022. https://gandhara.rferl.org/a/taliban-rifts-exposed-afghanistan/31880018.html

48. See Secunder Kermani, "Taliban leader makes first visit to capital city Kabul," *BBC*, July 1, 2022, at: https://www.bbc.com/news/world-asia-62015606; "Taliban supreme leader addresses major gathering in Kabul," *Al Jazeera*, July 1, 2022, at: https://www.aljazeera.com/news/2022/7/1/taliban-supreme-leader-addresses-gathering

49. Mullah Habitullah's complete speech audio with English subtitles, July 1, 2022, at: https://www.youtube.com/watch?v=Ft5ap4FDE7Y

50. For detailed analysis, see Fazelminalllah Qazizai, "For now, ideology trumps pragmatism in Afghanistan, *New Lines Magazine*, July 13, 2022, at: https://newlinesmag.com/newsletter/for-now-ideology-trumps-pragmatism-in-afghanistan/

51. For a detailed analysis of the content of the speech and a full transcript in English, see Sara Hakimi and C. Christine Fair, "The Taliban's Amir on the 'victory' in Afghanistan," *Hudson Institute*, September 12, 2022, at: https://www.hudson.org/research/18180-the-taliban-s-amir-on-the-victory-in-afghanistan

52. Interview with Kathy Gannon, Boston, December 1, 2022.

53. Akram, *Hum, Taliban Aur Afghanistan*, pp. 258–259.

54. Ibid., pp. 260–261.

55. Interview with Z in Tashkent, Uzbekistan, December 2022.

56. Ibid.

57. Navbahor Imamova, "Uzbekistan seeks to engage Taliban without alienating the west," *VOA*, May 4, 2022, at: https://www.voanews.com/a/uzbekistan-seeks-to-engage-taliban-without-alienating-west/6557338.html

58. For pictures of the occasion, see: https://twitter.com/navbahor/status/1553167869826957313

59. For instance, see: "U.S. delegation meeting with Taliban representatives," July 1, 2022, at: https://www.state.gov/u-s-delegation-meeting-with-taliban-representatives-2/

60. See Michael Rubin, "Did Pakistan give up Ayman Zawahiri for cash?" *19fortyfive.com*, August 2, 2022, at: https://www.aei.org/op-eds/did-pakistan-give-up-ayman-zawahiri-for-cash/

61. Quoted in Eric Schmitt, "U.S. says Al Qaeda has not regrouped in Afghanistan," *The New York Times,* August 13, 2022, at: https://www.nytimes.com/2022/08/13/us/politics/al-qaeda-afghanistan.html

62. "Tashkent Summit: Muttaqi urges the world to recognize IEA as new govt," *Ariana News*, July 26, 2022, at: https://www.ariananews.af/tashkent-summit-muttaqi-urges-the-world-to-recognize-iea-as-new-govt/

4 Deobandism, Islam and the Religious Narratives of the Taliban

1. Olivier Roy, "Has Islamism a future in Afghanistan?" in William Maley (ed.), *Fundamentalism Reborn? Afghanistan and the Taliban*, NYU Press, 1998, p. 211.

2. For details, see Barbara D. Metcalf, *Islamic Revival in British India: Deoband, 1860–1900*, Princeton University Press, 1982.

3. For details, see "A reading list on Deobandi studies," at: https://attahawi.com/2020/04/30/a-reading-list-on-deoband-studies/

4. The two founders of this school of thought are Muhammad Qasim Nanutavi and Rashid Ahmad Gangohi. For details, see Kamran Bokhari, "The long shadow of Deobandism in South Asia," *New Lines Magazine*, November 23, 2021, at: https://newlinesmag.com/essays/the-long-shadow-of-deobandism-in-south-asia/

5. For definition of Hanafi, see: https://www.britannica.com/topic/Hanafiyah

6. Lauren Frayer, "The Taliban's ideology has surprising roots in British-ruled India," *NPR*, September 8, 2021, at: https://www.npr.org/2021/09/08/1034754547/taliban-ideology-roots-deobandi-islam-india

7. Barbara D. Metcalf, " 'Traditionalist' Islamic activism: Deoband, Tablighis, and Talibs," *Social Science Research Council*, November 1, 2001, at: https://items.ssrc.org/after-september-11/traditionalist-islamic-activism-deoband-tablighis-and-talibs/

8. For details about Pashtunwali, see Lutz Rzehak, "Pashtunwali—tribal life and behaviours among the Pashtuns," *Afghanistan Analysts Network*, March 21, 2011, at: https://www.afghanistan-analysts.org/en/special-reports/pashtunwali-tribal-life-and-behaviour-among-the-pashtuns/

9. Metcalf, " 'Traditionalist' Islamic Activism: Deoband, Tablighis, and Talibs."

10. For details, see Simon Wolfgang Fuchs, "A direct flight to revolution: Maududi, divine sovereignty, and the 1979-moment in Iran," *Journal of the Royal Asiatic Society*, vol. 32, no. 2 (2022): 333–354, at: https://www.cambridge.org/core/journals/journal-of-the-royal-asiatic-society/article/direct-flight-to-revolution-maududi-divine-sovereignty-and-the-1979moment-in-iran/469BE06D4D083FB575608BB909C40EB7

11. See Bokhari, "The long shadow of Deobandism in South Asia."

12. For instance, see Umair Jamal, "Zia-ul-Haq and the 'Islamization' of Pakistan's public universities," *The Diplomat*, March 28, 2017, at: https://thediplomat.com/2017/03/zia-ul-haq-and-the-islamization-of-pakistans-public-universities/; also see Mariam Abou Zahab, *Pakistan: A Kaleidoscope of Islam*, Oxford University Press, 2020.
13. Brannon D. Ingram, *Revival from Below: The Deoband Movement and Global Islam*, University of California Press, 2018.
14. For instance, see "Lashkar-e-Jhangvi," *DNI*, at: https://www.dni.gov/nctc/groups/lj.html
15. Javid Ahmad, "The Taliban's religious roadmap for Afghanistan," *Middle East Institute*, January 26, 2022, at: https://www.mei.edu/publications/talibans-religious-roadmap-afghanistan
16. Dawood Azami, "The home of Sufi saints: The role and contribution of Afghan Sufis and the mystical message of love and tolerance in Pashto poetry," in Mahmoud Masaeli and Rico Sneller (eds.), *Responses of Mysticism to Religious Terrorism: Sufism and Beyond*, Gompel & Svacina, 2020, p. 85.
17. Ibid., p. 86.
18. Ibid., p. 100.
19. For definition, see "new religious movement," *Britannica*, at: https://www.britannica.com/topic/new-religious-movement
20. Roel Meijer, *Global Salafism: Islam's New Religious Movement*, Oxford University Press, 2014.
21. Farrukh Saleem, "New Afghanistan," *The News*, August 22, 2021, at: https://www.thenews.com.pk/print/881206-new-afghanistan
22. Brian R. Wilson, *The Social Dimensions of Sectarianism: Sects and New Religious Movements*, Clarendon Press, 1990.

5 Allies and Enemies of the Taliban: The Pakistani Taliban and the Islamic State in Khorasan (ISK)

1. Iftikhar A. Khan, "Terror attacks in Pakistan surge by 51 pc after Afghan Taliban victory," *Dawn*, October 20, 2022, at: https://www.dawn.com/news/1715927
2. "A call for bloodshed," *Dawn*, November 30, 2022, at: https://www.dawn.com/news/1723943/a-call-for-bloodshed
3. For details, see Steve Coll, *Ghost Wars: The Secret History of the CIA, Afghanistan, and Bin Laden, from the Soviet Invasion to September 10, 2001*, Penguin, 2004.
4. "Pakistan pays tribe al-Qaeda debt," *BBC News*, February 9, 2005, at: http://news.bbc.co.uk/2/hi/south_asia/4249525.stm
5. For details, see Abbas, *Taliban Revival: Violence and Extremism on the Pakistan–Afghanistan Frontier*, pp. 108–116.
6. Asad Munir, "How FATA was won by the Taliban," *Express Tribune* (Pakistan), June 21, 2010, at: https://tribune.com.pk/story/22601/how-fata-was-won-by-the-taliban
7. For background, see Hassan Abbas, "A profile of Tehrik-i-Taliban Pakistan," *CTC Sentinel*, vol. 1, no. 2 (2008), at: https://ctc.usma.edu/a-profile-of-tehrik-i-taliban-pakistan/

8. See Hassan Abbas, "Defining the Punjabi Taliban network," *CTC Sentinel*, vol. 2, no. 4 (2009), at: https://ctc.westpoint.edu/defining-the-punjabi-taliban-network/

9. Parts of this section are borrowed from Hassan Abbas, "Extremism and terrorism trends in Pakistan: Changing dynamics and new challenges," *CTC Sentinel*, vol. 14, no. 2 (February 2021): 44–53, at: https://ctc.usma.edu/extremism-and-terrorism-trends-in-pakistan-changing-dynamics-and-new-challenges/

10. For a discussion about the broader impact of the US drone campaign, see Hassan Abbas, "Are drone strikes killing terrorists or creating them?" *Atlantic*, March 31, 2013.

11. According to the ISIL and Al-Qaida Sanctions Committee of the UN Security Council, the attack was conducted by the Tariq Gidar Group (TGG) in association with Al-Qaeda and in conjunction with or on behalf of Jamaat ul Ahrar, TTP and Lashkar-e-Jhangvi. See https://www.un.org/securitycouncil/content/tariq-gidar-group-tgg

12. Syed Raza Hasan, "India, Afghanistan gave help to Pakistani Taliban, says group's ex-spokesman," *Reuters*, April 26, 2017, at: https://www.reuters.com/article/us-pakistan-militants/india-afghanistan-gave-help-to-pakistani-taliban-says-groups-ex-spokesman-idUSKBN17S1VN

13. "Allegiance of two popular North Waziristan's Jihadi organizations' leaders, Maulvi Aleem Khan and Commander Ghazi Omar Azzam, to TTP leader Mufti Noor Wali Mehsud," Umar Media video, November 27, 2020. For a detailed assessment of this development, see Abdul Sayed, "Waziristan militant leader Aleem Khan Ustad joins Tehreek-e-Taliban," *Militant Leadership Monitor*, vol. 11, no. 12 (2021), at: https://jamestown.org/brief/waziristan-militant-leader-aleem-khan-ustad-joins-tehreek-e-taliban/

14. For details, see: UN Security Council, Thirtieth Report of the Analytical Support and Sanctions Monitoring Team, July 15, 2022, https://www.ecoi.net/en/file/local/2075689/N2239429.pdf

15. Daud Khattak, "Whither the Pakistani Taliban: An assessment of recent trends," *New America*, August 31, 2020, at: https://www.newamerica.org/international-security/blog/whither-pakistani-taliban-assessment-recent-trends/

16. On the TTP celebrations in Afghanistan, see Abdul Sayed, "The evolution and future of Tehrik-e-Taliban Pakistan," *Carnegie Endowment for International Peace*, December 21, 2021, at: https://carnegieendowment.org/2021/12/21/evolution-and-future-of-tehrik-e-taliban-pakistan-pub-86051

17. Ismail Khan, "Islamabad, TTP agreed on indefinite ceasefire," *Dawn*, May 31, 2022, at: https://www.dawn.com/news/1692383/islamabad-ttp-agree-on-indefinite-ceasefire

18. Author interview, Imtiaz Ali, December 2020. For details on the change in FATA's legal status through a merger into KPK province, see Imtiaz Ali, "Mainstreaming Pakistan's Federally Administrative Tribal Areas: Reform initiatives and roadblocks," *USIP Special Report 421*, March 2018, at: https://www.usip.org/publications/2018/03/mainstreaming-pakistans-federally-administered-tribal-areas

19. "Radio Pak claims MNAs Dawar, Wazir 'fulfilling vested Indian agenda through Afghanistan,'" *Dawn*, March 10, 2020, at: https://www.dawn.com/news/1539808

20. Quoted in Ali Wazir, "What does the Pashtun Tahafuz movement want?" *The Diplomat*, April 27, 2018, at: https://thediplomat.com/2018/04/what-does-the-pashtun-tahafuz-movement-want/

21. Safiullah Padshah, Christina Goldbaum and Ihsanullah Tipu Mehsud, "Death toll from Pakistani airstrike rises to 45, Afghan officials say," *The New York Times*, April 17, 2022, at: https://www.nytimes.com/2022/04/17/world/asia/afghanistan-airstrikes-pakistan.html

22. Ibid.

23. Ibid.

24. Asfandyar Mir, "Pakistan's twin Taliban problem," *USIP*, May 4, 2022, at: https://www.usip.org/publications/2022/05/pakistans-twin-taliban-problem

25. Tahir Khan, "In letter to Taliban chief, Mufti Taqi Usmani urges reopening girls' schools," *Dawn*, April 21, 2022, at: https://www.dawn.com/news/1686106

26. Shahabullah Yousafzai, "Pakistani ulema fail to soften TTP in Kabul meetings," *Express Tribune* (Pakistan), July 27, 2022, at: https://tribune.com.pk/story/2367953/pakistani-ulema-fail-to-soften-ttp-in-kabul-meetings

27. "Afghanistan: ISIS group targets religious minorities," *Human Rights Watch*, September 6, 2022, at: https://www.hrw.org/news/2022/09/06/afghanistan-isis-group-targets-religious-minorities

28. "Facing critical human rights challenges, Afghanistan at a crossroads, says UN expert in Kabul," *OHCHR*, May 26, 2022, at: https://www.ohchr.org/en/press-releases/2022/05/facing-critical-human-rights-challenges-afghanistan-crossroads-says-un

29. Adnan Aamir, "The uncertain fate of Islamic State in Pakistan," *Interpreter*, November 7, 2019, at: https://ctc.westpoint.edu/the-revival-of-the-pakistani-taliban/

30. For details, see Abdul Sayed and Tore Hamming, "The revival of the Pakistani Taliban," *CTC Sentinel*, vol. 14, no. 4 (April/May 2021): 28–38, at: https://ctc.westpoint.edu/the-revival-of-the-pakistani-taliban/

31. For details, see Abbas, "Defining the Punjabi Taliban network."

32. Don Rassler, "Situating the emergence of the Islamic State of Khorasan," *CTC Sentinel*, vol. 8, no. 3 (March 2015), at: https://ctc.usma.edu/situating-the-emergence-of-the-islamic-state-of-khorasan/

33. Barbara Kelemen, "How the rise of Islamic State Khorasan in Afghanistan feeds Uyghur militancy," *The Diplomat*, February 17, 2022, at: https://thediplomat.com/2022/02/how-the-rise-of-islamic-state-khorasan-in-afghanistan-feeds-uyghur-militancy/

34. Sayed and Hamming, "The revival of the Pakistani Taliban."

35. Amira Jadoon, Abdul Sayed and Andrew Mines, "The Islamic State threat in Taliban Afghanistan: Tracing the resurgence of Islamic State Khorasan," *CTC Sentinel*, vol. 15, no. 1 (January 2022): 33–45, at: https://ctc.westpoint.edu/the-islamic-state-threat-in-taliban-afghanistan-tracing-the-resurgence-of-islamic-state-khorasan/

36. Ibid.
37. Ibid. For the 2021–22 figure, see Christina Goldbaum, "Suicide Attack Hits Russian Embassy in Afghanistan, Killing 2 Employees," *The New York Times*, September 5, 2022, at: https://www.nytimes.com/2022/09/05/world/asia/kabul-russian-embassy-suicide-attack.html
38. Interview, Abu Dhabi, June 2022.
39. Interview, Tampa, July 21, 2022.
40. Joshua White, "Non-state threats in Taliban's Afghanistan," *Brookings*, February 1, 2022, at: https://www.brookings.edu/blog/order-from-chaos/2022/02/01/nonstate-threats-in-the-talibans-afghanistan/amp/
41. "Memorandum for Department of Defense: Department of the Treasury's programs to combat terrorist financing and activities to disrupt the Islamic State of Iraq and Syria's (ISIS) financing," January 4, 2021, at: https://oig.treasury.gov/sites/oig/files/2021-01/OIG-CA-21-012.pdf
42. Umar Cheema and Azaz Syed, "The inside story of latest engagement between #Afghanistan and #Pakistan," *Talk Shock*, December 20, 2022, at: https://youtu.be/RUmoWpyvbJ0

6 The International Relations of the Taliban

1. Quoted in "Taliban say Afghanistan is secure enough for big projects," *Los Angeles Times*, October 12, 2022, at: https://www.latimes.com/world-nation/story/2022-10-12/taliban-say-afghanistan-secure-enough-for-big-projects
2. Farooq Yousaf, "Ghani seeks balance through China visit," *Global Times*, November 3, 2011, at: https://www.globaltimes.cn/content/889773.shtml
3. "HPC, Taliban and mediators set to meet in Doha," *TOLO News*, May 2, 2015, at: https://tolonews.com/afghanistan/hpc-taliban-and-mediators-set-meet-doha
4. Hamid Shalizi, "Afghans arrested Chinese Uighurs to aid Taliban talks bid: Officials," *Reuters*, February 20, 2015, at: https://www.reuters.com/article/us-afghanistan-taliban-china/afghans-arrested-chinese-uighurs-to-aid-taliban-talks-bid-officials-idUSKBN0LO18020150220
5. Ministry of Foreign Affairs of the People's Republic of China, "Wang Yi: Chinese, Afghan and Pakistani foreign ministers reach eight-point consensus," June 4, 2021, at: https://www.fmprc.gov.cn/mfa_eng/gjhdq_665435/2675_665437/2757_663518/2759_663522/202106/t20210604_9168735.html
6. Amy Chew, "China a 'welcome friend' for reconstruction in Afghanistan: Taliban spokesman," *South China Morning Post*, July 9, 2021, at: https://www.scmp.com/week-asia/politics/article/3140399/china-welcome-friend-reconstruction-afghanistan-taliban
7. Joel Gunter, "China committed genocide against Uyghurs, independent tribunal rules," *BBC News*, December 9, 2021, at: https://www.bbc.com/news/world-asia-china-59595952
8. Franz J. Marty, "Project to exploit Afghanistan's giant copper deposit languishes," *China Dialogue*, April 25, 2018, https://chinadialogue.net/en/

business/10577-project-to-exploit-afghanistan-s-giant-copper-deposit-languishes/

9. Zhou Bo, "In Afghanistan, China is ready to step into the void," *The New York Times*, August 20, 2021, at: https://www.nytimes.com/2021/08/20/opinion/china-afghanistan-taliban.html

10. Ministry of Foreign Affairs of the People's Republic of China, "Foreign ministry spokesperson Wang Wenbin's regular press conference on February 25, 2022," February 25, 2022, at: https://www.fmprc.gov.cn/mfa_eng/xwfw_665399/s2510_665401/2511_665403/202202/t20220225_10645705.html

11. Quoted in "Taliban say Afghanistan is secure enough for big projects," *Los Angeles Times*, October 12, 2022, at: https://www.latimes.com/world-nation/story/2022-10-12/taliban-say-afghanistan-secure-enough-for-big-projects

12. Gul Yousafzai, "Two killed in suicide bombing targeting Chinese nationals in Pakistan," *Reuters*, August 20, 2021, at: https://www.reuters.com/world/asia-pacific/two-killed-suicide-bombing-targeting-chinese-nationals-southwest-pakistan-2021-08-20/; also see "Foreign ministry spokesperson's remarks on the terrorist attack on a van of the Confucius Institute at the University of Karachi," April 27, 2022, at: https://www.fmprc.gov.cn/mfa_eng/xwfw_665399/s2510_665401/2535_665405/202204/t20220427_10674272.html; as regards controversial aspects of Chinese projects in Pakistan, see S. Khan, "Why Chinese investment is stoking anger in Pakistan's Balochistan province," *Deutsche Welle*, July 15, 2020, at: https://www.dw.com/en/why-chinese-investment-is-stoking-anger-in-pakistans-balochistan-province/a-54188705

13. Danna Harman, "Backstory: The royal couple that put Qatar on the map," *Christian Science Monitor*, March 5, 2077, at: https://www.csmonitor.com/2007/0305/p20s01-wome.html

14. For details, see Mounir Bouchenaki, "Safeguarding the Buddha statues in Bamiyan and the sustainable protection of Afghan cultural heritage," in Masanori Nagaoka (ed.), *The Future of the Bamiyan Buddha Statues*, Springer, 2020.

15. See Dannia Akkad, "How Qatar became the US–Taliban mediator—and what happens next," *Middle East Eye*, September 13, 2021, at: https://www.middleeasteye.net/news/qatar-us-taliban-how-became-mediator-talks

16. Interview with the late Robert D. Crane in August 2015, who at the time was based in Doha advising the government of Qatar and establishing the Center for the Study of Islamic Thought and Muslim Societies in Doha.

17. David D. Kirkpatrick, "Persian Gulf rivals competed to host Taliban, leaked emails show," *The New York Times*, July 31, 2017, at: https://www.nytimes.com/2017/07/31/world/middleeast/uae-qatar-taliban-emails.html

18. Andrew England and Benjamin Parkin, "Qatar urges West to engage with Taliban to stem crisis in Afghanistan," *Financial Times*, May 29, 2022, at: https://www.ft.com/content/0a9f41c3-b3ab-4c2d-81a2-c7b40169683d

19. For details, see Alex Marquardt, "First on CNN: Top US officials hold first in-person meeting with the Taliban since the US killed al Qaeda's leader in July," *CNN*, October 8, 2022, at: https://www.cnn.com/2022/10/08/politics/us-taliban-talks-wasiq-qatar

20. Suzanne Mcgee, "Why the Soviet Union invaded Afghanistan," *History.com*, March 4, 2022, at: https://www.history.com/news/1979-soviet-invasion-afghanistanSuz

21. Mariya Y. Omelicheva, "Shanghai Cooperation Organization and Afghanistan: Old fears, old barriers to counterterrorism cooperation," *Italian Institute for International Political Studies*, August 26, 2021, at: https://www.ispionline.it/en/pubblicazione/shanghai-cooperation-organization-and-afghanistan-old-fears-old-barriers-counterterrorism-cooperation-31398#:~:text=In%202005%2C%20the%20SCO%20established,agenda%20for%20the%20SCO%20members.

22. Henry Meyer, "Russia backs Afghan Taliban demand to withdraw foreign troops," *Bloomberg*, March 31, 2017, at: https://www.bloomberg.com/news/articles/2017-03-31/russia-backs-afghan-taliban-demand-to-withdraw-foreign-troops#xj4y7vzkg

23. Nathan Hodge, "Taliban representatives in Moscow signal Russia's rising diplomatic clout," *CNN*, November 9, 2018, at: https://www.cnn.com/2018/11/09/europe/russia-taliban-talks-intl/index.html

24. Sheikh Shabir Kulgami, " 'Moscow Format': An attempt in right direction," *The Geopolitics*, November 19, 2018, at: https://thegeopolitics.com/moscow-format-an-attempt-in-right-direction/

25. Vladimir Isachenkov, "Taliban visit Moscow to say their wins don't threaten Russia," *AP News*, July 8, 2021, at: https://apnews.com/article/taliban-moscow-europe-russia-51327432f1455020352826281c6c4e73

26. Mark Galeotti, "Narcotics and nationalism: Russian drug policies and futures," *Brookings*, July 2016, at: https://www.brookings.edu/wp-content/uploads/2016/07/galeotti-russia-final.pdf

27. Julia Yampolskaya, "Zhirinovsky advised the United States to 'get the hell out' of all countries of the world," *Lenta.ru*, August 17, 2021, at: https://lenta.ru/news/2021/08/17/predrek/

28. "Putin says Russia is mulling excluding Taliban from list of extremist groups," *Reuters*, October 20, 2021, at: https://www.reuters.com/world/europe/putin-says-russia-is-mulling-excluding-taliban-list-extremist-groups-2021-10-21/

29. "Russia says no plan to evacuate embassy," *Moscow Times*, August 16, 2021, at: https://www.themoscowtimes.com/2021/08/15/russia-says-no-plan-to-evacuate-kabul-embassy-a74793

30. "Russia calls Taliban 'rational', blames Afghan gov't for blocking talks," *Moscow Times*, July 23, 2021, at: https://www.themoscowtimes.com/2021/07/23/russia-calls-taliban-rational-blames-afghan-govt-for-blocking-talks-a74599

31. "Trans-Afghan railway line," *RailFreight.com*, at: https://www.railfreight.com/tag/trans-afghan-railway-line/

32. Ministry of External Affairs—Government of India, "Suo Motu statement by minister of external affairs in Parliament on the hijacking of Indian Airlines flight IC-814," March 1, 2000, at: https://mea.gov.in/in-focus-article.htm?5471/Suo+Motu+Statement+by+Minister+of+External+Affairs+in+Parliament+on+the+Hijacking+of+Indian+Airlines+Flight+IC814

33. Ministry of External Affairs—Government of India, "India and neighbours," December 12, 2012, at: https://mea.gov.in/india-and-neighbours.htm

34. "India says it brought development projects to Afghanistan, world knows what Pakistan brought," *Economic Times*, June 24, 2021, at: https://economictimes. indiatimes.com/news/defence/india-says-it-brought-development-projects-to-afghanistan-world-knows-what-pakistan-brought/articleshow/83813171. cms?from=mdr

35. "Touched that new Afghan parliament has an Atal Block: PM Modi," *Times of India*, December 25, 2015, at: https://timesofindia.indiatimes.com/ india/touched-that-new-afghan-parliament-has-an-atal-block-pm-modi/ articleshow/50321446.cms

36. " 'Peace process must be led, owned and controlled by Afghan': India on historic talks between Taliban and Afghanistan," *Hindustan Times*, September 12, 2020, at: https://www.hindustantimes.com/india-news/ peace-process-must-be-led-owned-and-controlled-by-afghan-india-on-historic-talks-between-taliban-and-afghanistan-read-full-statement-here/ story-3Ew8ip6HxysvHUBkNDLuzI.html

37. H.S. Panag, "Taliban dropped India from its thank you list: Delhi should face new Afghanistan realities," *The Print*, March 5, 2020, at: https:// theprint.in/opinion/taliban-dropped-india-from-its-thank-you-list-delhi-should-face-new-afghanistan-realities-2/376000/

38. Vineet Khare, "Afghanistan: Taliban says it will 'raise voice for Kashmir Muslims,'" *BBC News*, September 3, 2021, at: https://www.bbc.com/news/ world-asia-india-58419719

39. Ministry of External Affairs—Government of India, "Statement by Official Spokesperson on the bomb attack on Indian Embassy in Kabul," July 7, 2008, at: https://mea.gov.in/media-briefings.htm?dtl/3340/Statement+by+ Official+Spokesperson+on+the+bomb+attack+on+Indian+Embassy+in+ Kabul; also see Ministry of External Affairs—Government of India, "Q. No. 1713 attack on consulate in Herat, Afghanistan," Parliament Q & A, July 24, 2014, at: https://www.mea.gov.in/rajya-sabha.htm?dtl/23725/Q+NO1713+ ATTACK+ON+CONSULATE+IN+HERAT+AFGHANISTAN

40. Ministry of External Affairs—Government of India, External Publicity Division, "India and Afghanistan—A development partnership," p. 17, at: https://mea.gov.in/Uploads/PublicationDocs/176_india-and-afghanistan-a-development-partnership.pdf

41. Snehesh Alex Philip, "China's pressure tactics along LAC continue, aim to 'keep the pot simmering,'" *The Print*, July 25, 2022, at: https://theprint.in/ defence/chinas-pressure-tactics-along-lac-continue-aim-to-keep-the-pot-simmering/1054168/; and Ministry of External Affairs—Government of India, "Transcript of weekly media briefing by the Official Spokesperson," June 3, 2022, at: https://www.mea.gov.in/media-briefings.htm?dtl/35383/ Transcript_of_Weekly_Media_Briefing_by_the_Official_Spokesperson_ June_02_2022

42. Suhasini Haidar, "India reopens embassy in Kabul," *The Hindu*, June 24, 2022, at: https://www.thehindu.com/news/national/india-reopens-embassy-in-kabul/article65558557.ece

43. Quoted in Anjana Pasricha, "India returns to Afghanistan with small diplomatic presence," *VOA*, July 7, 2022, at: https://www.voanews.com/a/india-returns-to-afghanistan-with-small-diplomatic-presence/6648776.html

44. "Turkey takes over ISAF command," *New Humanitarian*, February 14, 2005, at: https://www.thenewhumanitarian.org/news/2005/02/14/turkey-takes-over-isaf-command

45. TIKA, "Overseas offices," Republic of Türkiye Ministry of Culture and Tourism—Turkish Cooperation and Coordination Agency, at: https://www.tika.gov.tr/en/overseasoffices

46. "Erdogan says Turkey still aims to maintain Kabul airport security," *Reuters*, August 18, 2021, at: https://www.reuters.com/world/asia-pacific/erdogan-says-turkey-still-aims-maintain-kabul-airport-security-2021-08-18/

47. "US imposes sanctions on Turkey of Russia weapons," *BBC News*, December 14, 2020, at: https://www.bbc.com/news/world-us-canada-55311099

48. "Turkey's Erdogan says Taliban should end 'occupation' in Afghanistan," *Reuters*, July 19, 2021, at: https://www.reuters.com/world/middle-east/turkeys-erdogan-says-taliban-should-end-occupation-afghanistan-2021-07-19/

49. "Turkey welcomes Taliban statements since their takeover in Afghanistan," *Reuters*, August 17, 2021, at: https://www.reuters.com/world/middle-east/turkey-talks-with-all-afghan-parties-welcomes-talibans-messages-minister-2021-08-17/

50. MÜSİAD Homepage, Independent Industrialists and Businessmen Association, at: https://www.musiad.org.tr/en

51. "Afghan Business Association in Turkey (AIAD)," Afghan Chamber of Commerce and Industry, at: https://aiadtr.com/

52. "Kajaki 100MW hydro power plan investment project," *77INSAAT*, at: https://www.77insaat.com/projects/commercial/energy-investment-projects-2/kajaki-100mw-hydro-power-plant-investment-project/

53. Ogulgozel Rejepova, "Lapis Lazuli corridor—Major trade route from Afghanistan to Europe," *Business Turkmenistan*, May 17, 2021, at: https://business.com.tm/post/7064/lapis-lazuli-corridor-major-trade-route-from-afghanistan-to-europe

54. Najibullah Lalzoy, "Turkey to resume visa issuance in Kabul and Mazar-e-Sharif," *Khaama Press News Agency*, February 10, 2022, at: https://www.khaama.com/turkey-to-resume-visa-issuance-in-kabul-and-mazar-e-sharif-76775765/

55. Aaron Y. Zelin, "Turkey calls for recognition of the Taliban's Emirate," *Washington Institute for Near East Policy*, March 17, 2022, at: https://www.washingtoninstitute.org/policy-analysis/turkey-calls-recognition-talibans-islamic-emirate; also see Suzan Fraser and Kathy Gannon, "Afghan Taliban delegation in Turkey for high-level talks," *AP News*, October 14, 2021, at: https://apnews.com/article/afghanistan-recep-tayyip-erdogan-qatar-doha-european-union-0c783ad346fc408aa5256fa62134bc7a

56. Akmal Dawi, "Turkey deports thousands to Taliban-controlled Afghanistan," *VOA*, June 16, 2022, at: https://www.voanews.com/a/turkey-deports-thousands-to-taliban-controlled-afghanistan/6620683.html

57. Tom Bateman, "Afghanistan: Qatar and Turkey become Taliban's lifeline to the outside world," *BBC*, September 2, 2021, at: https://www.bbc.com/news/world-middle-east-58394438

58. See Secretary-General Guterres addressing the media in Doha, UN News, February 19, 2024, at: https://news.un.org/en/story/2024/02/1146657

Conclusion

1. Hameed Hakimi and Gareth Price, "Afghanistan: One year of Taliban rule," *Chatham House*, August 15, 2022, at: https://www.chathamhouse.org/2022/08/afghanistan-one-year-taliban-rule

2. See Joanna Lilis, "Afghanistan pays electricity debts to Uzbekistan but still owes Tajikistan," *Eurasianet*, August 2, 2022, at: https://eurasianet.org/afghanistan-pays-electricity-debts-to-uzbekistan-but-still-owes-tajikistan

3. Catherine Putz, "Taliban again demands return of Afghan aircraft in Central Asia," *The Diplomat*, September 1, 2022, at: https://thediplomat.com/2022/09/taliban-again-demands-return-of-afghan-aircraft-in-central-asia/

4. Ibid.

5. For details, see Vinay Kaura, "Tajikistan's evolving relations with Taliban 2.0," *Middle East Institute*, December 1, 2021, at: https://www.mei.edu/publications/tajikistans-evolving-relations-taliban-20

6. For details, see "Taliban reach out to Shiite Hazara minority, seeking unity and Iran ties," *The Wall Street Journal*, September 2, 2021, at: https://www.wsj.com/articles/taliban-reach-out-to-shiite-hazara-minority-seeking-unity-and-iran-ties-11630599286

7. Interview, June 2022.

8. Interview, February 2022.

9. Ibid.

10. Interview, Washington DC, July 12, 2022.

Epilogue

1. "Taliban push for control of more Afghan diplomatic missions," *PBS*, March 25, 2023, https://www.pbs.org/newshour/world/taliban-push-for-control-of-more-afghan-diplomatic-missions

2. Quoted from William Byrd, "Two years into Taliban rule, new shocks weaken Afghan economy," *USIP*, August 2023, at: https://www.usip.org/publications/2023/08/two-years-taliban-rule-new-shocks-weaken-afghan-economy

3. For details, see Ayaz Gul, "UN: Opium cultivation in Afghanistan plunges by 95%," *Voice of America*, November 5, 2023, at: https://www.voanews.com/a/un-opium-cultivation-in-afghanistan-plunges-by-95-/7342235.html

4. UNODC Press Release on September 10, 2023, at: https://www.unodc.org/unodc/en/press/releases/2023/September/unodc_-methamphetamine-trafficking-in-and-around-afghanistan-expanding-rapidly-as-heroin-trade-slows.html

5. For details, see blog posts on *Tahqiqaat* (meaning research) run by Israr Madni, Islamabad, Pakistan, at: https://tahqiqaat.pk

6. Abubakar Siddique, "The Azadi briefing: Taliban minister under fire for alleged nepotism," *Radio Free Europe/Radio Liberty*, February 9, 2024,

at: https://www.rferl.org/a/azadi-briefing-taliban-nepotism-afghanistan/ 32812465.html

7. For background of Mullah Shereen Akhund, see John Foulkes, "Who is Taliban negotiator Mullah Sherin Akhund?," *Militant Leadership Monitor*, The Jamestown Foundation, April 1, 2021, at: https://jamestown.org/brief/who-is-taliban-negotiator-mullah-sherin-akhund/; also see Kamran Yusuf, "Taliban chief's top aide arriving tomorrow," *The Express Tribune*, January 1, 2024, at: https://tribune.com.pk/story/2451847/taliban-chiefs-top-aide-arriving-tomorrow

8. For details about the Eid message, see "Reclusive Taliban leader releases Eid message urging officials to set aside their differences," *Associated Press*, April 6, 2024, at: https://apnews.com/article/afghan-taliban-leader-eid-message-dda37680e57355b438766ab5eb821816

9. For details, see "Intelbrief: Back to the future in Afghanistan?," The Soufan Center, April 27, 2023, at: https://thesoufancenter.org/intelbrief-2023-april-28/

10. See A. Giustozzi, "Slowly and carefully, the Taliban are reining in Jihadists," *World Politics Review*, August 2, 2023, at: https://www.worldpoliticsreview.com/us-afghanistan-taliban-al-qaeda-war-on-terror-ttp/?

11. Ayaz Gul, "Afghan Taliban chief deems cross-border attacks on Pakistan forbidden," *Voice of America*, August 6, 2023, at: https://www.voanews.com/a/afghan-taliban-chief-deems-cross-border-attacks-on-pakistan-forbidden-/7213760.html

12. For details, see Organization of Islamic Cooperation, "Delegation of Muslim scholars visits Afghanistan," June 20, 2022, at: https://www.oic-oci.org/topic/?t_id=37102&t_ref=25739&lan=en

13. Ruchi Kumar, "Why has China recognized Taliban envoy to Beijing?," *Aljazeera*, February 14, 2023, at: https://www.aljazeera.com/news/2024/2/14/is-chinas-recognition-of-afghanistan-envoy-a-diplomatic-win-for-taliban

14. "Time to engage (very carefully) with the Taliban," *The Economist*, May 4, 2023, at: https://www.economist.com/leaders/2023/05/04/time-to-engage-very-carefully-with-the-taliban

15. Graeme Smith, "Rethinking talks with the Taliban," *International Crisis Group*, April 18, 2024, at: https://www.crisisgroup.org/asia/south-asia/afghanistan/rethinking-talks-taliban

Select Bibliography

Abbas, Hassan, "Extremism and terrorism trends in Pakistan: Changing dynamics and new challenges," *CTC Sentinel*, vol. 14, no. 2 (February 2021): 44–53, at: https://ctc.usma.edu/extremism-and-terrorism-trends-in-pakistan-changing-dynamics-and-new-challenges/
—— *Pakistan's Drift into Extremism: Allah, the Army, and America's War on Terror*, M.E. Sharpe, 2004.
—— *The Taliban Revival: Violence and Extremism on the Pakistan–Afghanistan Frontier*, Yale University Press, 2015.
Ahmad, Javid, "The Taliban's religious roadmap for Afghanistan," *Middle East Institute*, January 26, 2022, at: https://www.mei.edu/publications/talibans-religious-roadmap-afghanistan
Ahmadzai, Atal, "Dying to live: The 'love to death' narrative driving the Taliban's suicide bombings," *Perspectives on Terrorism*, vol. 15, no. 1 (February 2021): 17–38.
Aikins, Mathieu, "Inside the fall of Kabul," *The New York Times*, December 10, 2021, at: https://www.nytimes.com/2021/12/10/magazine/fall-of-kabul-afghanistan.html
Akbari, Farkhondeh, "The risks facing Hazaras in Taliban-ruled Afghanistan," *George Washington University Program on Extremism*, March 7, 2022, at: https://extremism.gwu.edu/risks-facing-hazaras-taliban-ruled-afghanistan
Ali, Imtiaz, "Mainstreaming Pakistan's Federally Administrated Tribal Areas: Reform initiatives and roadblocks," *USIP Special Report*, March 2018, at: https://www.usip.org/publications/2018/03/mainstreaming-pakistans-federally-administrated-tribal-areas
Atakpal, Haseeba, "Ghani's team had contact with Haqqani network in 2014 poll: Nabil," *TOLO News*, September 5, 2019, at: https://tolonews.com/afghanistan/ghani's-team-had-contact-haqqani-network-2014-poll-nabil
Azami, Dawood, "The home of Sufi saints: The role and contribution of Afghan Sufis and the mystical message of love and tolerance in Pashto poetry," in Mahmoud Masaeli and Rico Sneller (eds.), *Responses of Mysticism to Religious Terrorism: Sufism and Beyond*, Gompel & Svacina, 2020, pp. 85–135.

Barfield, Thomas, *Afghanistan: A Cultural and Political History*, Princeton University Press, 2010.

Basit, Abdul, "Future of the Afghan Taliban under Mullah Akhtar Mansoor," *Counter Terrorist Trends and Analyses*, vol. 7, no. 10 (November 2015): 9–13.

Bergen, Peter and Katherine Tiedemann (eds.), *Talibanistan: Negotiating the Borders between Terror, Politics and Religion*, Oxford University Press, 2013.

Bokhari, Kamran, "The long shadow of Deobandism in South Asia," *New Lines Magazine*, November 23, 2021, at: https://newlinesmag.com/essays/the-long-shadow-of-deobandism-in-south-asia/

Byrd, William, "Demands for prompt return of Afghan Central Bank reserves miss the full picture," *USIP*, August 15, 2022, at: https://www.usip.org/publications/2022/08/demands-prompt-return-afghan-central-bank-reserves-miss-full-picture

—— "One year later, Taliban unable to reverse Afghanistan's economic decline," *USIP*, August 8, 2022, at: https://www.usip.org/publications/2022/08/one-year-later-taliban-unable-reverse-afghanistans-economic-decline

Clark, Kate, "The release of Mullah Baradar: What's next for negotiations?" *Afghanistan Analysts Network*, September 13, 2013, at: https://www.afghanistan-analysts.org/en/reports/war-and-peace/the-release-of-mullah-baradar-whats-next-for-negotiations/

Coll, Steve, "A year after the fall of Kabul," *The New Yorker*, August 27, 2022, at: https://www.newyorker.com/news/daily-comment/a-year-after-the-fall-of-kabul

—— *Ghost Wars: The Secret History of the CIA, Afghanistan, and Bin Laden, from the Soviet Invasion to September 10, 2001*, Penguin Books, 2004.

Coll, Steve and Adam Entous, "The secret history of the U.S. diplomatic failure in Afghanistan," *The New Yorker*, December 20, 2021, at: https://www.newyorker.com/magazine/2021/12/20/the-secret-history-of-the-us-diplomatic-failure-in-afghanistan

Crile, George, *Charlie Wilson's War: The Extraordinary Story of How the Wildest Man in Congress and a Rogue CIA Agent Changed the History of Our Times*, Grove Press, 2003.

The Economist, "The Taliban government has proved surprisingly good at raising money," June 8, 2022, at: https://www.economist.com/asia/2022/06/08/the-taliban-government-has-proved-surprisingly-good-at-raising-money

Edwards, David. B., *Before Taliban: Genealogies of the Afghan Jihad*, University of California Press, 2002.

Farmer, Ben and Simon Townsley, "Middle-class Afghans facing starvation as aid runs out," *The Telegraph*, June 4, 2022, at: https://www.telegraph.co.uk/global-health/climate-and-people/middle-class-afghans-facing-starvation-aid-runs/

Fraser, Suzan and Kathy Gannon, "Afghan Taliban delegation in Turkey for high-level talks," *AP News*, October 14, 2021, at: https://apnews.com/article/afghanistan-recep-tayyip-erdogan-qatar-doha-european-union-0c783ad346fc408aa5256fa62134bc7a

Fuchs, Simon W., "A direct flight to revolution: Maududi, divine sovereignty, and the 1979-moment in Iran," *Journal of the Royal Asiatic Society*, vol. 32, no. 2 (2021): 333–354, at: https://www.cambridge.org/core/journals/journal-of-the-royal-asiatic-society/article/direct-flight-to-revolution-maududi-divine-

sovereignty-and-the-1979moment-in-iran/469BE06D4D083FB575608BB90
9C40EB7

Gannon, Kathy, "Afghan president was isolated before slipping into exile," *AP News*, August 15, 2021, at: https://apnews.com/article/race-and-ethnicity-2901e54d6268341d3caf936fef6313db

—— *I Is for Infidel: From Holy War to Holy Terror in Afghanistan*, Public Affairs, 2005.

George, Susannah, "Afghanistan's military collapse: Illicit deals and mass desertions," *The Washington Post*, August 15, 2021, at: https://www.washington post.com/world/2021/08/15/afghanistan-military-collapse-taliban/

—— "U.S. watchdog details collapse of Afghan security forces," *The Washington Post*, May 18, 2022, at: https://www.washingtonpost.com/world/2022/05/18/us-watchdog-details-collapse-afghan-security-forces/

Giustozzi, Antonio (ed.), *Decoding the New Taliban: Insights from the Afghan Field*, Columbia University Press, 2009.

Graham, Lindsey and Jack Keane, "We can't outsource our security to anyone—especially the Taliban," *The Washington Post*, August 28, 2019, at: https://www.washingtonpost.com/opinions/2019/08/28/afghan-war-must-end-our-terms-not-talibans/?noredirect=on

Hakim, Abdul, *Al-Imarah Al-Islamiah wa Nizamaha* [*The Islamic Emirate and its System*), Maktaba Dar al-aloom al-Sharia, 2022.

Hakimi, Hameed and Gareth Price, "Afghanistan: One year of Taliban rule," *Chatham House*, August 15, 2022, at: https://www.chathamhouse.org/2022/08/afghanistan-one-year-taliban-rule

Hansler, Jennifer and Kylie Atwood, "Senior Afghan official accuses US envoy of 'delegitimizing' Afghan government," *CNN*, March 14, 2019, at: https://www.cnn.com/2019/03/14/politics/mohib-khalilzad-afghanistan-row/index.html

Haroon, Sana, *Frontier of Faith: Islam in the Indo-Afghan Borderland*, Columbia University Press, 2007.

Human Rights Watch, "Afghanistan: Taliban forcibly evict minority Shia," *Human Rights Watch*, October 22, 2022, at: https://www.hrw.org/news/2021/10/22/afghanistan-taliban-forcibly-evict-minority-shia

Hussain, Mujahid, *Punjabi Taliban: Driving Extremism in Pakistan*, Pentagon Press, 2012.

Ingram, Brannon D., *Revival from Below: The Deoband Movement and Global Islam*, University of California Press, 2018.

International Crisis Group, *Taking Stock of the Taliban's Perspectives on Peace*, Report No. 113, August 11, 2020, at: https://www.crisisgroup.org/asia/south-asia/afghanistan/311-taking-stock-talibans-perspectives-peace

Jadoon, Amira, Abdul Sayed and Andrew Mines, "The Islamic state threat in Taliban Afghanistan: Tracing the resurgence of Islamic State Khorasan," *CTC Sentinel*, vol. 15, no. 1 (January 2022): 33–45 at: https://ctc.westpoint.edu/the-islamic-state-threat-in-taliban-afghanistan-tracing-the-resurgence-of-islamic-state-khorasan/

Jamal, Umair, "Zia-ul-Haq and the "Islamization" of Pakistan's public universities," *The Diplomat*, March 28, 2017, at: https://thediplomat.com/2017/03/zia-ul-haq-and-the-islamization-of-pakistans-public-universities/

Khattak, Daud, "Whither the Pakistani Taliban: An assessment of recent trends," *New America*, August 31, 2020, at: https://www.newamerica.org/international-security/blog/whither-pakistani-taliban-assessment-recent-trends/

Kirkpatrick, David D., "Persian Gulf rivals competed to host Taliban, leaked emails show," *York Times*, July 31, 2017, at: https://www.nytimes.com/2017/07/31/world/middleeast/uae-qatar-taliban-emails.html

Madi, Mohamed, Ahmad Khalid and Sayed A. Nizami, "Chaos and confusion: The frenzied final hours of the Afghan government," *BBC News*, September 8, 2021, at: https://www.bbc.com/news/world-asia-58477131

Malkasian, Carter, *The American War in Afghanistan: A History*, Oxford University Press, 2021.

Mashal, Mujib, "The president, the envoy and the Talib: 3 lives shaped by war and study abroad," *The New York Times*, February 16, 2019, at: https://www.nytimes.com/2019/02/16/world/asia/afghanistan-ghani-khalilzad-stanekzai.html

Mashal, Mujib and Taimoor Shah, "Taliban offer to reduce violence in Afghanistan ahead of deal with U.S.," *The New York Times*, January 16, 2020, at: https://www.nytimes.com/2020/01/16/world/asia/afghanistan-taliban-agreement.html

Matinuddin, Kamal, *The Taliban Phenomenon: Afghanistan 1994–1997*, Oxford University Press, 1999.

Meijer, Roel, *Global Salafism: Islam's New Religious Movement*, Oxford University Press, 2014.

Metcalf, Barbara D., *Islamic Revival in British India: Deoband, 1860–1900*, Princeton University Press, 1982.

—— "'Traditionalist' Islamic activism: Deoband, Tablighis, and Talibs," *Social Science Research Council*, November 1, 2001, at: https://items.ssrc.org/after-september-11/traditionalist-islamic-activism-deoband-tablighis-and-talibs/

Mir, Asfandyar, "Pakistan's twin Taliban problem," *USIP*, May 4, 2022, at: https://www.usip.org/publications/2022/05/pakistans-twin-taliban-problem

Mogelson, Luke, "The shattered Afghan dream of peace," *The New Yorker*, October 21, 2019, at: https://www.newyorker.com/magazine/2019/10/28/the-shattered-afghan-dream-of-peace

Mutma'in, Abdul H., *Mullah Mohammad Omar, Taliban and Afghanistan*, Afghan Publishing Community (Kabul), 2017.

—— *Taliban: A Critical History from Within*, edited by Alex Strick van Linschoten, Saba Imtiaz and Felix Kuehn, First Draft Publishing, 2019.

Mutmain, Nazr M., *Six Days with Taliban Leaders*, Danish Publishing Community (Kabul), 2019.

Nasr, Vali, *The Dispensable Nation: American Foreign Policy in Retreat*, Anchor, 2013.

O'Donnell, Lynne and Mirwais Khan, "Taliban leadership in disarray on verge of peace talks," *Foreign Policy*, May 29, 2020, at: https://foreignpolicy.com/2020/05/29/taliban-leadership-disarray-coronavirus-covid-peace-talks/

Qazi, Shereena, "Afghanistan: Taliban resume fighting as Eid ceasefire ends," *Al Jazeera*, June 18, 2018, at: https://www.aljazeera.com/news/2018/6/18/afghanistan-taliban-resume-fighting-as-eid-ceasefire-ends

Qaziziai, Fazel M. and Diaa Hadid, "Afghans who want teen girls back in school have new allies: Taliban-affiliated clerics," *NPR*, May 5, 2022, at: https://

newlinesmag.com/newsletter/for-now-ideology-trumps-pragmatism-in-afghanistan/

Rahman, Zia ur-, "Where Afghanistan's new Taliban leaders went to school," *The New York Times*, November 25, 2021, at: https://www.nytimes.com/2021/11/25/world/asia/pakistan-taliban-afghanistan-madrasa.html

Roy, Olivier, "Has Islamism a future in Afghanistan?" in William Maley (ed.), *Fundamentalism Reborn? Afghanistan and the Taliban*, NYU Press, 1998, pp. 199–211.

Sayed, Abdul, "How are Taliban organized?" *VOA*, September 5, 2021, at: https://www.voanews.com/a/us-afghanistan-troop-withdrawal_analysis-how-are-taliban-organized/6219266.html

—— "The evolution and future of Tehrik-e-Taliban Pakistan," *Carnegie Endowment for International Peace*, December 21, 2021, at: https://carnegieendowment.org/2021/12/21/evolution-and-future-of-tehrik-e-taliban-pakistan-pub-86051

Sayed, Abdul and Tore Hamming, "The revival of the Pakistani Taliban," *CTC Sentinel*, vol. 14, no. 4 (May 2021): 28–38, at: https://ctc.westpoint.edu/the-revival-of-the-pakistani-taliban/

Schroden, Jonathan, "Lessons from the collapse of Afghanistan's security forces," *CTC Sentinel*, vol. 14, no. 8 (October 2021): 45–61, at: https://ctc.westpoint.edu/lessons-from-the-collapse-of-afghanistans-security-forces/

Sciutto, Jim, Zachary Cohen and Kylie Atwood, "US intel assessments on Afghanistan warn of 'accelerating pace' of Taliban hold on country," *CNN*, July 16, 2021, at: https://www.cnn.com/2021/07/16/politics/us-intel-kabul-taliban/index.html

Stancati, Margherita and Ehsanullah Amiri, "Taliban reach out to Shiite Hazara minority, seeking unity and Iran ties," *The Wall Street Journal*, September 2, 2021.

Thomas, Clayton, "Afghanistan: Background and U.S. policy: In brief," *Congressional Research Service*, August 26, 2021, at: https://crsreports.congress.gov/product/pdf/R/R45122

Timberg, Craig and Cristiano Lima, "Today's Taliban uses sophisticated social media practices that rarely violate the rules," *The Washington Post*, August 18, 2021, at: https://www.washingtonpost.com/technology/2021/08/18/taliban-social-media-success/

Trofimov, Yaroslav and Margherita Stancati, "Taliban covert operatives seized Kabul, other Afghan cities from within," *The Wall Street Journal*, November 28, 2021, at: https://www.wsj.com/articles/taliban-covert-operatives-seized-kabul-other-afghan-cities-from-within-11638095401

Watkins, Andrew, "Five questions on the Taliban's caretaker government," *USIP*, September 9, 2021, at: https://www.usip.org/publications/2021/09/five-questions-talibans-caretaker-government

—— "Taliban fragmentation: A figment of your imagination?" *War on the Rocks*, September 4, 2019, at: https://warontherocks.com/2019/09/taliban-fragmentation-a-figment-of-your-imagination/

—— "Taliban fragmentation: Fact, fiction, and future," *USIP, Peaceworks*, no. 160 (March 2020), at: https://www.usip.org/sites/default/files/2020-03/pw_160-taliban_fragmentation_fact_fiction_and_future-pw.pdf

Whitlock, Craig, *The Afghanistan Papers: A Secret History of the War*, Simon & Schuster, 2021.

Wilson, Brian R., *The Social Dimensions of Sectarianism: Sects and New Religious Movements*, Clarendon Press, 1990.

Zahab, Mariam A., *Pakistan: A Kaleidoscope of Islam*, Oxford University Press, 2020.

Zelin, Aaron Y., "Turkey calls for recognition of the Taliban's emirate," *Washington Institute for Near East Policy*, March 17, 2022, at: https://www.washingtoninstitute.org/policy-analysis/turkey-calls-recognition-talibans-islamic-emirate

Zucchino, David, "Collapse and conquest: The Taliban strategy that seized Afghanistan," *The New York Times*, August 18, 2021, at: https://www.nytimes.com/2021/08/18/world/asia/taliban-victory-strategy-afghanistan.html

Acknowledgments

This book has been in the making for a very long time even though the period of writing was comparatively short. When the Taliban returned to power in Afghanistan in August 2021, Heather McCallum at Yale University Press asked me if I would write a new epilogue to my earlier work *The Taliban Revival* (2014), as there was demand for the book given recent developments. I said I would prefer not to update my earlier work but maybe I would write another book—she instantaneously agreed, and introduced me to another brilliant editor, Joanna Godfrey, who really facilitated the development of the idea of this book and was always available to offer support and valuable feedback.

Early on I approached my three former professors—Professors Richard Shultz and Andrew Hess of the Fletcher School at Tufts University, and Professor Jessica Stern, now at Boston University—to share what I had in mind as well as the tentative title for this work then: *The New Taliban*. It was as if I was a student again, pitching my thesis to them, and ultimately, their critique and encouragement convinced me to complete the story I had started writing a decade ago. Shultz invited me back to the Fletcher School to test my thesis by giving a talk at the International Security Studies Program forum, which proved to be very helpful, as the students there asked me brilliant questions, making me rethink the title as well the core ideas of the book. I am indebted to my former professors for helping me to refine the idea, and for encouraging and cautioning me. What a blessing to have such figures who continue to guide you throughout your career.

I am incredibly grateful to my lovely wife Benish and three daughters, who are always supportive and tremendously patient as I jump from one book to the next!

Thirdly, I must thank my employer, Near East South Asia Center for Strategic Studies (NESA) at the National Defense University in Washington DC, where my colleagues and center leaders are very supportive of my research endeavors. NESA offered me great opportunities to travel worldwide, teach,

ACKNOWLEDGMENTS

research and organize seminars that allowed me to learn and meet so many people from all over. NESA interns as well as some Fulbright scholars from South Asia helped with various aspects of my research and I am especially grateful to Christopher Mills, Gabriel Blais, Theodore Bennett, Meesum Alam and Simran Sharma. Then Fletcher School student (now alum) Simran spent significant time supporting the research and writing of the chapter "The International Relations of the Taliban."

I am also very grateful to many journalists, scholars and practitioners with whom I had numerous conversations about all things Taliban and who graciously shared their insights and wisdom with me. These include Kathy Gannon, Dawood Azami, Kamran Bokhari, Asfandyar Mir, Harold Ingram, Greta Holtz, Thomas West, Mathew Dearing, Thomas Marks, Rameez Abbas, Kavita Nair, Ali Jalali, Abdul Basit, Omar Daudzai, Ali Mustafa, Syed Adnan Bokhari, Hassan Ahmadian and Robin Raphel.

In Pakistan, I am grateful to Ambassador Aziz Chaudry, and especially Amina Khan at the Institute of Strategic Studies Islamabad for organizing a book workshop for me in September 2022, where I had a useful discussion with many retired diplomats, generals and experts helping me better understand Pakistani perspectives on Afghanistan. Other Pakistanis with whom I had valuable conversations include Senator Mushahid Hussain Syed, Ambassador Mohammad Sadiq, Major General (ret'd) Isfandiyar Pataudi, Inspector General of Police (ret'd) Syed Kaleem Imam, Mohammad Ismail Khan, Qamar Cheema, Aamir Ghauri, Major General (ret'd) Tariq Quddus and Amir Rana. I am also thankful to London's International Institute for Strategic Studies which, through some of its programs, facilitated my research engagements with South Asian experts. Some individuals I interviewed, especially in Afghanistan, wish to remain anonymous, due to their understandable security concerns. Their insights and courage are highly appreciated.

One friend in Pakistan, who is also mentioned in the Introduction, and with whom I had a series of conversations on many aspects of the Taliban worldview, is Mohammad Israr Madani. He is a former teacher at Darul Uloom Haqqania at Akora Khattak and a respected counter-extremism practitioner in Pakistan. I am indebted to him for his time and guidance.

Finally, I am truly appreciative of Zahra Hassan, my research assistant for this book who conducted extensive research for the chapter on the Deobandi school and spent innumerable hours fulfilling various task requests including editing. The outstanding support I received from my editor and the support team at the YUP London office deserves special mention. Joanna Godfrey's help was instrumental, and others including Rachael Lonsdale, Sophie Richmond, Frazer Martin and Lucy Buchan were also always kind and very supportive.

All opinions expressed are solely my own and do not express the views or opinions of my employer.

Index

Note: page numbers in italics indicate mentions in cabinet charts.

INDEX

INDEX

cloak of the Prophet Muhammad
160–1
Doha negotiations 41
Pakistani Taliban 182
secrecy over death 29–30, 33, 41–2
status as founder 168
Taliban resurgence 29
Omari, Mohammad Nabi 55
Operation Zarb-e-Azb 184
opium 225

Pakistan
coal imports 117, 120, 121
Deobandi thinking 158
FATA (Federally Administered
Tribal Areas) 8–9, 34, 179–81,
186
FATA Reforms Bill (2018) 188
and Hidayatullah Badri 91
and India 16–17, 51, 197–8
intelligence services see Inter-
Services Intelligence (ISI)
(Pakistan)
Jaish-e-Mohammed (JeM) 158, 228
Khyber Pukhtunkhwa (KPK)
province 18, 24, 186
and non-Taliban Afghan leaders
193–4
Operation Zarb-e-Azb 184
peace negotiation strategy 51
relations with Taliban 17–18, 19
relations with Taliban interim
government 91–2, 97, 139–40,
194–5
relations with US 145
Shakai Agreement (2004) 180–1
Taliban sanctuary during
insurgency 8–9, 32, 37, 40, 240
tribal institutions 180–1
US drone strikes 33–4, 181
US policy 45
al-Zawahiri drone strike 145
Pakistan–Afghan border 183–4, 186,
191, 193
Pakistani Taliban (Tehrik-i-Taliban)
(TTP) 179–89
Afghan and Indian intelligence
funding 185

in Afghanistan 185–6, 192–3
background 179–82
ceasefire deal brokered by Hameed
187
demands to Pakistan 195
faction consolidation 184–5
ideology 152, 182, 183
military offensive against 18, 183
origins 183
relations with Afghan Taliban
177–8, 182, 186–7, 194, 207
resurgence 18, 183
siege of Bannu counterterrorism
center 187–8
sources 23–4
terror attacks 18, 177, 182–3, 184,
186
US drone attacks 184
Pashteen, Manzoor 188
Pashtun areas 18–19
Pashtun poetry and language 162,
164–5
Pashtun Tahafuz (Protection)
Movement (PTM) 188–9
Pashtunistan 17
Pashtuns, in government 89–90, 97
Pashtunwali (Pashtun code of honor)
44
peace negotiations
intra-Afghan dialogue 26, 27,
58–9, 67–8
Moscow talks 224, 228
see also Doha negotiations; tribes,
Taliban deals; US–Taliban
peace deal (Feb 2020)
Peshawar 8, 95, 177, 184, 185, 189
police
Afghan police 8, 15, 46, 55, 74,
77, 88, 106
Pakistan, 24
Taliban morality police, 9, 15
political succession
for prime minister 130
for supreme leader 127–8, 129, 168
Pompeo, Mike 51–2, 62, 65
pragmatists see moderate pragmatists
press conference, August 2021 83–5
Price, Gareth 237